Best Dog Hikes
South Carolina

Melissa Watson

FALCONGUIDES

GUILFORD, CONNECTICUT

FALCONGUIDES®

An imprint of Globe Pequot

Falcon and FalconGuides are registered trademarks and Make Adventure Your Story is a trademark of Rowman & Littlefield.

Distributed by NATIONAL BOOK NETWORK

British Library Cataloguing-in-Publication Information available

Library of Congress Cataloging-in-Publication Data available

ISBN 978-1-4930-3024-8 (paperback)
ISBN 978-1-4930-3025-5 (e-book)

∞™ The paper used in this publication meets the minimum requirements of American National Standard for Information Sciences—Permanence of Paper for Printed Library Materials, ANSI/NISO Z39.48-1992.

Printed in the United States of America

The author and Globe Pequot Press assume no liability for accidents happening to, or injuries sustained by, readers who engage in the activities described in this book.

Best Dog Hikes
South Carolina

For my big sister Sue

Dolly!
Where to start? You put me in the trash can and
the toilet. Hung me over the railing two flights
up. Made me ride the Dragon Coaster, and
run down to Stanton House with a note from
"mom." Who could forget the party when I was
six?! Or the night Aunt Terry was babysitting! Or
"Crash"?! The stories go on and on. And through
it all, I survived . . . and I wouldn't change a thing!
So many good times, so much laughter and
love. Now my dear big sister, it's your turn
to survive! And thrive! We have many more
memories to create! Plus no one can do "Cousin
It" like you can. Or the Martian Lady!
I love you!

Contents

The Lowcountry—Coast

◀   *Despite the tiny package, this poodle was extremely agile (hike 44).*

The Midlands—Piedmont

Clinton

Spartanburg

Blacksburg

The Upcountry—Mountains

Gaffney

Greenville

Pickens

Lake Jocassee

Walhalla

Walhalla to Cashiers, NC

Westminster

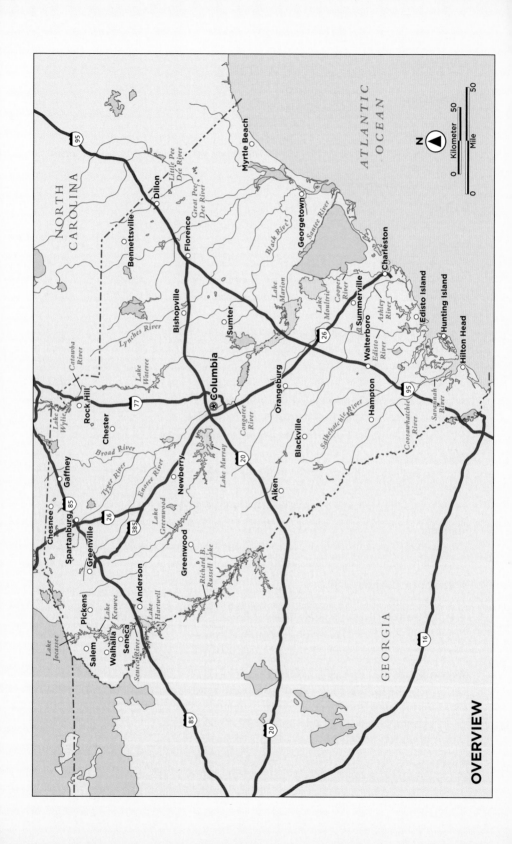

OVERVIEW

Acknowledgments

To my family, who has been so supportive in *every* way and has always been there unconditionally, I love you! Terri Sansonetti, Maria, Frazier, Christina, Cory and Parker Payton, Doug Watson, Sue, Tom, Frank, Amy, Thomas, Luana, Joe, Dena, Kristen, Rebecca, Nathaniel, Katilee, Mark, Jonathon, Joshua, Silas, Micah, Grace and Giulia Strazza, Michelle, Roland, Lucas, Zackary Arisolo, and Doug and Claire Watson. I love you all!

To Cheryl Arcand. For one, thank you for all the time and effort you put into researching the hotels and restaurants. But most importantly, for being patient, tolerant, understanding, and for picking up a *lot* of the slack while I diligently worked on this book. I love you!

To my friends, Dawn McKinney, Shari Santos, Cheryl Giovagnorio, Liz Martinez, Irene Freer, Jenn Getter, Susie Castro, Maris Herold, Terri Bennett: Thanks for your patience. I love you all!

To my canine kids, Mikey, Bandit, Blue, and Alley, for bringing pure joy to my life!

To my dog sitter and friend, Bruce Easton, for taking such good care of the pups on the occasions that they are unable to travel with me.

To my crew at Station 51, John Schultz, Chris Uzzo, Robert Burns, David Adams, and Dan Vera, for all the fun times and support.

For all of my canine and human "models": Kevin, Stephanie, and Banjo; Pat and Holly; Catherine and Little D-O-G; The Riker Family; Rhiannan, Avery, and Tucky; Tammy and Calvin; Avery, Brian, Wendy, and Suzie; Tony, Pat, and Leo; Hal and Casey; Mary and Dixie; Ella, Olivia, Linda, Buck, and Punkin; Brian and Jake; Autumn, Joey, and Miya, plus Toots the Cat; Lisa, Ian, Colin, and Cal; Roy and Pepe; and John, Tamara, Jackie, and the entire family of Chihuahuas: Grace, Justice, Maggie, Myles, and Tank. Cooper Payton. Thanks for taking the extra time along the trail to let me snap some photos.

To those at the state parks, national forests, and Park Service for ensuring accuracy: David Gilson, Everett Ernst, Brian Robson, J. W. Weatherford, Eddie Richburg, Scott Teodorski, Avery Joiner, Sadaris Benjamin, Noah Letter, Noel Simons, Keelie Robinson, and Bren Harmer. And to Steven and Scott with Oconee County Fire Rescue. Thank you!

To all the folks at Falcon Guides who helped work on the maps, photos, and manuscript. Without your hard work and expert ability, this book would not be the final product that we are able to present today. Among others, David Legere and Ellen Urban. Thank you!

Introduction

Whether you have one dog, or ten, whether they're inseparable or independent, they'll love getting outdoors on the trails of South Carolina. Within these pages I've compiled sixty of the best dog hikes in the state. Lakes, rivers, creeks, and waterfalls, from mountain views to the coveted coast—I've covered them all. Whether your dogs are experienced hikers or new to the trail, whether you're looking for an easy stroll or a strenuous trek, there's a trail for you. And what better way to enjoy the great outdoors than with your best friends, your pampered pups, your canine companions at your side? While you enjoy stunning scenery, flowing waterfalls, and pristine lakes, they get to explore the new sights, scents, and sounds of the forest. And more importantly, they get to be with you—romping around, sniffing new smells, splashing in the creeks, and making new friends along the way. Any dog can do it, from Maltese to mastiffs and every breed in between. The key is knowing your dogs, and their limitations. Just as you do when hiking with human companions, you simply need to find the right trail. If your pups aren't in fantastic shape, you can still take them on a short hike. And they'll be grateful for it. Also, if your hounds have any medical conditions, check with your vet before taking them out on the trail. It's important to use common sense with your canine kids, and it's up to you to know what they can and cannot handle. Dogs will go, go, go to a fault to spend the day with their best friend. But you need to know their limitations, and your own, so you can enjoy hike after hike for years to come, with your trusty pups at your side.

How to Use This Guide

Before you begin your endeavor, here's some important information on how to use this guide.

You'll see the hikes have been divided into geographic area. This way, when you visit an area, you can see what hikes are nearby. Each hike has its own coinciding trail map. Every hike in this book follows the same format, which begins with a brief description of the hike. Next you'll see the hike "specs." This section provides you with important information about where the trail starts, distance (round-trip), blaze color, difficulty, elevation, when to visit, trail surface, other trail users, whether a leash is required, land status, and fees.

Recommended maps, trail contacts, and nearest towns are also listed. Lastly, you'll find "trail tips." Here you'll find pertinent information about whether there are restrooms or trash cans near the trailhead, or whether you need a hiking stick or extra drinking water. Following the hike specs, you'll see "Finding the trailhead." This includes explicit driving directions, using a main intersection as your starting point. The driving distances are given in mileage rounded to the nearest tenth of a mile.

◀ *Blazes mark the trail, keeping you on track.*

Please note, whenever parking near a Forest Service gate, don't block the gate. GPS coordinates are provided for the trailhead and any highlights along the trail. Next, you'll find "The Hike." This is where you'll get a general description, what to expect along the hike, and some entertaining facts about the trail, area, and history. The "Miles and Directions" are next. Here you'll find step by step trail directions, guiding you through every fork and every T. You'll see the distance from the trailhead at which you reach them, and then left/right directions with corresponding compass directions. I've made every effort to keep you and your pups from getting lost, but trails do change over time and with the seasons. This is why I return time and time again and am always greeted with a fabulous new experience. Following the Miles and Directions, you'll find hotels, campgrounds, and restaurants where your dogs are welcomed with open arms. Each hike concludes with "Puppy paws and golden years." Not all dogs can hike some of the trails in this book, especially the very young and very old. But this doesn't mean you have to leave them at home. In this section, you'll find easy alternative options that are suitable for dogs of all ages and fitness levels. They'll simply enjoy getting outdoors, breathing the fresh air, and spending quality time with you.

For You and Your Dog's Safety

Preparation is the best way to keep you and your four-legged friends safe. Here are a few friendly reminders to help you both enjoy your time on the trail to the fullest.

Make sure you keep your dogs cool in the hot summer months.

Weather

The weather in South Carolina can range from super hot on the coast in summer to snow on the mountaintops in winter. Do your homework before you go. Dress in layers, so you can adapt to any fluctuations that Mother Nature throws your way. And always carry rain gear, just in case. Zip-off pants and wool socks are ideal. The pants are thin but still keep you warm, and they double as shorts by zipping off the legs. Wool socks retain heat when needed and dry quickly. Cotton is the worst material to wear in the woods. Once cotton gets wet, it stays wet, which is dangerous in colder climates. I recommend wearing quick-dry materials. They wick moisture, keeping you dry and comfortable as you hike. While most of the trails are shaded, when necessary, use sunscreen.

Water and Hydration

It's essential that you bring enough drinking water for both you and your canine compadres, and a bowl for them too. You may forget you are exercising while surrounded by beautiful scenery, but it's important to stay hydrated. A good rule of thumb is to drink every 15 minutes. And, if you drink, have the dogs drink too. I recommend wearing a hydration pack. Then you can ice it down, and hike hands free. It's natural for your pups to sip from the cool mountain creeks, but don't let them gulp it down. Even the clearest creek carries tiny bacteria. Prevention is the best medicine. If you notice your dog is vomiting or has diarrhea after a hike, they may have drank from a bad source. If it continues, call your veterinarian. Also, don't let your dogs drink saltwater. They will get sick, and can become dehydrated, which is a serious condition.

Leashes, Collars, and Harnesses

Even if a trail is leash free, always bring one along. It's also a great idea to keep an extra leash in the car, in case one snaps. If a trailhead is near a roadway, or the hike is heavily populated, keep the dogs on lead even if it's not required—at least until you move away from the road or crowd. Also, it's up to you to keep them away from steep dropoffs and to be cautious of swift currents. Leash them as needed, for their own safety.

Collars with tags are essential! With an up-to-date tag, dogs at least have a chance of being returned if they get lost. And remember, a microchip is no substitute for a dog tag. Harnesses are good if your dogs are pullers. Clip them in the front, and it will help alleviate pulling. But harnesses and collars can get caught up on branches and bushes if the dogs wander off-trail. Always keep a close eye on your pooches as you would your children. And bring a copy of their current vaccination records, just in case.

Dog Packs

If your pooch wears a pack, it's important that it fits properly. An ill-fitted pack can cause chafing on the armpits and belly. Also, start with an empty pack so they can

Top: If you get a pack for your dog, make sure it fits comfortably. Never exceed 25 percent of their body weight.

adjust to this strange coat on their back. As they adapt, you can add weight, up to 25 percent of their body weight, but no more or they'll be prone to injury.

Body Language

Knowing your dogs' body language is key. Are they panting? Limping? Slowing down? Just not being themselves? It's up to you to notice these signals when you take your furry friends on the trail. Remember: Dogs can't sweat like we do. They eliminate excessive heat by panting. If you're tired, panting, and working up a sweat, they feel the same way. Overheating is a serious condition for dogs. If you notice your dogs are panting excessively, cool them down immediately. Give them water, cool them in a creek, pour water over their heads, keep them shaded, and wait until they cool down before you continue hiking.

Stance

Pay attention to your dogs' stance, ears, and tail. These are telltale signs of what they see, hear, and smell. They may alert you that there's a deer up ahead, or an owl up above. Their keen senses can help you spot wildlife, and will give you a chance to see it before they spook it off.

Booties

When people hike, foot care is essential. It's just as important to your four-legged friends. Your pooches are out to please, at all costs, so they may push beyond their limits. It's up to you to know your dogs' limits. If they're limping, check their pads and joints. Buffered aspirin may help with pain, but you need to find the problem. And *never* give them Advil or Tylenol. If they've strained something, call it a day, and apply ice when you can. Bring a first-aid kit for you both. If they've injured a pad, you can bandage it and use booties to keep the bandage in place. Better yet, have them wear booties to prevent problems in the first place, especially on rough or gravel terrain. Booties are also helpful in winter, allowing them to hike year-round.

Poison Ivy, Oak, and Sumac

All of these plant irritants are found in South Carolina. If you know how to identify them, you may save yourself some unpleasant itching. A good rule of thumb is "leaves of three, let it be," since poison ivy and oak both have three leaflets to a leaf.

Alligators

South Carolina presents a special challenge when hiking with dogs, the American alligator. Unfortunately, alligators do see our canine companions as prey. With this in mind, it's very important that you heed all warnings. I've seen alligators firsthand while researching this book. It's virtually impossible to avoid when hiking near water in the coast and Piedmont. If you're aware of the potential hazard, and your surroundings, you can keep your puppies safe. Do not let them in or near the water if

Use caution: Alligators do inhabit the Jarvis Creek Park Lake (hike 1).

Bufo toads are poisonous to dogs.

alligators may be present. Gators can blend in with their surroundings, and they can hold their breath for extended periods. Just because you don't see an alligator doesn't mean they're not there. Keep your pups on a leash and at your side any time there may be alligators present.

Bugs, Bees, and Ticks

Depending on when and where you hike, you may encounter mosquitoes, horseflies, ticks, or chiggers. Insect repellent with DEET helps keep mosquitoes and horseflies at bay. Mosquitoes carry heartworm, so keep current on your pup's preventative medicine. If you get chiggers, it's an experience you'll *never* forget. They itch ten times more than poison ivy. The solution is clear nail polish. Cover the red bumps completely, and reapply often. As for ticks, give your dogs preventive medicine such as NexGuard *before* you hike, and protect yourself as well. Insect repellent may help, but also wear light colors so the ticks are easy to spot. Tuck your shirt in, and tuck your pants into your socks. Most important: Do a thorough tick check on you *and* your dogs at the end of each hike.

In late summer bees can inhabit underground nests alongside mountain creeks. These bees are vicious when provoked. Whether you have an allergy or not, carrying an antihistamine such as Benadryl is essential. If you have a known allergy, always carry an EpiPen.

Snakes

South Carolina is home to four species of venomous snakes. Treat all snakes, venomous or not, with respect. Prevention is the best medicine. Before letting the dogs explore on their own, do a quick snake check on sunny rocks near creeks. If you or your dog get bitten, *stay calm* and seek medical attention *immediately*. Don't delay care trying to identify the snake. If your dog is playing in the brush and you hear a yelp, check them for wounds and fang marks. It's unlikely, but if you think your dog was bitten by a snake, clean the wound immediately and mark the margins of the bite. If you're able, carry your dog out of the forest. Antivenin is the *only* treatment for a venomous snake bite, so don't try to suck the venom out. Do *not* elevate the limb, and do *not* apply ice. Call 911.

Poison

Damp cool creeks create the perfect environment for mushrooms and fungi to grow. Although some are edible, many are poisonous. If your dogs put everything in their mouth, watch them closely. Also, choose wisely before throwing a stick for them. Mountain laurel, rhododendron, and azalea are common in the mountain region and can be toxic if ingested. Poison Control is available 24/7: (800) 222-1212.

Blaze Orange

When hiking in national forests, always wear blaze orange during hunting season. And of course put some on your dogs too.

Courtesy

Not everyone loves your cute and cuddly canines as much as you do. If a hike is leash free, don't let your dogs run amok. They must remain under voice control. It's fun for them to have freedom, but it's up to you to keep them safe. Just as with children, you're responsible for their behavior. Always yield to other hikers and equestrians. And always pick up after your dogs, carrying extra waste bags just in case.

If You Have a Dog...

In the national forest, you and your dog could meet people, horses, mountain bikes, ATVs, other dogs and/or wild animals. Help make the outdoor experience enjoyable for you, your dog and all the forest's users by following these safety rules:

- Keep your pet under physical restraint at all times.
- Give your dog plenty of water and rest, and watch for signs of stress and fatigue.
- Keep your dog leashed and under control in campgrounds. Secure your pet in a shady spot and give it lots of attention to minimize barking.
- If you encounter wild animals, respect them by restraining your dog.

Heed all instructions when hiking with your happy hound.

Wildlife

You're a guest in the forest, where many animals make their home. Some are cute and furry, like otters and beavers, others not so much, like snakes and spiders. No matter what you encounter, please *do not feed the wildlife*. Often these cuddly critters cannot digest people food. If you feed them, you may be doing more harm than good. Also, they may begin to associate people with food, and someone may inadvertently get bitten as a result. Keep wildlife wild.

Leave No Trace

The last thing I'd like to share with you is the concept of No Trace hiking. Simply put, when you leave the forest, it should be just as you arrived. "Take nothing but pictures, leave nothing but footprints." Every stone in the creek and every wildflower along the path has a purpose within the ecosystem. Please don't remove anything from the forest, except litter. Instead, bring a camera, and you can preserve the memory while allowing others to appreciate them as well. Also, "pack it in, pack it out," meaning everything you bring into the forest, you should also bring out. This puts less impact on the environment and allows other hikers to appreciate it as well.

Features of a Good Dog Hike

So what is it that makes a great dog hike? Water for one thing. Almost every trail in this book has some sort of natural water source—whether it's a clear mountain stream, a crisp clean lake, or waves lapping on the sand. But heed all alligator warnings. Shade is another key component so your dogs don't overheat. Trails that are less populated, or open to foot traffic only, make ideal dog hikes. Encountering fewer people makes it a bit easier on you.

Fill your pack with water, grab the leash, and load 'em up. It's time for a new adventure, with your proud and playful pups at your side.

> *Hiking Waterfalls in Georgia and South Carolina* and *Camping South Carolina* make fantastic companion books. They'll give you specific details on campgrounds across the state and offer more hiking options for you and your dogs to explore.

Trail Finder

Author's Favorites

2-Lagoon Access/Nature Center Scenic Trail
4-Spanish Mount Trail
5-History Trail
10-Sandpiper Pond Trail
11-Yaupon Trail/Sculptured Oak Trail Loop
15-Boardwalk Trail
19-Coquina Trail
29-Little Gap Trail
33-Caney Fork Falls Trail
34-Nature Trail/River Trail Loop
36-Nature Trail
42-Jones Gap Trail
45-CCC Lakeside Trail
46-Carrick Creek Falls Trail
47-Twin Falls Trail
50-Oconee Bells Nature Trail
51-Station Cove Falls Trail
52-Yellow Branch Falls Trail
54-Pigpen Falls Trail
56-Chattooga River Trail
59-Opossum Creek Falls Trail

Cooper is ready to run.

Lakeside Hikes

1-Leisure Loop Trail
15-Boardwalk Trail
17-Sandhills Trail
19-Coquina Trail
20-Bike Trail
22-Dogwood Interpretive Trail
29-Little Gap Trail
30-Desportes Nature Trail
32-Garden of the Waxhaws Trail
33-Caney Fork Falls Trail
40-Lake Placid Trail
45-CCC Lakeside Trail
53-Lake Trail

Blue and Bandit are best of friends.

Waterfall Hikes

Mikey and Bandit patiently wait at the entrance to the fort at Colonial Dorchester (hike 6).

Leash Free Hikes (Voice Control)

Easy Hikes

1-Leisure Loop Trail
2-Lagoon Access/Nature Center Scenic Trail
3-Lighthouse Nature Trail
4-Spanish Mount Trail
5-History Trail
6-Colonial Dorchester Walking Tour
7-River Bluff Trail
8-Cypress Swamp Nature Trail
9-Awendaw Passage
10-Sandpiper Pond Trail
11-Yaupon Trail/Sculptured Oak Trail Loop
12-Mill Pond Nature Trail
13-Nature Trail/Riverwalk Trail Loop
14-Beaver Pond Trail
15-Boardwalk Trail
16-Big Pine Tree Nature Trail
17-Sandhills Trail
21-Fit Trail/Interpretive Trail Loop
22-Dogwood Interpretive Trail
23-Hopeland Gardens Trail
26-Beaver Run Trail
27-Mariner Nature Trail
30-Desportes Nature Trail
31-Nature Trail/Canal Trail
32-Garden of the Waxhaws Trail
33-Caney Fork Falls Trail
38-Cowpens Battlefield Trail
40-Lake Placid Trail
47-Twin Falls Trail
51-Station Cove Falls Trail
58-Falls on Little Brasstown Creek Trail

Nearly 200 breeds of dogs are recognized by the American Kennel Club.

Strenuous and Moderate-to-Strenuous Hikes

41-Sulphur Springs Trail
44-Coldspring Branch-Jones Gap-Tom Miller Trail Loop
49-Natural Bridge Trail
52-Yellow Branch Falls Trail
53-Lake Trail
57-Riley Moore Falls Trail
59-Opossum Creek Falls Trail

MAP LEGEND

Municipal

▬🄰95🄰▬	Freeway/Interstate Highway	⏝	Bridge/Footbridge
▬(25)▬	US Highway	⦀⦀⦀⦀⦀⦀	Boardwalk/Steps
▬(46)▬	State Road	🏠	Cabin
▬[632]▬	County/Secondary/Forest Road	🔺	Campground
------	Trail	🏛	Church
▬▬▬▬	Featured Trail	🏊	Designated Swim Area
		→	Direction of Trail

Water Features

⬭	Pond/Lake	•─•	Gate
∿	River or Creek	☐	General Point of Interest
∿	Medium River	🏛	Monument
🌊	Waterfall/Spillway	🅿	Parking
		▲	Peak

Land Management

🌲	State/County/Local Park	🎏	Picnic Area
		👫	Ranger Station/Park Office
		🚻	Restroom

Symbols

✈	Airport	◰	Shelter
▲	Backcountry Camping	🔭	Scenic View/Overlook
🚤	Boat Ramp	①	Trailhead
		?	Visitor/Information Center
		🚰	Water

A paved path loops around the lake at Jarvis Creek Park (hike 1). ▶

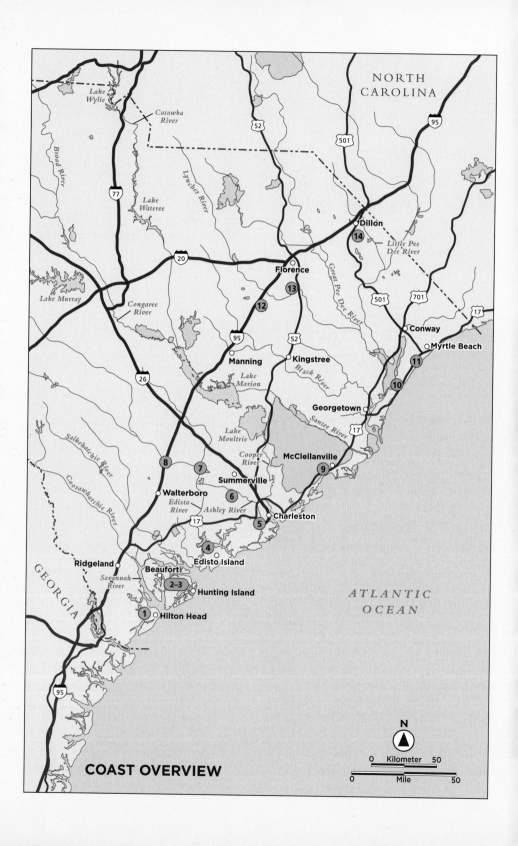

COAST OVERVIEW

The Lowcountry—Coast

From Hilton Head to Myrtle Beach, Francis Marion to Florence, the coast has a trail for you. Although the topography may not be tough, the scenery is outstanding. Where else can you hike past a lighthouse and end with the dogs taking a dip in the deep blue sea? You'll journey back through time taking historic self-guided tours in Charleston and Dorchester. Visit an old shell mound in Edisto Island and see a Carolina bay near Florence. Hike along rivers, lakes, and even the ocean as you travel around the fabulous coast, or leave your footprints on the Palmetto Trail, the longest trail in the state. The options are endless as you discover all the coast of South Carolina has to offer.

The bottlenose dolphin is the South Carolina state marine mammal.

Hilton Head

1 Leisure Loop Trail–Jarvis Creek Park

Aptly named, this primarily paved path makes a pleasant leisurely loop around the park's lake. The trail is lined with lush grass, so the pups can enjoy this hike even in the summer months when the pavement heats up. Be forewarned, alligators *are present* in this lake. Please use caution, keep the dogs on a leash, and away from the water's edge. Near the end of the loop, take notice of the enormous live oak tree standing between the walkway and the water. You're sure to be impressed.

Start: 50 Jarvis Park Rd., Hilton Head; at the southeast side of the lake, near the fishing pier
Distance: 0.9-mile loop
Hiking time: About 25 minutes
Blaze color: None
Difficulty: Easy
Trailhead elevation: 8 feet
Highest point: 81 feet
Best season: Year-round
Schedule: 6 a.m. to 9 p.m., wintertime 6 a.m. to 6 p.m.
Trail surface: Paved path
Other trail users: Bicycles, in-line skaters
Canine compatibility: Leash required

Land status: Hilton Head Parks & Facilities
Fees: No fee
Maps: *DeLorme: South Carolina Atlas & Gazetteer:* Page 63, D7
Trail contacts: (843) 341-4600; www.hilton headislandsc.gov/ourisland/parks/parksand facdetails.cfm?FacilityID=14
Nearest town: Hilton Head
Trail tips: Water fountain, bathrooms, and trash cans near the trailhead
Special considerations: Alligators do live in the lake. Do *not* let the dogs in or near the water.

Finding the trailhead: From the junction of US 278 (Cross Island Parkway) and US 278 Business (William Hilton Parkway) in Hilton Head, drive east on US 278 Business for approximately 0.7 mile to the park on the right (past the stoplight at Gum Tree Road). Follow Jarvis Park Road for 0.2 mile and park near the lake. **Trailhead GPS:** N32 12.759'/W80 44.112'

The Hike

The drive to the park is rather mundane, that is until you reach the bridge leading onto the island. As you cross, a sprawling scenic waterway greets you, and you instantly see why people are drawn to the illustrious island of Hilton Head. Beaches, resorts, and championship golf courses are all part of the allure, as is a harbor, a lighthouse, and a tradition steeped in history. During its formative years, after the Civil War, Hilton Head was one of the first communities of freed men in the South. In the wake of the war, hundreds of people flocked to the island. Heritage tours are available,

The whole family will enjoy a day on Hilton Head.

and you can gain insight into the traditions of the Gullah people, whose descendants still inhabit the island. Hilton Head also houses an astounding number of local parks that are open to the public. Among them is the delightful Jarvis Creek Park. Picnic shelters, playgrounds, charcoal grills, and open grassland border the park's lake, and the Leisure Loop Trail circles around it. Following the loop clockwise quickly leads you over an elevated boardwalk. You'll see cypress knees and ferns, and a variety of trees keep you shaded. Beyond the boardwalk, a paved path follows the water's edge. Locals walk their dogs, in-line skate, run, and ride their bikes. Randomly placed benches offer a peaceful place to enjoy the view. Doggy bag dispensers and trash cans are also dispersed along the path, making it easy to clean up after your pampered pooches. You may spy osprey, hawks, or herons hunting for fish in the wonderful water. Turtles and alligators also inhabit this lake. So keep the dogs on a leash, and away from the water *at all times.* Although you hear traffic from US 278, it's still a very serene setting. In summertime the pavement may be hot. But lush grass lines the pathway, keeping your puppy's paws protected. Following the shoreline around the lake you'll see open fields big enough to toss a football or Frisbee. On the final leg of the loop, the trail leads you past a massive live oak tree. Its long, sturdy branches reach out far from the base, with the weight of them dipping down to the ground. It's truly an amazing specimen. Arrive early. Parking is limited, and you'll beat the heat of the day.

Miles and Directions

- **0.0** Begin near the bathroom and hike south past the fishing pier.
- **0.05** Cross a boardwalk. Continue hiking southwest.
- **0.4** Bypass the Honey Horn Trail on your left (north). Continue hiking straight ahead (southeast) on the Leisure Loop.
- **0.8** Hike past the live oak tree on the right (west) (N32 12.812'/W80 44.120').
- **0.9** Arrive at the trailhead.

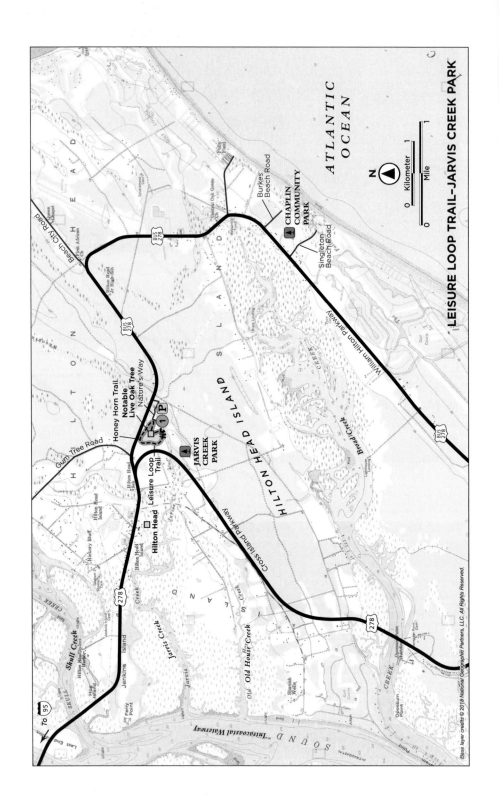

LEISURE LOOP TRAIL–JARVIS CREEK PARK

This mighty oak is certainly a highlight.

Resting up

Park Lane Hotel and Suites, 12 Park Ln., Hilton Head Island, (843) 686-5700; pet fee required.

Ramada, 200 Museum St., Hilton Head, (843) 681-3655; pet fee required.

Camping

Hilton Head Island Motorcoach Resort, 133 Arrow Rd., Hilton Head Island, (843) 593-9755; RV sites only.

Fueling up

Black Marlin Bayside Grill, 86 Helmsman Way, Ste. 103, Hilton Head Island, (843) 785-4950.

Skull Creek Boathouse, 397 Squire Pope Rd., Hilton Head Island, (843) 681-3663.

Puppy Paws and Golden Years

This hike is suitable for all dogs. Or take them to the beach before 10 a.m. or after 5 p.m. Leash required.

Beaufort

2 Lagoon Access Trail/Nature Center Scenic Trail– Hunting Island State Park

The park map makes this look like a wonderful waterfront hike. While the trail is wonderful, it leads through a magnificent forest rather than following the shoreline of the lagoon. Pines and palm trees fill the forest, and you'll catch a glimpse of the water along the way. The trees offer shade, and a steady breeze is present. But what makes this one a favorite is the highlight at the end, a sandy oceanfront beach with massive downed trees enhancing the scenery.

Start: 2555 Sea Island Pkwy., Hunting Island; begin west of Parking J, on the west side of the road that loops back toward the visitor center
Distance: 3.3 miles out and back
Hiking time: About 1 hour, 45 minutes
Blaze color: Pale blue (sparsely placed)
Difficulty: Easy
Trailhead elevation: 44 feet
Highest point: 46 feet
Best season: Year-round
Schedule: 6 a.m. to 6 p.m. (extended to 9 p.m. during Daylight Saving Time)
Trail surface: Hard-packed sand and shell rock
Other trail users: None

Canine compatibility: Leash required
Land status: South Carolina Department of Natural Resources
Fees: Fee required
Maps: *DeLorme: South Carolina Atlas & Gazetteer:* Page 63, A10
Trail contacts: (843) 838-2011; www.south carolinaparks.com/huntingisland/introduction .aspx
Nearest town: Hunting Island, Beaufort
Trail tips: Vault toilet near the trailhead; bring bug spray in summer, and lots of water for you and the pups.

Finding the trailhead: From the junction of US 21 (Sea Island Parkway) and SC 802 East in Beaufort, drive east on US 21 for 15.0 miles to a left into the park. Follow the park road to the end. Beyond S. Beach Drive, follow signs to "Fishing/Parking J." After making the left toward Parking J, follow the lagoon for approximately 0.2 mile and park near the road that shortcuts west to the trailhead.

From I-95 get off at exit 33. Drive east on US 17 for 8.3 miles to a right onto US 21 South toward Beaufort. Follow US 21 for 32.4 miles to the park on the left. Follow directions above.
Trailhead GPS: N32 21.696'/W80 26.711'

Note that the colors of the spectrum are always a mirror image on a double rainbow.

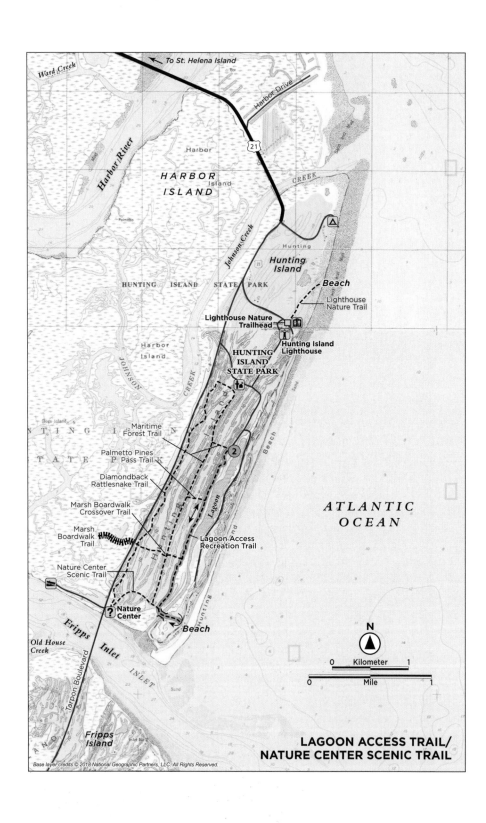

To St. Helena Island

Ward Creek

Harbor River

Harbor Drive

21

Harbor

HARBOR ISLAND
Island

CREEK

Johnson Creek

Hunting Island

HUNTING ISLAND STATE PARK

Hunting

Beach

Lighthouse Nature Trail

Lighthouse Nature Trailhead

Hunting Island Lighthouse

Harbor Island

HUNTING ISLAND STATE PARK

JOHNSON

CREEK

Hogs Island

NTING ISLAND

Maritime Forest Trail

STATE

Palmetto Pines Pass Trail

2

Diamondback Rattlesnake Trail

Marsh Boardwalk Crossover Trail

Marsh Boardwalk Trail

Lagoon

Beach

Lagoon Access Recreation Trail

ATLANTIC OCEAN

Nature Center Scenic Trail

? **Nature Center**

Hunting

Beach

Old House Creek

Fripps Inlet

Tarpon Boulevard

INLET

N

0   Kilometer   1
0   Mile   1

Fripps Island

Inlet No. 2

Sand

LAGOON ACCESS TRAIL/ NATURE CENTER SCENIC TRAIL

Downed trees add to the oceanfront scenery.

The Hike

A maze of narrow roadways weaves throughout this park. When you finally park, the long, narrow lagoon comes into view. The lagoon is saltwater, not fresh, and ties into Fripps Inlet at the south end. As you follow the Lagoon Access Trail, you'll see several trails intersect it, forming a network of pathways. If you wanted to change the distance, there are several options. Tall pine trees wave in the wind, like flags on a flagpole, as they bend and bow to the might of Mother Nature. Pines, palmettos, and palms form this maritime forest, and even the tallest palm trees are dwarfed by the lofty pines. The occasional big oak adds to the scenery, as does the lagoon when it comes into view. Seagulls soar overhead, while fishermen cast their lines from the banks. There are a few twists and turns early on, but in general, the trail leads you southwest as it parallels the wide waterway. The park map is deceiving, making it look like you hike right next to the water. In reality, a buffer of brush stands between you and the salty seawater. The trees offer plenty of shade, a steady breeze keeps you cool, and the occasional bench offers a place to sit. The farther you go on the trail, the closer you come to the lagoon, giving you better and better views. On the eastern shore, a sea of grass greets you from afar, and the occasional virgin sandy beach stands out from the scenery. The breeze helps deter them, but there are mosquitoes in summertime, especially after it rains. The Lagoon Access Trail ends at a T, where the blue-blazed Nature Center Scenic Trail runs east and west. Head left (east), and this scenic trail leads you to a long footbridge over the lagoon, and then out to the beach. This part of the hike is a *must do*. The view from the bridge is phenomenal, and the dogs will run, play, dig, and dash about in the waves as they crash down on the sand. The remnants of large trees in the shallows of the ocean are quite a sight. The trees are joined by an old stilt cabin, known by locals as "Little Blue." Some say it's haunted. Luckily, this local landmark survived the mayhem of Hurricane Matthew in 2016.

Miles and Directions

0.0 Hike northwest and immediately come to a fork. Straight (northwest) is the Maritime Forest Trail. Go left (south southwest) on the Lagoon Access Trail.

0.5 Bypass the Palmetto Pines Pass Trail on the right (west). Continue straight (south), paralleling the lagoon.

1.1 Bypass the Marsh Boardwalk Crossover Trail to the right (west). Continue hiking straight (southwest).

1.4 The Lagoon Access Trail ends at a T with the Nature Center Scenic Trail. Go left (east) on the Nature Center Scenic Trail.

1.45 Cross a footbridge over the lagoon. Several narrow paths lead toward the ocean.

1.65 Arrive at the beach (N32 20.531'/W80 27.150'). Backtrack to the trailhead.

3.3 Arrive at the trailhead.

Option: Begin at the Nature Center and follow the Nature Center Scenic Trail for 0.7 mile out to the beach.

Resting up

Days Inn, 1660 S. Ribaut Rd., Port Royal, (843) 524-1551; pet fee required.
City Loft Hotel, 301 Carteret St., Beaufort, (843) 379-5638; pet fee required.

Camping

Onsite.

Fueling up

Shrimp Shack, 1925 Sea Island Pkwy., Saint Helena Island, (843) 838-2962.
Johnson Creek Tavern, 2141 Sea Island Pkwy., Saint Helena Island, (843) 838-4166.

Puppy Paws and Golden Years

Visit the park's lighthouse, and then take them less than 0.1 mile to the beach.

3 Lighthouse Nature Trail–Hunting Island State Park

This short and easy hike first leads past the park's lofty lighthouse. A simple two-toned color scheme of black and white distinguishes this lovely lighthouse from others in the state. Beyond the lighthouse, the path parallels the seashore with nothing but a small sand dune separating you from the ocean. When the trail ends, a small pond sits to your left and the ocean lies in front of you. The dogs will have a blast digging in the sand and dodging the waves as they tumble in.

Start: 2555 Sea Island Pkwy., Hunting Island; The trail begins on the grassy field on the east side of the lighthouse.
Distance: 0.8 mile out and back
Hiking time: About 20 minutes
Blaze color: None
Difficulty: Easy
Trailhead elevation: Sea level
Highest point: 7 feet
Best season: Year-round
Schedule: 6 a.m. to 6 p.m. (extended to 9 p.m. during Daylight Saving Time)
Trail surface: Hard-packed sand
Other trail users: None
Canine compatibility: Leash required

Land status: South Carolina Department of Natural Resources
Fees: Fee required
Maps: *DeLorme: South Carolina Atlas & Gazetteer:* Page 63, A10
Trail contacts: (843) 838-2011; www.south carolinaparks.com/huntingisland/introduction .aspx
Nearest town: Hunting Island, Beaufort
Trail tips: Restrooms, outdoor showers, trash cans, and a water fountain are on the north side of the lighthouse.
Special considerations: Alligators may inhabit the pond near the trail's end. Let the dogs swim in the ocean only.

Finding the trailhead: From the junction of US 21 (Sea Island Parkway) and SC 802 East in Beaufort, drive east on US 21 for 15.0 miles to a left into the park. Travel for 1.5 miles to a left onto N. Beach Road. Travel for 0.2 mile to a fork. Go right and drive another 0.4 mile to the parking area near the lighthouse.

From I-95 get off at exit 33. Drive east on US 17 for 8.3 miles to a right onto US 21 South toward Beaufort. Follow US 21 for 32.4 miles to the park on the left. Follow directions above.
Trailhead GPS: N32 22.551'/W80 26.250'

The Hike

The simple black and white color scheme isn't the only thing that distinguishes this lovely lighthouse from others in the state. The Hunting Island Lighthouse is over 150 years old. And, it's the only lighthouse in the state open for tours. For a nominal fee, you can climb the steep staircase all the way to the top. The panoramic views are unmatched. Unfortunately, dogs are not allowed inside the structure, so you'll have to appreciate it from ground level. After admiring the celebrated structure, follow the sidewalk northeast toward the restrooms. Between the lighthouse and the restrooms,

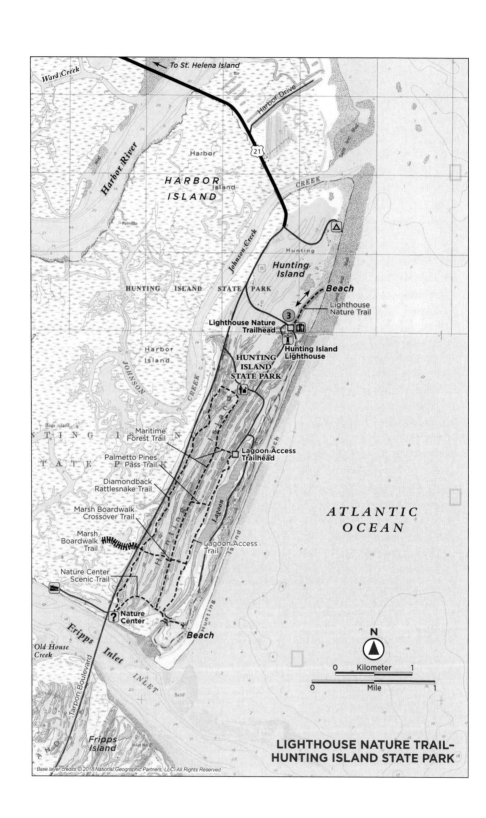

To St. Helena Island

Ward Creek

Harbor River

Harbor Drive

21

Harbor

HARBOR
ISLAND

Island

Palmetto

Johnson Creek

CREEK

Hunting
Island

HUNTING   ISLAND   STATE   PARK

Hunting

Beach

Lighthouse
Nature Trail

Lighthouse Nature
Trailhead

3

Hunting Island
Lighthouse

Harbor
Island

JOHNSON

HUNTING
ISLAND
STATE PARK

Hogs Island

UNTING   ISLAN

CREEK

STATE

Maritime
Forest Trail

Lagoon Access
Trailhead

Palmetto Pines
Pass Trail

Diamondback
Rattlesnake Trail

ATLANTIC
OCEAN

Marsh Boardwalk
Crossover Trail

Lagoon

Marsh
Boardwalk
Trail

Lagoon Access
Trail

Hunting

Nature Center
Scenic Trail

Nature
Center

?

Beach

Fripps   Inlet

Old House
Creek

Tarpon Boulevard

INLET

Sand

N

0   Kilometer   1

0   Mile   1

Fripps
Island

Inlet No 2

LIGHTHOUSE NATURE TRAIL–
HUNTING ISLAND STATE PARK

you'll find showers, and a water fountain with a low basin for the dogs to drink from. This is ideal, since they can't drink the salty seawater. Beyond the restrooms you'll walk through an alternate parking lot. You could park here, but then you'd miss out on the lighthouse. However, the lighthouse area is very populated. If your dogs aren't good with people, park in this lot to avoid the crowds. At the northeast end of this lot, the trail continues on hard-packed sand. You'll follow a tree line on your left, and on the right stands a short sand dune with trees growing out of it as well. This dune is all that separates you from the ocean, and it's low enough to see over. The dogs enjoy the sound of the waves crashing in as much as you do. Near the trails end, you may see a pond to the left (west), depending on water levels. This is freshwater. Do *not* let the dogs swim here; alligators may be present. When the trail ends, you'll be standing on the shore alongside the glorious ocean. The beach here is far less populated than near the lighthouse. The dogs can swim, run, dig, frolic, and play at will. They'll scamper on the soft sand, with

The two-toned lighthouse at Hunting Island towers over the trail.

Dogs are allowed on the beach at Hunting Island, as long as they remain on a leash.

If you time it right, you can watch sea turtles nesting on the beach at Hunting Island.

the energy of a puppy. The park has a fabulous campground. If you spend the night, you can enjoy stunning sunrises in the morning. Then, finish the day with dazzling sunsets over the many acres of marshland also present in the park.

Miles and Directions

0.0 Hike north along the grass on the east side of the Hunting Island Lighthouse.

<0.1 At the northwest corner of the lighthouse, follow the sidewalk northeast past the restrooms. Walk through an alternate parking lot.

0.15 At the northeast end of the alternate parking lot, the hard-packed sand trail leads northeast between a tree line and a small sand dune.

0.4 The trail ends at the beach (N32 22.767'/W80 26.073'). Backtrack to the trailhead.

0.8 Arrive at the trailhead.

Resting up

Days Inn, 1660 S. Ribaut Rd., Port Royal, (843) 524-1551; pet fee required.
City Loft Hotel, 301 Carteret St., Beaufort, (843) 379-5638; pet fee required.

Camping

Onsite.

Fueling up

Shrimp Shack, 1925 Sea Island Pkwy., Saint Helena Island, (843) 838-2962.
Johnson Creek Tavern, 2141 Sea Island Pkwy., Saint Helena Island, (843) 838-4166.

Puppy Paws and Golden Years

Visit the park's lighthouse, and then take them less than 0.1 mile to the beach.

Charleston

4 Spanish Mount Trail—Edisto Island State Park

The Spanish Mount Trail is the longest in the park, and leads you deep within a marvelous maritime forest. Impressive oak trees enhance the scenery, while an abundance of palmettos grace the understory. Sheer and utter peace awaits. Hiking along the wooded pathway, you'll hear nothing but nature and the pitter patter of your puppy's paws. At trail's end, you'll find an ancient shell mound whose origins remain a mystery.

Start: 8377 State Cabin Rd., Edisto Island; at the northeast end of the parking lot
Distance: 3.6 miles out and back
Hiking time: About 1 hour, 45 minutes
Blaze color: Red arrows
Difficulty: Easy
Trailhead elevation: 62 feet
Highest point: 62 feet
Best season: Year-round
Schedule: 8 a.m. to 6 p.m. (extended during Daylight Saving Time)
Trail surface: Hard-packed dirt
Other trail users: Mountain bikers

Canine compatibility: Leash required
Land status: South Carolina Department of Natural Resources
Fees: Fee required
Maps: *DeLorme: North Carolina Atlas & Gazetteer:* Page 60, G2
Trail contacts: (843) 869-2156; www.south carolinaparks.com/edistobeach/introduction .aspx
Nearest town: Edisto Beach, Edisto Island
Trail tips: The trail is shaded; bring lots of water for you and the pups.

Finding the trailhead: From the junction of SC 174 and US 17 in Osborn, drive south on SC 174 for 20.9 miles to a right onto State Cabin Road at the entrance to the park. Drive 0.15 mile to the office and park across the street in the parking lot for the Spanish Mount Trail.

Note: At 2.5 miles, stay right, continuing to follow SC 174 south. **Trailhead GPS:** N32 30.702'/ W80 18.164'

The Hike

A number of trails intersect the Spanish Mount Trail from the right and left. Ignore them all, staying with the red blazes. The trail system is very well marked, and this enjoyable stroll is among my favorites. The wide and well-groomed path leads through a high canopy of trees. The surface is flat, smooth, and perfect for trail running too. As you explore this marvelous maritime forest, you'll hear the constant buzz of crickets, chirping birds, and a breeze blowing through the trees: nature at its best, along with the panting of your pups, and your own footsteps. The air is clean, crisp,

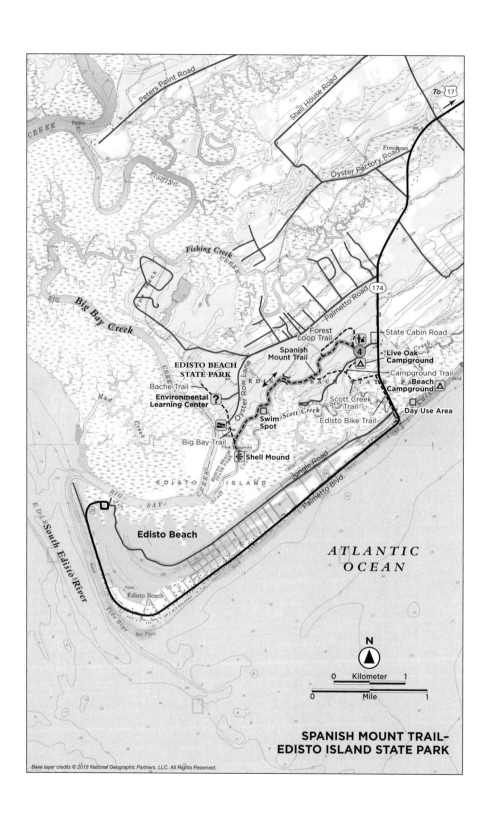

CREEK

Peters Point Road

Shell House Road

To 17

Peters Pt.

FISHING

Oyster Factory Road

Freedman

CREEK

Fishing Creek

BIG

Big Bay Creek

The Neck

Palmetto Road

174

Forest
Loop Trail

State Cabin Road

Spanish
Mount Trail

Live Oak
Campground

EDISTO BEACH
STATE PARK

Campground Trail

Bache Trail

Oyster Row Lane

Beach
Campground

Environmental
Learning Center

?

Scott Creek
Trail

Swim
Spot

Scott Creek

Day Use Area

Edisto Bike Trail

Mud

Creek

Big Bay Trail

Shell Mound

ED

S

O

ISLAND

Jungle Road

Palmetto Blvd.

BIG

BAY

ATLANTIC
OCEAN

Edisto Beach

South Edisto River

Edisto Beach

Tide Rips

Bay Point

N

0   Kilometer   1

0   Mile   1

**SPANISH MOUNT TRAIL–
EDISTO ISLAND STATE PARK**

A variety of wildlife can be found along the coast of South Carolina.

and peaceful. No signs of civilization, no traffic, horns, or airplanes—just you and nature. The farther you hike, the closer you get to Scott Creek. But there are no water stops for the dogs, so bring enough water for you and your happy hounds. The trail is mostly shaded, and brings you alongside a muddy, pluff-filled marshy area. Pluff is a type of shoe-sucking mud unique to the South Carolina lowcountry. At low tide, it can have a distinct, unpleasant odor. So don't blame it on the dog. Impressive oak trees enhance the scenery. As their large limbs branch out, an abundance of palmettos grace the understory. The closer you get to the end, the more the breeze picks up. At 1.3 miles, take the side trail to a lovely picnic spot alongside Scott Creek. Fiddler crabs scurry, running for cover in the cracked muddy banks of the creek. Please have the dogs tread lightly; this is their home. Beyond the picnic site, the trail parallels Scott Creek, but you can't see the water. A thicket of saw palmetto stands between you and the waterway, until you reach trail's end and get the grandest view of Scott Creek. A placard explains the mystery of the shell mound, and an observation deck give you a good viewing point. This shell mound is thousands of years old, and its exact origin is unknown. Edisto Island has a great oceanfront campground, the beach is lined with seashells, and birdlife is abundant. There's a paved bike path, volleyball, picnic areas, playgrounds, and of course . . . the beach! Swim, fish, collect shells, bird watch, bike, run, walk, or wade. Take a river cruise, kayak tour the salt marsh, or rent a fishing charter on the Atlantic. The aquatic opportunities are endless.

Miles and Directions

0.0 Hike north into the forest.

<0.1 Come to a fork. The blue-blazed Forest Loop Trail leads right (north). Go left, following the Spanish Mount Trail west.

0.4 Come to a second fork. The Forest Loop Trail leads right (north). Continue hiking forward (west).

Grand views of Scott Creek greet you as you hike.

Option: Shorten the hike to 1.0 mile by following the Forest Loop Trail and returning to the trailhead.

0.6 Come to a fork. The Scott Creek Trail heads left (south). Continue straight (west).

0.9 Cross a footbridge over a marshy area.

1.3 A side path leads 100 feet to a picnic spot near Scott Creek (N32 30.286'/W80 19.034'). Return to the trail; continue southwest.

1.7 Come to a fork. The Big Bay Trail goes right (north). Follow the Spanish Mount Trail left (south).

1.8 Arrive at the shell mound along Scott Creek (N32 29.953'/W80 19.224'). The banks are high, so the dogs can't swim here. Backtrack to the trailhead.

3.6 Arrive at the trailhead.

Resting up

Sleep Inn, 3043 Hiers Corner Rd., Walterboro, (843) 539-1199; pet fee required.
Best Western, 1428 Sniders Hwy., Walterboro, (843) 538-3600; pet fee required.

Camping

Onsite.

Fueling up

McConky's Jungle Shack, 108 Jungle Rd., Edisto Beach, (843) 869-0097.
Seacow Eatery, 145 Jungle Rd., Edisto Island, (843) 869-3222.

Puppy Paws and Golden Years

Bring the pups to the park's day use area where they can romp in the sand and toil with the ocean waves.

5 History Trail–Charles Towne Landing State Historic Site

What a treat! The people of Charleston are fortunate to have this lovely park in their backyards. The paved path takes you back through time, exploring exhibits that date back to the 17th century. A variety of trees offer shade, and the dogs love sniffing around the grass lining the pathway. A gentle breeze from Oldtown Creek adds the final touch, and you can see why this hike makes the Author's Favorites list.

Start: 1500 Old Towne Rd., Charleston; begin on the northeast side of the visitor center
Distance: 1.5-mile loop
Hiking time: About 1 hour, 30 minutes
Blaze color: None
Difficulty: Easy
Trailhead elevation: Sea level
Highest point: Sea level
Best season: Year-round
Schedule: 9 a.m. to 5 p.m.; closed Christmas Eve and Day
Trail surface: Paved path
Other trail users: Bicycles
Canine compatibility: Leash required
Land status: South Carolina Department of Natural Resources

Fees: Fee required
Maps: *DeLorme: South Carolina Atlas & Gazetteer:* Page 61, B6
Trail contacts: (843) 852-4200; www.south carolinaparks.com/ctl/introduction.aspx
Nearest town: Charleston
Trail tips: Bring lots of water for you and the dogs. A trash can and doggy waste bags are near the trailhead. Try to get the puppies to poop before hiking. Trash cans are few and far between. A water fountain sits at 0.2 mile, and restrooms near 0.3 mile.
Special considerations: Alligators inhabit the park ponds. *Do not* let the dogs in or around the water.

Finding the trailhead: From I-26 in North Charleston get off at exit 216A (Cosgrove Road). Cosgrove Road leads to SC 7 South (Sam Rittenburg Blvd.). Follow SC 7 south for 1.8 miles and bear left onto SC 171 (to Folly Beach). Travel on SC 171 (Old Towne Road) for 0.5 mile to the park on the left. Follow the signs to the visitor center.

From the junction of SC 171 (Old Towne Road) and SC 61 in Charleston, drive north on SC 171 for 1.0 mile to the park on the right. Follow directions above. **Trailhead GPS:** N32 48.423'/W79 59.208'

The Hike

Sitting in the center of Charleston, you'll find the fabulous Charles Towne Landing. This large historic site encompasses nearly 700 acres, and sits across the Ashley River from the world famous Citadel. Driving through the park, it's hard to believe that you're in the sprawling city of Charleston. Tall trees canopy the roadway, like you're driving through a perfect little forest. If you arrive before or after hours, you can enter through a gate on the east side of the visitor center, but you'll miss out on the opportunity to rent a headset. The park offers headsets for a nominal fee, enabling you to

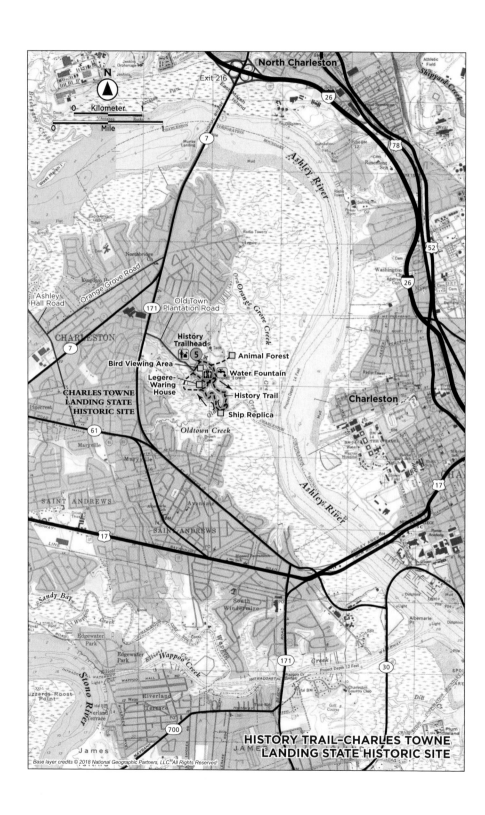

N

0   Kilometer   1

0   Mile

North Charleston

Exit 216

Ashley River

CHARLES TOWNE LANDING STATE HISTORIC SITE

CHARLESTON

Ashley Hall Road

Orange Grove Road

Old Town Plantation Road

History Trailhead

Bird Viewing Area

Legere-Waring House

Animal Forest

Water Fountain

History Trail

Ship Replica

Oldtown Creek

Orange Grove Creek

Charleston

SAINT ANDREWS

SAINT ANDREWS

Maryville

Avondale

Sandy Bay

Edgewater Park

Wappoo Creek

Stono River

Riverland Terrace

James

South Windermire

Creek

Charleston Country Club

HISTORY TRAIL–CHARLES TOWNE LANDING STATE HISTORIC SITE

Charles Towne Landing is fun for all ages.

take an audio tour as you hike. This may not sound thrilling, but the audio tour adds a wealth of knowledge. Placards also educate you on the many exhibits found here. It's easy to see why locals flock to this park. The well-marked paved path forms a figure eight, and birds serenade you over the length of the hike. Grass lines the pavement, and there are plenty of scents to keep the dogs entertained. Oak and magnolia trees offer some shade, but it's best to hike early or late in the day, when it's a bit cooler. Randomly placed benches give you a place to sit and enjoy the tranquility. The farther you go the closer you get to the water, and a lovely breeze picks up. You'll hike past stockades, a fort, and cannons that are fired monthly just for show. Near the halfway mark, you'll reach the *Adventure*, an amazing replica of a 17th-century sailing ship. Tours are available, but no dogs are allowed in this portion of the park. You'll also have to skip the park's Animal Forest. Bison, bobcats, and black bears are among the animals housed here, and dogs are *not* allowed. Beyond the ship, an elevated boardwalk takes you over the marsh, where wading birds and vast views greet you. You'll see glorious gardens hiking past the Legere-Waring House, and the trail ends back at the visitor center. You can shortcut through the building with the dogs, or double the length of the hike by backtracking to the trailhead.

Miles and Directions

0.0 Hike southeast into the park.

0.1 Come to a fork. Left leads northeast to the Animal Forest. Stay right, following the paved path south.

0.27 Arrive at a large roundabout. Go left (south) following the roundabout for about 200 feet.

0.31 Go left (south), off of the roundabout toward the fort.

Option: Shorten the hike by cutting west across the roundabout.

0.36 Reach a fork at the "Palisade Wall" (N32 48.214'/W79 59.051'). Go left (southeast) alongside the wall.

Above: The park hosts monthly live cannon firings.
Below left: You'll hike past the Adventure, *a replica of a 17th-century ship.*
Below right: An exhibit along the path shows how the Adventure *trading vessel was built.*

0.41 Enter the fort; continue following the paved path.

0.6 Near post #11, arrive at a small roundabout. Go left, following Old Towne Creek.

0.65 Head left off of the roundabout, following the pavement west.

0.7 Arrive at the *Adventure* (N32 48.048'/W79 59.004'). Continue hiking west.

0.75 Cross a footbridge over the marsh; continue hiking north.

1.1 Come to a T. Left (west) is the English Garden Trail. Go right (east) on the paved History Trail.

Option: Follow the English Garden Trail. It loops back onto the History Trail beyond the Legere-Waring House.

1.13 Hike past the Legere-Waring House (N32 48.218'/W79 59.157').

1.18 Bypass the restrooms. Continue hiking forward (northwest) on the History Trail.

1.22 The trail leads past a pond. Alligator alert–do *not* let the dogs swim here.

1.35 Hike past an iron gate and come to an intersection. Left (west) is the English Garden Trail. Straight leads north toward the park exit. Go right (east) on the narrow path toward the visitor center.

1.42 Bypass a trail to the right, leading to the bird viewing area (N32 48.382'/W79 59.205'). Hike northeast toward the visitor center.

1.5 Arrive at the visitor center. Walk through the building to the trailhead.

Option: Double the hike distance by backtracking to the trailhead.

Resting up

La Quinta Inn and Suites, 11 Ashley Pointe Dr., Charleston, (843) 556-5200; no pet fee.

Holiday Inn Express, 250 Spring St., Charleston, (800) 315-2621; pet fee required, must call ahead.

Camping

James Island County Park, 871 Riverland Dr., Charleston, (864) 795-4386.

Fueling up

Fuel Charleston, 211 Rutledge Ave., (843) 737-5959.

Blue Rose Cafe, 652 St. Andrews Blvd., Charleston, (843) 225-2583.

Puppy Paws and Golden Years

Stroll around near the visitor center, or visit the bird viewing area.

North Charleston

6 Colonial Dorchester Walking Tour Trail–Colonial Dorchester State Historic Site

This unique hike takes you back in time, exploring the remains of a bustling riverfront town. From tannery to tavern, seamstress to schoolhouse, Dorchester was a thriving 18th-century pre-war town. Walking from one exhibit to the next, follow along with the park's interpretive brochure. While you educate yourself on colonial history, the dogs enjoy a pleasant stroll in the park.

Start: 300 State Park Rd., Summerville; at the east end of the parking lot near the information kiosk
Distance: 0.6-mile loop
Hiking time: About 20 minutes
Blaze color: None
Difficulty: Easy
Trailhead elevation: 86 feet
Highest point: 116 feet
Best season: Year-round
Schedule: 9 a.m. to 5 p.m. (9 a.m. to 6 p.m. during Daylight Saving Time)
Trail surface: Grass
Other trail users: None
Canine compatibility: Leash required

Land status: South Carolina Department of Natural Resources
Fees: Fee required
Maps: *DeLorme: South Carolina Atlas & Gazetteer:* Page 55, G8
Trail contacts: (843) 873-1740; www.south carolinaparks.com/colonialdorchester/introduction.aspx
Nearest town: Summerville, North Charleston
Trail tips: Restrooms and a picnic area are near the trailhead. Before you visit, print the self-guided walking tour brochure from the link on the park's website.
Special considerations: Alligators may be present in the Ashley River; use caution with the dogs near the banks.

Finding the trailhead: From I-526 in North Charleston, get off at exit 15 and travel north on SC 642 for 11.8 miles to a left onto State Park Road. Travel for 0.3 mile to the end of the road.

From the junction of SC 642 (Dorchester Road) and SC 165 (Bacons Bridge Road) in Summerville, drive east on SC 642 for 1.9 miles to a right onto State Park Road. Follow directions above.
Trailhead GPS: N32 56.890'/W80 10.159'

The Hike

Within easy reach of Charleston, you'll find the peaceful Colonial Dorchester State Historic Site. The park proudly sits upon the registry of National Historic Places, and as you delve into the details, you'll see why. Hundreds of years ago, Dorchester was a bustling hub of trade and commerce. Today, only remnants of the town remain. Hiking

A model exhibit near the trailhead shows what the town of Dorchester once was.

around the property is a pleasant walk in the park for the dogs. Lush grass, squirrels, birds, and raccoons gain their interest. But for you, it's the educational and historical significance that keeps you entertained. Before you visit, go online and print the self-guided tour brochure to enjoy the full experience. (They may have some copies at the trailhead, but sometimes they run out.) The "trail" follows alphabetical exhibits on a clockwise loop around the park. Each lettered post has a story behind it. Perhaps the most important is exhibit A, a mini-replica of the town. This acts as a visual aid, showing you how industrious this riverfront town was. At B, you'll reach the river. At low tide you can view the tattered timber remains of the wharf. Merchants sold their wares here, while ships came and went. Use caution near the banks; alligators inhabit the Ashley River. Moving away from the water, you'll hike through the tabby fort, which was built in the mid-1700s, as was St. George's Bell Tower. Remarkably, both survived the Revolutionary War, and endured a 7.0 earthquake in 1886. You can see the oyster shells mixed in with mud and stucco to form the fort walls. Placards add information not found on the tour brochure. You'll pass an excavation site, where archaeologists continue to find artifacts from colonial times. The park offers educational programs, where you can learn about the excavation process here at the dig site. The faded brick remains of St. George's Monument is a highlight. An old cemetery stands out nearly as much as the tower does. Some

Raccoons are typically nocturnal, but you may get lucky and see one in the daytime too.

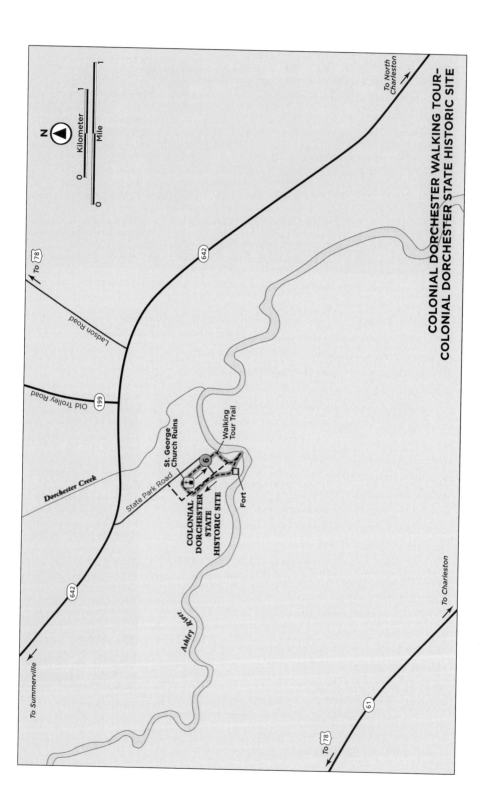

COLONIAL DORCHESTER WALKING TOUR–
COLONIAL DORCHESTER STATE HISTORIC SITE

stones leaning, some stones cracked, here lies the remains of four generations of residents who prospered here hundreds of years ago. A self-guided tour of the cemetery is also available by printing a separate online brochure. All in all, it's a peaceful hike, with plenty of shade, lush green grass, and a steady breeze blowing off the river.

Miles and Directions

0.0 Hike south across the grass toward the Ashley River.

100' Arrive at exhibit A, a mini-replica of Dorchester. Continue hiking south toward the river.

0.05 Exhibit B; at low tide you can see the remains of the wharf. Go right, following the shoreline southwest.

0.13 Come to a fork. Left leads 0.05 mile to the river. Enjoy the view, then head right (north) toward the fort and pass by exhibit C.

0.26 Enter the fort at the southeast corner, then exit on the north side. Follow the posts in the grass generally north.

0.32 Exhibit D, the brick remnants of an old structure. Follow the posts and placards north toward exhibit E. Hike northwest on the gravel road.

0.42 When you reach exhibit F, the gravel road continues straight (northwest). Go right (northeast) here, following the tree line along the grass toward exhibit G.

0.47 When you reach exhibit G, go right (southeast) following the grassy path between the cemetery and St. George's Bell Tower. Both date back to the 1700s. Continue hiking southeast.

0.52 Arrive at exhibit H, gaining more insight on the church ruins. Continue hiking southeast.

0.54 Exhibit I; continue hiking southeast.

0.6 Arrive at the trailhead.

Resting up

Wyndham Garden, 120 Holiday Dr., Summerville, (843) 875-3300; pet fee required.
Econo Lodge, 110 Holiday Dr., Summerville, (843) 875-3022; pet fee required.

Camping

Givhans Ferry State Park, 746 Givhans Ferry Rd., Ridgeville, (843) 873-0692.

Fueling up

Dog and Duck, 1580 Old Trolley Rd., Summerville, (843) 821-3056.
Montreux Bar and Grill, 127 W. Richardson Ave., Summerville, (843) 264-1200.

Puppy Paws and Golden Years

If they can't hike the full loop, simply stroll along the river's edge, or pop in to get a closer look at the bell tower.

Walterboro

7 River Bluff Trail–Givhans Ferry State Park

Popular with the locals, this quaint state park offers swimming, paddling, picnicking, volleyball, and camping. As for hiking, the River Bluff Trail is designed as an out-and-back, but I like making a loop along the park road. The road is lined with grass, so you can keep the pups away from traffic, and a steady breeze almost always greets you. But most importantly, this route leads past the park's amazing swim area. Dogs are allowed, and it's not to be missed.

Start: 746 Givhans Ferry Rd., Ridgeville; The trailhead is due north of the sand volleyball court, on the north side of the road between the Overlook and Magnolia shelters.
Distance: 1.6-mile loop
Hiking time: About 50 minutes
Blaze color: Green arrows
Difficulty: Easy
Trailhead elevation: 70 feet
Highest point: 82 feet
Best season: Year-round
Schedule: Apr–Sept 9 a.m. to 9 p.m.; mid Sept-Oct, Mon–Thurs 9 a.m. to 6 p.m., Fri–Sun 9 a.m. to 9 p.m.; Nov–Mar 9 a.m. to 6 p.m.
Trail surface: Hard-packed dirt, grass
Other trail users: None on the trail, but cars and bicycles use the park road

Canine compatibility: Leash required
Land status: South Carolina Department of Natural Resources
Fees: Fee required
Maps: *DeLorme: South Carolina Atlas & Gazetteer:* Page 54, F5
Trail contacts: (843) 873-0692; www.south carolinaparks.com/givhansferry/introduction .aspx
Nearest town: Walterboro, St. George, Summerville
Trail tips: There's a water fountain near the trailhead at the Magnolia Shelter. Bring lots of drinking water for you and the dogs. Apply bug spray in summertime.
Special considerations: Alligators do inhabit the Edisto River; use caution with the dogs.

Finding the trailhead: From I-95, get off at exit 68 (Canadys exit/SC 61) and follow SC 61 east for 17.2 miles to a left onto Givhans Ferry Road (SR 30). Travel for 0.1 mile to the park on your left. Follow the park road for 0.6 mile to the end and park near the Magnolia Shelter.
From the junction of SC 61 and SC 27 in Givhans, drive west on SC 61 for 3.0 miles to a right onto Givhans Ferry Road. Follow directions above. **Trailhead GPS:** N33 01.964'/W80 23.182'

The Hike

Givhans Ferry State Park is best known for the long-running Edisto River. This rustic river covers a full 250 miles and borders the western edge of the park. But that's just one perk of this pleasant park. They also have large open play fields, volleyball, picnic shelters, cabins, and a campground. On the east side of Givhans Ferry Road,

Portions of the River Bluff Trail are wide enough to hike two by two.

RIVER BLUFF TRAIL–GIVHANS FERRY STATE PARK

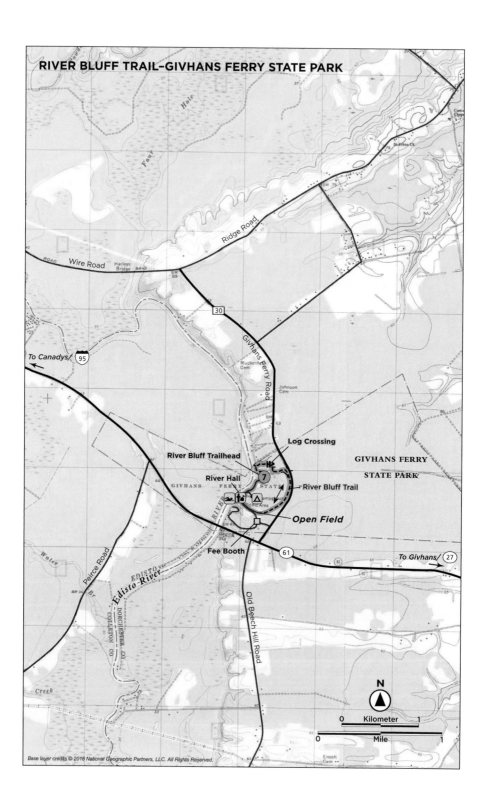

the Old Loop Trail follows a service road for 5 miles. It's open to hikers, mountain bikes, and equestrian use seasonally. But for strictly hiking, the River Bluff Trail is it. This forested path leads you up and down some fairly steep slopes, which is surprising this far south in the coastal region. Within 0.1 mile, you'll be standing high on a limestone bluff above the Edisto River. People travel from miles around to paddle here. Following the winding waterway by land, you'll come to a narrow creek. You can hear the creek well before you see it rushing down the steep banks into the river. Foam gathers on the surface, covering the narrow creek as you follow it upstream. Moving away from the sudsy water, you leave the sound of it behind as well. That sound is soon replaced with the jovial voices of visitors off in the distance, especially on weekends. But if you hike during the week, you may have the park to yourself, except in summertime. A small ravine adds diversity, and the trees keep you shaded, even at high noon. Birds chirp and sing in the background, and woodpeckers rapidly knock against the pines. After cross-

The South Carolina flag proudly presents a palmetto tree under the crescent moon.

ing the ravine, the path widens, and parallels Givhans Ferry Road. The trail officially ends at an open field near the fee booth. You could backtrack from here, but I like to make a loop instead. I don't often recommend hiking alongside the road, but this is an exception. The park is lovely, and the park road is lined with grass, so you can keep the dogs away from traffic. There's almost always a steady breeze, and this route leads past the swim area, which sits below the River Hall building and is a must see. A low stone wall separates a large grassy area from the sandy "beach" along the river. It gives you the best of both worlds. You can picnic on the grass, sunbathe on the sand, or swim in the river. Your playful pups will love splashing around in the water. It's certainly a highlight of this hike. Continuing past the River Hall leads back to the trailhead.

Miles and Directions

0.0 Hike north into the forest through an opening in the split rail fence.

0.15 Come to a fork. Left leads north toward the river where a tributary flows into it. Go right (east), following the tributary upstream.

0.25 Cross a log over a wet weather area. The trail bends right (south) away from the tributary.

0.45 Cross a footbridge over a ravine. Continue hiking south.

0.9 The River Bluff Trail ends at an open field (N33 01.732'/W80 23.185'). Hike west across the field toward the road.

Option: Backtrack to the trailhead from here to make this a 1.8 mile hike.

0.95 When you reach the park road, go right (northwest) toward the trailhead.

1.15 Arrive at the River Hall/Park Office (N33 01.822'/W80 23.365'). Go left, following the side street south and downhill toward the river.

1.25 Arrive at the swim area (N33 01.829'/W80 23.416'). Backtrack to the River Hall.

1.35 Arrive back at the River Hall. Go left (north), following the park road toward the trailhead.

1.6 Arrive at the trailhead.

Resting up

Country Inn and Suites, 220 Holiday Dr., Summerville, (843) 285-9000; pet fee required.
Wyndham Garden, 120 Holiday Dr., Summerville, (843) 875-3300; pet fee required.

Camping

Onsite.

Fueling up

Dog and Duck, 1580 Old Trolley Rd., Summerville, (843) 821-3056.
Montreux Bar and Grill, 127 W. Richardson Ave., Summerville, (843) 264-1200.

Puppy Paws and Golden Years

Park closer to the swim area, and take the pups directly there.

Dogs and people alike will love the swim area at Givhans Ferry.

8 Cypress Swamp Nature Trail–Colleton State Park

Although it's short, this hike offers unique insight into the life and diversity of the park's cypress swamp. Following along with the brochure for this interpretive trail, you'll realize how amazing this damp forest truly is. You'll appreciate long-range views of the peaceful Edisto River and then hike near a stand of mighty cypress trees. Enjoy the shade as the branches and boughs stretch far overhead.

Start: 147 Wayside Ln., Walterboro; on the north side of the road, northwest of the Park Office/Resource Center, across from the picnic area

Distance: 0.4-mile loop

Hiking time: About 15 minutes

Blaze color: Posts with arrows on them

Difficulty: Easy

Trailhead elevation: 123 feet

Highest point: 138 feet

Best season: Year-round

Schedule: 9 a.m. to 6 p.m. (extended to 9 p.m. during Daylight Saving Time)

Trail surface: Hard-packed dirt

Other trail users: None

Canine compatibility: Leash required

Land status: South Carolina Department of Natural Resources

Fees: No fee

Maps: *DeLorme: South Carolina Atlas & Gazetteer:* Page 54, E2

Trail contacts: (843) 538-8206; www.south carolinaparks.com/colleton/introduction.aspx

Nearest town: Walterboro, St. George

Trail tips: Trail maps and interpretive brochures are at the trailhead. Apply bug spray in summertime.

Special considerations: Alligators do inhabit the Edisto River. Use caution with the dogs near the banks.

Finding the trailhead: From I-95 near Walterboro, get off at exit 68 (SC 61). Follow SC 61 south for 2.8 miles to a left onto US 15. Follow US 15 north for 0.3 mile to a left onto Wayside Lane. Travel 0.1 mile to the Park Office/Resource Center. Pass the office, make a U-turn, and park near the trailhead on the north side of the road. **Trailhead GPS:** N33 03.773'/W80 36.949'

The Hike

Covering a mere 35 acres, Colleton State Park is slight in size, but quite enjoyable. A picnic area, campground, swing sets, volleyball, and an open field are among the activities available. But the spectacular Edisto River is the highlight here. The river begins well into the Piedmont and covers 250 miles, making it the longest free-flowing blackwater river in North America. The term *blackwater* doesn't mean the water itself is black. As a matter of fact, it's quite clear. It's simply stained by the brown tannins from all the leaves that have fallen into the water. If you look at the surface, it may appear dark, but scoop it up, and you'll see how clear it really is. You'll get a firsthand look at this wonderful waterway when you head out on the Cypress Swamp Nature Trail. First, pick up a brochure at the trailhead, since it's an interpretive trail with numbered posts along the way. Following along with the brochure gives insight

Pick up a brochure at the trailhead and follow along as you hike.

into the flora that's found here. The posts are not in numerical order, but with the brochure in hand, it's easy enough to educate yourself as you hike. The trail begins amid a dry forested high ground. Tall trees and a thick underbrush line the path. But the closer you get to the river, the damper the area becomes. A variety of birds keep you company, and in the background you'll hear voices of campers and kids playing in the playground. When you reach the canoe dock, you'll see why they call it "black-water." The reflection of the clouds and sky on the water is stunning, and a gentle breeze chimes in. Although this is a popular paddling spot, the park doesn't rent canoes or kayaks. You can bring your own though, or rent one from across the river at Carolina Heritage Outfitters. Exploring the park's cypress swamp, you'll find enormous cypress trees with their wide trunks and "knees" protruding up from the damp ground below. Lush green hues line the path as a variety of ferns join the cypress. But the flora is not limited to ferns and cypress. On the contrary, there's an amazing amount of diversity for such a short hike. Hardwoods like maple, oak, and poplar are mixed in with hickory, birch, and sweet-scented magnolia. It's a magnificent mix. A

Left: A variety of birdlife inhabits Colleton State Park.
Right: A large American alligator suns himself on a log along the Edisto River.

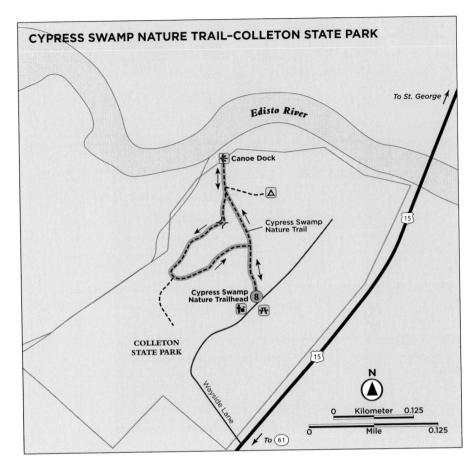

CYPRESS SWAMP NATURE TRAIL–COLLETON STATE PARK

Edisto River

To St. George

Canoe Dock

Cypress Swamp
Nature Trail

15

Cypress Swamp
Nature Trailhead (8)

COLLETON
STATE PARK

15

Wayside Lane

To (61)

N

0   Kilometer   0.125

0   Mile   0.125

wide variety of birds are drawn to this forest, and you'll hear them singing during the hike. You may also spy deer, raccoons, and if you're very lucky, river otters. The only downside of this hike is that it can be a bit buggy in the summertime.

Miles and Directions

0.0 Hike north into the forest.

0.05 Come to a fork near interpretive post #13. Left (west) is where the loop ends. Go straight (north), toward the canoe dock and river.

0.1 Come to an intersection. Right is a social trail leading east toward the campground. Left (southwest) is the continuation of the Cypress Swamp Nature Trail. Go straight (north) as you take a detour to the canoe dock.

0.13 Arrive at the canoe dock alongside the river (N33 03.879'/W80 36.977'). Backtrack to the intersection.

0.16 Arrive back at the intersection. Follow the Cypress Swamp Nature Trail southwest.

0.21 Cross a footbridge. Continue hiking southwest.

0.27 Come to a fork. Right leads west to an open field. Go left (southeast) looping back toward the trailhead.

The Edisto River covers over 250 miles as it winds across the state.

0.35 Arrive at the fork from 0.05 mile. Go right (south), backtracking to the trailhead.

0.4 Arrive at the trailhead.

Resting up

Sleep Inn, 3043 Hiers Corner Rd., Walterboro, (843) 539-1199; pet fee required.
Best Western, 1428 Sniders Hwy., Walterboro, (843) 538-3600; pet fee required.

Camping

Onsite.

Fueling up

Dog and Duck, 1580 Old Trolley Rd., Summerville, (843) 821-3056.
Montreux Bar and Grill, 127 W. Richardson Ave., Summerville, (843) 264-1200.

Puppy Paws and Golden Years

If 0.4 mile is too long for your pups, hike out to the canoe dock and back.

9 Awendaw Passage–Francis Marion National Forest

This rustic hike is one of the longest in this region, and far less traveled. It begins at Buck Hall Recreation Area, on the eastern edge of Francis Marion National Forest. Pine trees and palmettos offer plenty of shade, but there are no swim spots for the dogs. Make sure you bring *lots* of water so you and the pups can stay hydrated. A light breeze helps keep you cool, and the long-range views are spectacular.

Start: Buck Hall Recreation Area; at the southeast end of the recreation area
Distance: 6.6 miles out and back
Hiking time: About 3 hours, 20 minutes
Blaze color: White
Difficulty: Easy
Trailhead elevation: Sea level
Highest point: 29 feet
Best season: Year-round
Trail surface: Hard-packed dirt
Other trail users: Mountain bikers
Canine compatibility: Voice control, but leashes are requested by the Forest Service
Land status: Francis Marion National Forest
Fees: Fee required

Maps: *DeLorme: North Carolina Atlas & Gazetteer:* Page 56, F5
Trail contacts: (843) 336-3248; www.fs .usda.gov/recarea/scnfs/recreation/hiking/ recarea/?recid=47313&actid=50; www .palmettoconservation.org/passage/ awendaw-passage/
Nearest town: Awendaw, McClellanville
Trail tips: Bathrooms, water fountain, and trash cans are at Buck Hall Campground. Bring lots of drinking water for you and the dogs.
Special considerations: Alligators may be present in Awendaw Creek. Use caution near the water.

Finding the trailhead: From the junction of US 17 and SC 41 near Whitehall Terrace, drive north on US 17 for 19.8 miles to a right onto Buck Hall Landing Road (FR 242). Travel for 0.5 mile to the stop sign. Get your pass, and drive south 0.1 mile to a second stop sign. Go left toward the picnic area, and drive less than 0.1 mile to the parking loop at the end of the road.

From the junction of US 17 and SC 45 in McClellanville, drive south on US 17 for 6.2 miles to a left onto Buck Hall Landing Road (FR 242). Follow directions above. **Trailhead GPS:** N33 02.384'/W79 33.639'

The Hike

Stretching across the length of the state, from the coast to the mountains, you'll find the proud Palmetto Trail. The trail is made up of many shorter sections known as "passages." Some people pop in for a day hike, while others spend weeks on the trail. Hiking from south to north, the Awendaw Passage is the first you'll find. The full length of this passage is 14 miles round-trip, but that's a little excessive for the dogs.

Left: You'll cross several footbridges on the Awendaw portion of the Palmetto Trail.
Right: Take advantage of the shady spots to help keep the dogs cool in summertime.

I've highlighted a nice portion of the passage and given you a good landmark to use as a turnaround point. Adapt the length to suit your needs. Buck Hall Landing sits along the shores of Bulls Bay, part of Cape Romain National Wildlife Refuge. The refuge is home to nearly 300 species of birds. Black skimmers, American oystercatchers, and the endangered piping plover are among them, as are a variety of wading birds, pelicans, and raptors. I'd say bring your binoculars, but dogs aren't allowed out in the refuge. That's okay; birds are abundant on the trail as well. And that just scratches the surface of wildlife found within the national forest. From beavers to boars, otters to osprey, many species make their home here, although you're more likely to come across deer, raccoon, snakes, turtles, and fiddler crabs. There's an array of wildflowers, so bring your camera. The trail can be a bit buggy in summertime, and there may be ticks too. Bug spray should do the trick, and make sure you pre-medicate the dogs as well. The trail crosses several footbridges, but they aren't over creeks, so the dogs can't cool off in them. Make sure you bring *lots* of drinking water for you both. The trail is well groomed, and mostly shaded, except for high noon. Magnolia, maple, oak, and pine all form this fabulous forest, with an understory of palms, palmetto, and holly, hundreds of years in the making, just waiting for you to explore. Mile markers help you keep track of your progress. A scent of pine fills the air over the first 2 miles, but as you delve deeper, a light breeze and long-range views are the highlight. Passing the 3.0-mile mark, the trail leads you closer to the creek, with less of a grass buffer between you and the water. A lovely picnic spot at 3.3 miles makes a good turnaround.

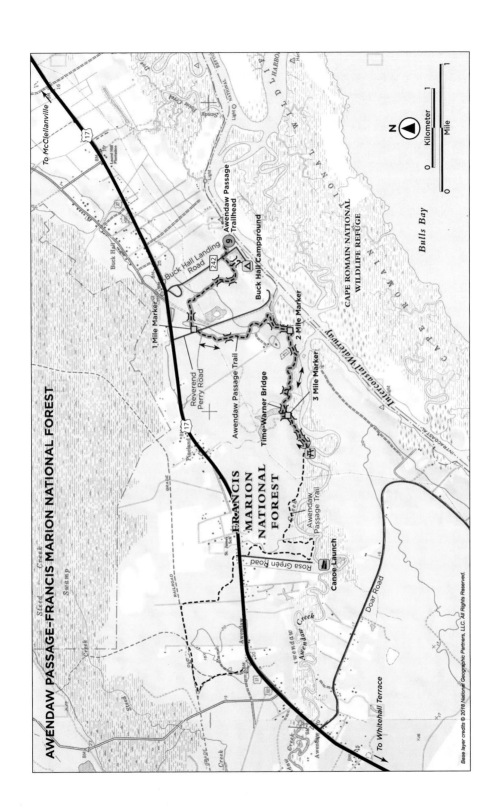

AWENDAW PASSAGE–FRANCIS MARION NATIONAL FOREST

To McClellanville

Steed Creek

Creek

Swamp

Sandy

Buck Hall Creek

17

17

1 Mile Marker

Reverend Perry Road

Awendaw Passage Trail

242

9 Awendaw Passage Trailhead

Buck Hall Landing Road

Buck Hall Campground

Time-Warner Bridge

2 Mile Marker

3 Mile Marker

FRANCIS MARION NATIONAL FOREST

Awendaw Passage Trail

Rosa Green Road

Canoe Launch

Awendaw Creek

Doar Road

To Whitehall Terrace

Intracoastal Waterway

CAPE ROMAIN NATIONAL WILDLIFE REFUGE

Bulls Bay

N

0 Kilometer 1
0 Mile

Miles and Directions

0.0 Hike north on the wooden boardwalk.

0.1 Cross FR 242. Continue hiking into the forest.

0.2 Bypass the trail to your left. It crosses a footbridge south and leads into the campground. Continue straight (west).

0.35 Cross a footbridge. Continue hiking north.

0.45 Cross a footbridge. Continue hiking north.

0.7 Follow the power lines west for about 100 feet and hike back into the forest.

0.75 Come to a fork. Straight is a wide unmanicured trail. Go left (west) on the white-blazed Palmetto Trail.

0.9 Cross a footbridge over a narrow creek; continue hiking northwest.

1.0 Pass the 1-mile marker.

1.04 Hike west across Reverend Perry Road.

1.15 Cross under power lines.

1.3 Cross a footbridge; continue hiking south.

1.9 Cross a bridge over a muddy creek (look for fiddler crabs). Continue hiking west.

1.97 Cross a footbridge; continue hiking south-southwest.

2.0 Pass the 2-mile marker.

2.2 Cross a footbridge; continue hiking west.

2.65 Cross a footbridge; continue hiking west.

2.9 Cross the Time-Warner Bridge.

2.92 Cross a footbridge near a tiny pond.

Long-range views are exquisite along the Awendaw Passage.

Cape Romain National Wildlife Refuge is said to have the largest wintering population of American oystercatchers on the East Coast.

2.97 Cross a footbridge; continue hiking south.

3.0 Pass the 3-mile marker; continue hiking west.

3.2 Cross another footbridge; continue hiking southwest.

3.25 Cross another footbridge; continue hiking southwest.

3.3 Arrive at a lovely picnic spot near the water (N33 01.833'/W79 35.284'). A large oak tree offers plenty of shade. Backtrack to the trailhead.

6.6 Arrive at the trailhead.

Resting up

Hampton Inn, 255 Sessions Way, Mt. Pleasant, (843) 881-3300; no pet fee.
Residence Inn, 1116 Isle of Palms Connector, Mt. Pleasant, (843) 881-1599; pet fee required.

Camping

Onsite.

Fueling up

See Wee Restaurant, 4808 US 17, Awendaw, (843) 928-3609.
The Rusty Rudder, 3563 N. Hwy. 17, Mount Pleasant, (843) 388-3177.

Puppy Paws and Golden Years

The Awendaw Passage is relatively flat and easy terrain. Just shorten the distance to suit your needs.

10 Sandpiper Pond Trail–Huntington Beach State Park

This wide and well-maintained path is surprisingly wooded, considering how close you are to the beach. Rolling hill topography is an added plus, and the farther you go, the louder the sound of the ocean becomes. Viewing platforms give you a glimpse of the Sandpiper Pond, which is much larger in life than it appears on the map. The trail ends at an overlook, where you'll view the full expanse of the pristine pond you just hiked beside.

Start: 16148 Ocean Hwy., Murrells Inlet; on the south side of the park road, across the street from the parking lot

Distance: 2.0 miles out and back

Hiking time: About 1 hour

Blaze color: White

Difficulty: Easy

Trailhead elevation: 14 feet

Highest point: 23 feet

Best season: Year-round

Schedule: Jan 1–Mar 6, 6 a.m. to 6 p.m.; Mar 7–Apr 3 6 a.m. to 8 p.m.; Apr 4–Nov 6 6 a.m. to 10 p.m.; Nov 7–Dec 4 6 a.m. to 8 p.m.; Dec 5–31 6 a.m. to 6 p.m.

Trail surface: Hard-packed dirt, some sandy sections

Other trail users: None

Canine compatibility: Leash required

Land status: South Carolina Department of Natural Resources

Fees: Fee required

Maps: *DeLorme: South Carolina Atlas & Gazetteer:* Page 50, F1

Trail contacts: (843) 237-4440; www.south carolinaparks.com/huntingtonbeach/introduction.aspx

Nearest town: Pawley's Island, Murrells Inlet, Myrtle Beach

Trail tips: Bring lots of drinking water for you and the pups.

Special considerations: The beach sand can be hot in summer. If you need sandals then the dogs need booties too.

Finding the trailhead: From the junction of US 17 and SC 707 in Murrells Inlet, drive south on US 17 for 4.5 miles to the park on your left. Follow the park road for 0.6 mile across the causeway, and then go left. Travel for 0.2 mile to the parking lot on the left next to the Nature/Education Center.

From the junction of US 17 and US 701 in Georgetown, drive north on US 17 for 18.0 miles to the park on your right. Follow directions above. **Trailhead GPS:** N33 30.568'/W79 03.753'

The Hike

From the minute you enter this fabulous state park you'll be impressed with the beauty and diversity that it has to offer. Driving across the causeway gives you spectacular views of the freshwater lagoon to the right and the saltwater marsh to the left,

Left: Be on the lookout as you drive across the causeway at Huntington Beach State Park.
Right: The long-billed curlew is among the largest in the sandpiper family.

two unique habitats. You're likely to spy an alligator sunning itself, a great white egret wading in the water, or an osprey soaring overhead. The park boasts more than 300 bird species. If you're an ornithological enthusiast, print out the bird list, and bring your binoculars. As you begin the hike, you're greeted by a chorus of birdsong, beating to the drum of woodpeckers tapping on the trees. Bright red cardinals chirp, and painted buntings rush by as you hike through the maritime forest. Although they're stunted by the salty air, the trees offer plenty of shade. It's really quite amazing how wooded this portion of the park is, considering you're right next to the ocean. And rolling hill topography adds to the astonishment. As you hike along the wide path, the sound of the ocean joins in with the birds. A few elevated platforms grant you superb views of the Sandpiper Pond. The pond is much bigger than it looks on the map. As you parallel the pond, bypass any side trails that lead toward it. The platforms give you the best view. The trail ends at a sidewalk T. Head right, and you'll come to one final overlook. From here you'll see the full expanse of the pond you just hiked beside. This is certainly a favorite. Plus you can take the pups to the beach at the south end of the park. The dogs will love it, and so will you!

Miles and Directions

0.0 Hike south into the maritime forest.

0.05 Come to a fork. Right leads west toward the campground. Go left (east) on the Sandpiper Pond Trail.

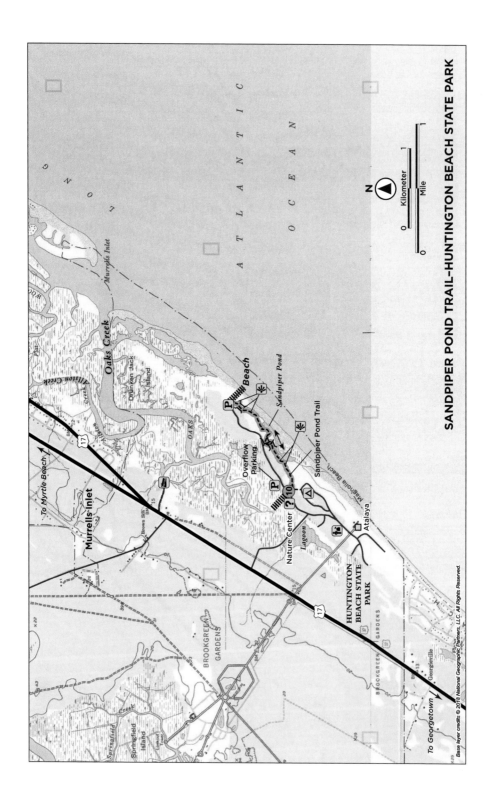

SANDPIPER POND TRAIL–HUNTINGTON BEACH STATE PARK

If you wake up early enough, you'll see a stunning sunrise at Huntington Beach.

0.2 Come to a viewing platform (N33 30.603'/W79 03.539'). Continue hiking northeast.

0.25 Come to a viewing platform (N33 30.635'/W79 03.516'). Continue hiking northeast.

0.4 Come to a T. The trail makes a small loop. Left leads across two footbridges. Right leads to an overlook and then loops back, skipping the first of the two footbridges.

0.85 Come to an overlook (N33 30.842'/W79 03.127'); continue hiking north.

0.9 Come to another overlook (N33 30.884'/W79 03.110'); continue hiking north.

0.95 Cross a footbridge. The trail ends at a sidewalk T. Go right (south).

1.0 Arrive at an overlook (N33 30.925'/W79 03.059'). Backtrack to the trailhead.

2.0 Arrive at the trailhead.

Resting up

Garden City Inn, 1120 Waccamaw Dr., Murrells Inlet, (843) 651-5600; pet fee required.
Motel 6, 7903 Ocean Hwy., Pawleys Island, (843) 237-4261; no pet fee.

Camping

Onsite.

Fueling up

Graham's Landing, 5225 Business Hwy. 17, Murrells Inlet, (843) 947-0520.
The Spotted Dog, 3415 Hwy. 17 South, Murrells Inlet, (843) 652-3116.

Puppy Paws and Golden Years

Take the dogs to the beach at the south end of the park.

11 Yaupon Trail/Sculptured Oak Trail Loop—Myrtle Beach State Park

By combining the Yaupon and Sculptured Oak Trails, you'll make a nice loop through a surprisingly wooded portion of the park. This dense stretch of seaside forest is home to a variety of wildlife. Deer, raccoons, rabbits, and an abundance of birds live within. If you can keep the pups from spooking them off, you may be lucky enough to catch a sighting, especially at dusk and dawn. You'll also find dusk and dawn are perfect to let the dogs play on the beach.

Start: 4401 S. Kings Hwy., Myrtle Beach; just east of Picnic Shelter #B6
Distance: 1.4-mile loop
Hiking time: About 40 minutes
Blaze color: Red—Yaupon Trail, Yellow—Sculptured Oak Trail
Difficulty: Easy
Trailhead elevation: Sea level
Highest point: 4 feet
Best season: Year-round
Schedule: Mar–Nov, 6 a.m. to 10 p.m.; Dec–Feb, 6 a.m. to 8 p.m.
Trail surface: Hard-packed dirt
Other trail users: None
Canine compatibility: Leash required
Land status: South Carolina Department of Natural Resources

Fees: Fee required
Maps: *DeLorme: South Carolina Atlas & Gazetteer:* Page 50, D3
Trail contacts: (843) 238-5325; www.south carolinaparks.com/myrtlebeach/introduction .aspx
Nearest town: Myrtle Beach
Trail tips: Restrooms and trash cans are near the trailhead. Dogs are allowed on the beach from 10 a.m. to 5 p.m. May 1–Labor Day, and anytime during the rest of the year.
Special considerations: The pavement between the trail's end and trailhead may be very hot in summertime. Booties are recommended.

Finding the trailhead: From the junction of US 17 and US 501 in Myrtle Beach, drive south on US 17 for 3.7 miles to the park on the left. Drive 0.5 mile to the fee booth. Continue another 0.3 mile to a fork. Go right and travel less than 0.1 mile to a T. Turn right again, and travel 0.3 mile to the trailhead near Picnic Shelter #B6.

From the junction of US 17 Business and SC 544 in Surfside Beach, drive north on US 17 Business for 1.9 miles to the park on the right. Follow directions above. **Trailhead GPS:** N33 38.780'/W78 55.965'

The Hike

This wonderful hike is among my favorites, and begins by following the Yaupon Trail into the thick forest. It was named for the Yaupon holly (*ilex vomitoria*), which is one of nearly twenty species of holly. The bright red berries it produces provide food for a

Sunrise over the pier at Myrtle Beach is magnificent.

number of birds and mammals during fall and winter. But as the Latin name suggests, you don't want to eat them. The colorful fruit is toxic to dogs and will make a human vomit. This festive flora is suited to the salty air and does well in drought conditions. The Yaupon is joined by a diverse variety of trees. Cherry, oak, sweet gum, tupelo, hickory, and pine all keep company within this coastal patch of forest, and interpretive signs help you identify them. Randomly placed benches give you a place to sit and enjoy the peaceful sounds of nature. You can hear traffic in the distance, but the sweet serenading birdsongs override it. The farther you go on this flat, easy trail, the taller the trees become. This dense forest is home to deer, raccoons, and rabbits, and a wide variety of birds. Loblolly pines with impressive diameters drop pinecones on the path, and flowering dogwood, poplar, and elm add to the diversity. When you reach the Sculptured Oak Trail, follow it out to see the Oak Pond. The pond isn't that impressive, especially when you have the ocean nearby in comparison. But it adds a little distance to the hike. Holly lines the Sculptured Oak Trail, and the trees seem smaller here. You'll exit the forest in the parking lot, about 0.2 mile north of the trailhead.

Miles and Directions

0.0 Hike north into the forest.

0.05 Cross a footbridge; continue hiking north.

0.5 Come to a well-marked intersection. Sculptured Oak leads right (south) toward the park road. Go left on the red-blazed Yaupon Trail.

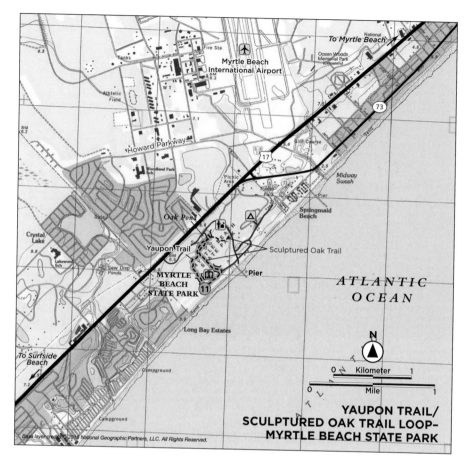

YAUPON TRAIL/
SCULPTURED OAK TRAIL LOOP-
MYRTLE BEACH STATE PARK

0.6 The Yaupon Trail ends at a T with the yellow-blazed Sculptured Oak Trail. Right leads south toward the trailhead. Go left (north) toward the Oak Pond.

0.65 Come to another T. Right (east) is the continuation of the Sculptured Oak Trail leading to an alternate trailhead. Go left (northwest) to the Oak Pond.

0.7 Arrive at the Oak Pond (N33 39.128'/W78 55.947'). Backtrack to the intersection at 0.5 mile.

0.9 Arrive back at the intersection. Go left, following the yellow-blazed Sculptured Oak Trail south toward the park road.

1.2 The trail ends at the park road. Go right, following the road southwest to the trailhead.

1.4 Arrive at the trailhead.

Resting up

La Quinta Inn and Suites, 4709 N. Kings Hwy., Myrtle Beach, (843) 449-5231; pet fee required.

Best Western Plus, 9551 N. Kings Hwy., Myrtle Beach, (843) 213-1440; pet fee required.

Top left: A dog's nose print is just as unique as our fingerprints.
Top right: These brilliant blanket flowers blanket the dunes with color.
Bottom left: Lilies line the roadway as you drive through Myrtle Beach State Park.
Bottom right: Bunny rabbits make their home along the Yaupon Trail.

Camping

Onsite.

Fueling up

Liberty Pub and Grill, 7651 N. Kings Hwy., Myrtle Beach; (843) 839-4677.
8th Ave Tiki, 706 N. Ocean Blvd., Myrtle Beach, (843) 712-2340.

Puppy Paws and Golden Years

Take the dogs to the beach near the trailhead.

Florence

12 Mill Pond Nature Trail–Woods Bay State Park

First and foremost, I must warn you that large alligators do inhabit this park. Please keep the dogs on a leash, and away from the water *at all times!* Beyond the threat of alligators this is a wonderful unpopulated park. Birdlife is abundant, and you'll gain insight into a unique natural feature known as a Carolina bay. Hickory, pine, and cypress offer shade, and although you're hiking through a damp marshland, you're able to keep your feet dry.

Start: 11020 Woods Bay Rd., Olanta; at the southwest corner of the park, just south of picnic shelter WBS1. A sign reads "Boardwalk, Nature Trail, Fishing."
Distance: 0.75-mile loop
Hiking time: About 20 minutes
Blaze color: None
Difficulty: Easy
Trailhead elevation: 118 feet
Highest point: 136 feet
Best season: Year-round
Schedule: 9 a.m. to 6 p.m.
Trail surface: Hard-packed dirt
Other trail users: None
Canine compatibility: Leash required

Land status: South Carolina Department of Natural Resources
Fees: No fee
Maps: *DeLorme: South Carolina Atlas & Gazetteer:* Page 38, G5
Trail contacts: (843) 659-4445; www.south carolinaparks.com/woodsbay/introduction .aspx
Nearest town: Sumter, Lake City, Florence
Trail tips: Restrooms are near the trailhead. There's a water spigot at the picnic shelter. Bring drinking water for you and the dogs.
Special considerations: Alligators *are present* in this park. Do *not* let the dogs in, or near any water on this property. Do *not* bring the dogs on the boardwalk.

Finding the trailhead: From the junction of US 301 and SC 341 in Olanta, drive south on US 301 for 1.1 miles to a right onto Woods Bay Road (SR 48). Travel for 2.0 miles to the park on the left. Follow the park road for 0.3 mile to the end of the road.

From I-95 near Shiloh, get off at exit 141. Drive northeast on SC 53 (Narrow Pave Road) for 1.3 miles to a right onto SR 597. Travel for 1.6 miles to a left onto Woods Bay Road (SR 48). Travel for 1.9 miles to the park on the right. Follow directions above. **Trailhead GPS:** N33 56.713'/W79 58.766'

The Hike

If you visit the park's website, it tells you that Woods Bay is "one of the last remaining large Carolina bays." But what is a Carolina bay? I thought a bay was a big body of water. Actually, a Carolina bay may or may not be holding water. Unlike a typical bay, basin, or bight, a Carolina bay is an elliptical depression in the ground.

Oddly enough, these depressions are always oriented in a northwest–southeast direction. They also tend to be found in clusters, and are often lined up in a linear fashion from one another. Carolina bays are not limited to the Carolinas. As a matter of fact, they span the eastern seaboard from New Jersey south to Florida. But the highest concentration is in the Carolinas, hence the name. There are a number of scientific theories on how they were formed, but they're just that, theories. There's no emphatic proof, and no concrete evidence on how they came to be. The origins of this ovate natural phenomenon remain a mystery. Woods Bay covers nearly 1,600 acres. The Mill Pond Trail circles around the park's comparatively small Mill Pond, which sits on the eastern edge of the bay. As you head into the forest, keep the dogs on a tight leash. You'll

Keep your dogs safe by heeding all warning signs.

hike past the canoe launch, and then the park's boardwalk. The boardwalk juts about a quarter-mile into the water, and parallels the canoe trail. I do not recommend hiking this boardwalk with dogs. Large alligators are present! It's simply not worth the risk. Beyond the boardwalk, you'll hike on a small levee, keeping your feet dry from the damp marshland. You're greeted by tall cypress trees with their knees reaching out in all directions. A chorus of birds serenade you. And you may hear an occasional splash

Large alligators do live at Woods Bay State Park, so please use extreme caution with your canine companions.

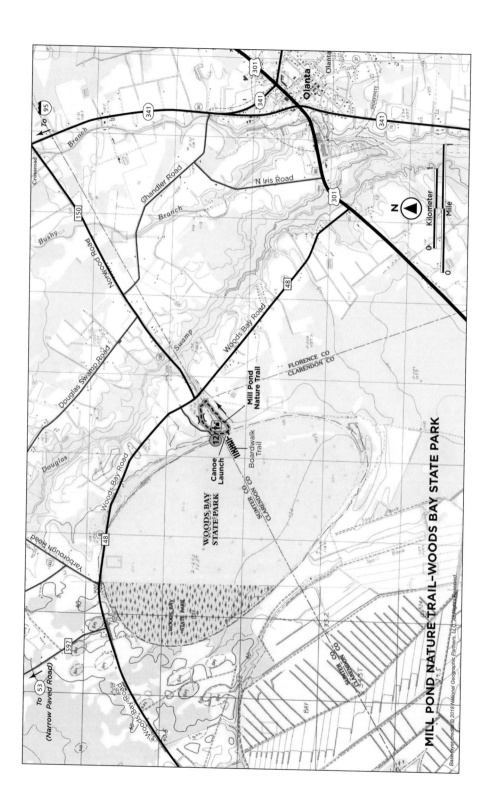

MILL POND NATURE TRAIL–WOODS BAY STATE PARK

as a frog leaps into the water, or turtle plops down into the drink. The diversity is astonishing! Mud fish, birds, snakes, frogs, turtles, and alligators all thrive here. A variety of mammals also come to sip from the water's edge. Hickory, cypress, and pine shade the trail, but there are no water stops, so carry enough drinking water for you both. You'll gain insight into the life of a cypress swamp, while hiking on an earthen surface rather than an elevated boardwalk. There was some bee activity along the trail

The white underside is a telltale sign of the tricolored heron.

in June. If you have a known bee allergy, skip this hike as a precaution, and carry an EpiPen at all times.

Miles and Directions

- **0.0** Hike south into the forest.
- **0.05** Pass the canoe launch. The trail bends left (southeast) toward the boardwalk.
- **0.1** Bypass the Boardwalk Trail. Continue hiking south; the path narrows and bends left (north).
- **0.6** Cross a footbridge; continue hiking southwest.
- **0.75** The trail ends just north of the park office. Walk across the grass toward the trailhead.

Option: Double the distance by backtracking to the trailhead.

Resting up

Quality Inn, 2390 Broad St., Sumter, (803) 469-9001; pet fee required.
La Quinta Inn and Suites, 2123 W. Lucas St., Florence, (843) 946-9956; no pet fee.

Camping

Lynches River County Park, 5094 County Park Rd., Coward, (843) 389-0550 or (843) 667-0920.
Lee State Park, 487 Loop Rd., Bishopville, (803) 428-5307.

Fueling up

The Clay Pot, 166 S. Dargan St., Florence, (843) 407-1646.
Mellow Mushroom, 120 Dunbarton Dr., Florence, (843) 407-1442.

Puppy Paws and Golden Years

Let the dogs sniff around the picnic area but keep them on leash so they don't wander over to the water's edge.

13 Nature Trail/Riverwalk Trail Loop–Lynches River County Park

This lovely loop begins and ends near the park's canoe launch. Wide, shallow steps line the length of the launch, making it easy for dogs to cool off in the river. Heading out on the Nature Trail, you'll find the forest offers shade and diversity. Then, returning on the boardwalk of the Riverwalk Trail, you're treated with views of Lynches River, with an abundance of cypress trees lining the banks below you. It's the best of both worlds.

Start: 5094 County Park Rd., Coward; northeast of the canoe launch. The Nature Trail is the dirt trail to the right. The Riverwalk Trail is the wooden boardwalk to the left.
Distance: 1.3-mile loop
Hiking time: About 40 minutes
Blaze color: None
Difficulty: Easy
Trailhead elevation: 144 feet
Highest point: 156 feet
Best season: Year-round
Schedule: Open daily 9 a.m. to sunset; closed Thanksgiving, Christmas Eve, Christmas Day
Trail surface: Hard-packed sand, wooden boardwalk
Other trail users: Mountain bikes

Canine compatibility: Leash required
Land status: Florence County Parks and Recreation Commission
Fees: No fee
Maps: *DeLorme: North Carolina Atlas & Gazetteer.* Page 39, E7
Trail contacts: (843) 389-0550; www.lynches riverpark.com/hiking.php
Nearest town: Florence, Lake City
Trail tips: Trash can, poop bags, and an inaccurate trail map are near the trailhead. If you plan on altering the hike as described, print a map before you hike.
Special considerations: Alligators do inhabit Lynches River. Keep the dogs on a leash, and use caution at the canoe launch.

Finding the trailhead: From the junction of US 52 and US 301 in Effingham, drive south on US 52 for 1.3 miles to a right onto Old Highway Number 4. Travel for 1.8 miles to a right onto County Park Road (SR 1679). Travel for 0.6 mile to the entrance to the park. Drive less than 0.1 mile and park on the left near the Discovery Center.

From the junction of SC 541 and SC 403 at Byrds Crossroads, drive east on SC 541/Old Highway Number 4 for 0.6 mile. Bear left here, following Old Highway Number 4 for another 7.0 miles to a left onto County Park Road. Follow directions above. **Trailhead GPS:** N34 02.059'/W79 47.413'

The Hike

Just minutes south of Florence, you'll find the quaint Lynches River County Park, named for the river it borders upon. Popular with the locals, this park offers an abundance of activities. There's an archery range, ball field, splash pad, small campground, canoe/kayak rentals, and a canoe launch. The canoe launch sits near the shared

The dogs were on their best behavior hiking Lynches' River Nature Trail.

trailhead. I recommend taking the dogs for a dip before hitting the trail. Although there's no swimming allowed, they can cool off in the water, as long as they remain on a leash. The steps that form the launch site are ideal for dogs of all sizes. The park also houses the Environmental Discovery Center (EDC), which offers educational programs and activities for all ages. They even host a weekly "meet and greet," where they showcase indigenous species such as turtles, toads, and even an alligator. Dogs are not allowed in the EDC. That's okay; the hike will entertain you both. As you enter the forest, the hard-packed sandy surface of the Nature Trail parallels the Riverwalk Trail, and both offer plenty of shade. Placards help identify some of the plant life, and you may also spy a geocache along the way. You'll bypass the unmarked Historic Stagecoach Trail on the right, and the Riverwalk Trail on the left. Blueberry, wild azalea, dogwood, and sourgum add color, and the peeling bark of the birch stands out as well. When you reach a second fork with the Historic Stagecoach Trail, it's time to turn back. Looping back on the Riverwalk Trail, the boardwalk parallels Lynches River, but the river isn't within direct view yet. Massive cypress trees tower overhead, standing

The whole family will enjoy an easy stroll at Lynches River Park.

NATURE TRAIL/RIVERWALK TRAIL LOOP–LYNCHES RIVER COUNTY PARK

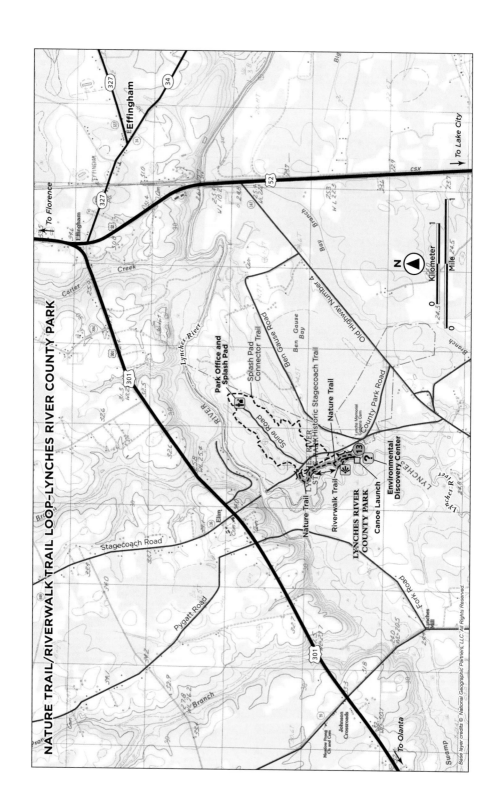

between you and the waterway. Once you reach the T, you'll stay with the shoreline for the remainder of the hike. Overall, it's a peaceful hike with an array of birds, a variety of flora, and views of Lynches River.

Miles and Directions

0.0 Hike north on the Nature Trail.

0.05 Cross a footbridge; continue hiking north.

0.1 Cross a footbridge; continue hiking north.

0.13 Come to a fork. Right (northeast) is the Historic Stagecoach Trail. Go straight (north) on the Nature Trail.

0.2 Come to a fork. The Riverwalk Trail leads left (southwest). For now, go straight (north) on the Nature Trail.

Option: To shorten the hike to 0.5 mile, go left on the Riverwalk Trail.

0.4 Cross a footbridge; continue hiking northwest.

0.5 Pass a series of outdoor lecterns.

0.6 Cross a footbridge and immediately come to a fork. The orange-blazed Splash Pad Trail is straight (northeast). Right (southeast) is the Stagecoach Trail. The Nature Trail ends here. Backtrack to the fork at 0.2 mile.

Option: To extend the hike, follow the Splash Pad Trail. It makes a 2.3-mile loop, ending on the Stagecoach Trail.

1.0 Arrive back at the fork from 0.2 mile. Go right (southwest) on the Riverwalk Trail.

1.1 Come to a T. Right leads about 100 feet to an overlook (N34 02.132'/W79 47.494'). Left leads south to the trailhead.

1.3 Arrive at the trailhead.

A long wooden boardwalk forms the Riverwalk Trail.

Resting up

La Quinta Inn and Suites, 2123 W. Lucas St., Florence, (843) 946-9956; no pet fee.
Days Inn, 2111 W. Lucas St., Florence, (843) 665-4444; no pet fee.

Camping

Onsite.

Fueling up

The Clay Pot, 166 S. Dargan St., Florence; (843) 407-1646.
Mellow Mushroom, 120 Dunbarton Dr., Florence; (843) 407-1442.

Puppy Paws and Golden Years

Take them for a stroll on the Riverwalk Trail.

14 Beaver Pond Trail–Little Pee Dee State Park

Vast farmland surrounds Little Pee Dee State Park. Cornfields and cows greet you as you near the Piedmont. Yet amid all this wide open space, you'll find a lovely patch of forest within the park. Pine trees and oaks are the primary sources of shade on this pleasant stroll. The trail forms a lollipop-style loop, leading you to a peaceful pond where an abundance of birds and frogs serenade you.

Start: 1298 State Park Rd., Dillon; across the street from the parking lot, on the south side of Park Access Road, southwest of the park office
Distance: 1.7 miles out and back
Hiking time: About 50 minutes
Blaze color: Blue
Difficulty: Easy
Trailhead elevation: 94 feet
Highest point: 95 feet
Best season: Year-round
Schedule: 9 a.m. to 6 p.m. (extended to 9 p.m. during Daylight Saving Time)
Trail surface: Hard-packed dirt
Other trail users: None
Canine compatibility: Leash required

Land status: South Carolina Department of Natural Resources
Fees: No fee
Maps: *DeLorme: South Carolina Atlas & Gazetteer:* Page 40, A4 & 31, H9
Trail contacts: (843) 774-8872; www.south carolinaparks.com/lpd/introduction.aspx
Nearest town: Dillon, Mullins, Marion, Latta
Trail tips: Apply bug spray in summertime. A soda machine that sells water is next to the park office.
Special considerations: Although there's no known population of alligators in Lake Norton, they may be present. Use caution.

Finding the trailhead: From the junction of SC 57 and SC 41 in Fork, drive northwest on SC 57 for 2.3 miles to a right onto State Park Road (SR 22). Travel for 1.9 miles to a right onto Park Access Road. Travel for 1.1 miles to the parking lot on the left (before reaching the park office).

From the junction of SC 9 and SC 57 in Dillon, drive southeast on SC 9 for 5.9 miles to a right onto State Park Road (SR 22). Travel for 4.0 miles to a left onto Park Access Road. Follow directions above.

Note: When driving on Park Access Road, bypass the parking lot on your right at 0.9 mile. This is an alternative trailhead. **Trailhead GPS:** N34 19.775'/W79 16.130'

The Hike

Surrounding this lovely park, fields of tall corn blow in the wind, and herds of cows greet you with their melancholy moos. Driving through the countryside, enormous pieces of farm equipment rest along the roadway. Yet, with Dillon to the north, and Marion and Mullins to the south, you're not completely isolated. Arriving at this

Families of Canada geese make their home on the park's peaceful Lake Norton.

peaceful park, you'll find families come to use the playground, and swing on the swing set. Couples holding hands walk the levee or feed the geese. A beautiful, moss-covered spillway sits at the south end of the lake and forms a narrow creek where fishermen cast their lines. The park encompasses over 800 acres, and the Beaver Pond Trail barely makes a dent in the overall scheme of things. The well-maintained path heads into a forest of oaks and pristine pines, leading you on a pleasant stroll. An abundance of birds inhabit the area. Whistles, hoots, tweets, chirps, and songs all fill the air, as does the loud, echoing knock of the red-bellied, pileated, and downy woodpecker. Pines are among their favorite habitat, so keep your eyes peeled. Loblolly, longleaf, and slash pines all make their home here, and a blanket of pine needles covers the firm forest floor. As you hike across the park road, you'll see a small parking lot nearby. To shorten the hike to 1.1 miles (round-trip), you could start here at the alternate trailhead instead. The dogs may pick up the scent of deer as you pass an open meadow. The loop of the lollipop is a full half-mile long and leads you downhill to a marshy area.

The sound of the birds singing is replaced by the loud croaking of frogs and toads. You'll soon reach an overlook, where the Beaver Pond comes into view. Tall wispy grass of cattails lines the banks, and out in the middle, you'll notice cypress knees popping up in the water. Turtles sun themselves, birds fly overhead, and a gentle breeze presents itself. There's no swimming here for the dogs; reserve that for the boat ramp. As you loop back around, the trail gently climbs. Oak, holly, pine, and sourgum all form the forest around you, and ivy covers the ground below. The hike is shaded, but with no water stops, bring enough along for you and the dogs.

The male and female anhinga take turns watching over their young.

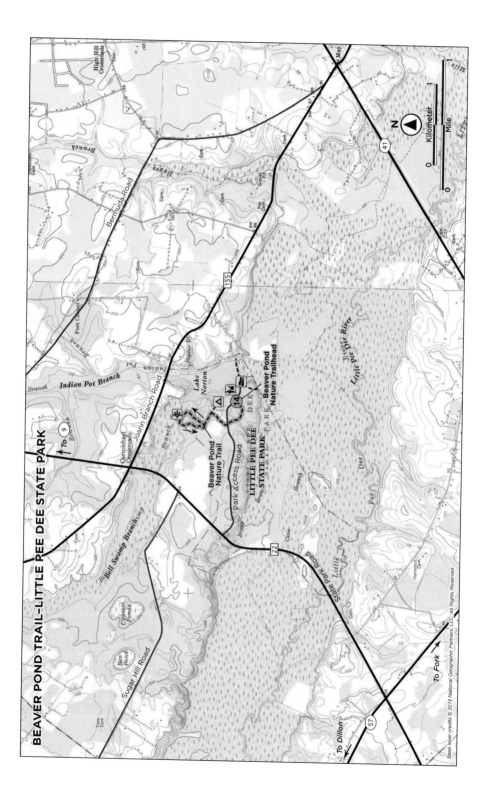

BEAVER POND TRAIL–LITTLE PEE DEE STATE PARK

Left: Sprawling farmland surrounds Little Pee Dee State Park.
Right: Fields full of cows greet you on the way to Little Pee Dee.

Miles and Directions

0.0 Hike southwest into the forest.

0.15 Hike across an old access road. Continue west on the Beaver Pond Trail.

0.2 Bypass a trail to your right that has posts with red markings. Stay right (north), following blue blazes.

0.3 Carefully cross the park road, stay left (west). Hike northwest back into the forest.

Option: Park here to shorten the hike to 1.1 miles (round-trip).

0.46 Come to a T. Right leads southeast to the campground (N34 19.834'/W79 15.959'). Go left (northwest).

0.6 Come to a fork where the loop begins. Go right (east), downhill to a marshy area.

0.85 Come to an overlook (N34 20.075'/W79 16.058'). Continue hiking west.

1.1 Arrive back at the fork where the loop began. Backtrack to the trailhead.

1.7 Arrive at the trailhead.

Resting up

America's Best Value Inn, 904 Radford Blvd., Dillon, (843) 664-2400; pet fee required.

Camping

Onsite.

Fueling up

Shulers BBQ, 419 Hwy. 38 West, Latta, (843) 752-4700.

Puppy Paws and Golden Years

Take them for a leisurely stroll on the levee at the south end of Lake Norton.

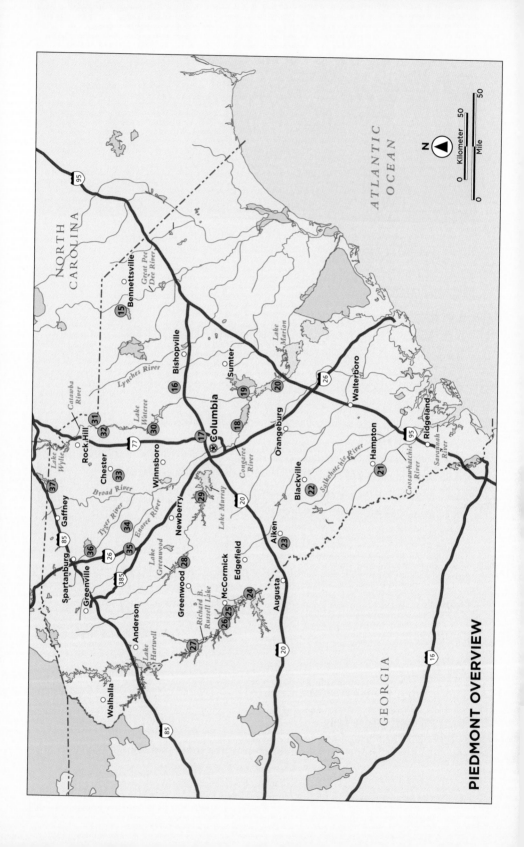

PIEDMONT OVERVIEW

The Midlands–Piedmont

This region stretches clear across the center of the state, from the Great Pee Dee River to the shores of Lake Hartwell, with the capital of Columbia sitting proudly in the center. Vast farmland spans the area, painting the Piedmont like a tapestry. Whether it's fields of corn or fields of flowers, they'll span as far as the eye can see. As you drive down the peaceful country roads, horses, cows, goats, and pigs greet you when you pass them by. Amid this sprawling agriculture, you'll find some of the most spectacular lakes in the state. Lakes Marion, Thurmond, and Russell cover over 200,000 acres between them, and you can hike along the shores of them all. You'll find just as much beauty gazing upon Lakes Warren, Wateree, and Juniper. Although they're not as big, they shouldn't be overlooked. If you prefer moving water, hike along the banks of the Enoree and Tyger Rivers, and then hop in for a dip. If you appreciate history, hike to Musgrove Mill, or the living history farm at Kings Mountain. Delve into the floodplain forest of Congaree National Park to see champion trees like no other. Or visit the colorful, glorious gardens at Rose Hill Plantation and Hopeland Gardens. Whatever you seek, there's a trail for you, here in the heartland, in the Piedmont of South Carolina.

Vast farmland stretches across the Piedmont.

Bennettsville

15 Boardwalk Trail–Cheraw State Park

The Boardwalk Trail gives you the best of both worlds. It begins near the park's populated swim area. The sandy beach is fantastic for the dogs to cool off before hitting the trail. Near the end of the hike, you'll find another great swim hole at the base of a man-made spillway. Between the swim spots, the trail crosses a boardwalk out over Lake Juniper. The serenity is unsurpassed.

Start: 100 State Park Rd., Cheraw; north of the park office, east side of the road
Distance: 1.2 miles out and back
Hiking time: About 35 minutes
Blaze color: None
Difficulty: Easy
Trailhead elevation: 112 feet
Highest point: 122 feet
Best season: Year-round
Schedule: Nov–Feb, 7 a.m. to 6 p.m.; Mar, Sept, and Oct, 7 a.m. to 8 p.m.; Apr–Aug, 7 a.m. to 9 p.m.
Trail surface: Hard-packed dirt, long wooden boardwalk

Other trail users: None
Canine compatibility: Leash required
Land status: South Carolina Department of Natural Resources
Fees: No fee
Maps: *DeLorme: South Carolina Atlas & Gazetteer:* Page 30, C1
Trail contacts: (843) 537-9656; www.south carolinaparks.com/cheraw/introduction.aspx
Nearest town: Cheraw, Bennettsville, Chesterfield
Trail tips: Restrooms, water fountain, swim beach, trash cans, and puppy waste bags are near the trailhead.

Finding the trailhead: From the junction of US 52 and US 1 near Cheraw, drive south on US 52 for 1.0 mile to the park on the right. Follow the park road for 0.8 mile to a stop sign. Go left and travel 0.25 mile to the parking lot near the park office.

From the junction of US 52 and US 15/US 401 in Society Hill, drive north on US 52 for 10.1 miles to the park on your left. Follow directions above. *Note:* When coming from the south, you'll pass the entrance to the park's campground at 9.8 miles. Continue driving another 0.3 mile to the main entrance. **Trailhead GPS:** N34 38.482'/W79 54.037'

The Hike

Cheraw State Park is outstanding. Activities include picnic areas, a playground, sand volleyball, swim beach, campground, eighteen-hole golf course, and a fantastic trail system dedicated to equestrians, mountain bikers, and hikers. In the middle of it all, you'll find the stunning scenery of Lake Juniper. This 360-acre lake spans 2.5 miles, running the length of the park. Boat rentals are available, or you can launch your own canoe, kayak, or johnboat. The park is popular with paddlers and nature photographers alike. A variety of rare species find their home here including carnivorous plants, and the endangered red-cockaded woodpecker. These stiff-tailed avian aerialists are supported by a large longleaf pine forest and blend in remarkably well. But once they take flight, a pale patch on their belly gives them away. Many other species inhabit the park, including cardinals, hummingbirds, chickadees, owls, osprey, hawks, and even bald eagles. The hike begins near the swim area. This splendid sandy beach is a perfect side trip for the dogs to take a dip before hitting the trail. A constant breeze off the lake is refreshing, and trees offer shade. Hiking along the sandy path, the views of the lake become more captivating. The occasional swing offers a place to perch and take in the scenery. By 0.2 mile a long wooden boardwalk leads directly over the water. A collection of color-

Dogs are welcome at Cheraw's swim area, as long as they remain on a leash.

ful lily pads float on the water like clouds in the sky. Green, yellow, red, and brown form a patchwork tapestry from these aquatic plants. The occasional white and yellow water lily blossom peeks out from below the brilliant green. Its mirrored reflection

A wooden boardwalk leads out and over Lake Juniper.

BOARDWALK TRAIL–CHERAW STATE PARK

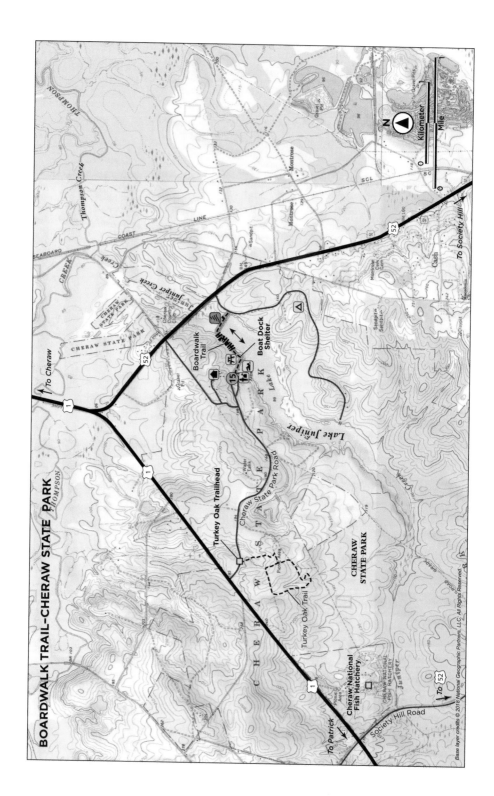

ripples on the water below. Although there's no shade here, the breeze is glorious. When you reach the levee, the hike across offers exceptional full-length views of the lake. Turtles sun themselves, and visitors fish from the banks. About halfway across the levee, a man-made spillway forms a wonderful waterfall. Follow the narrow path down to the creek at the base. The dogs will be in heaven, splashing around in the creek. With a swim beach, waterfall, and clear running creek, of course it's a favorite.

Miles and Directions

0.0 Hike east on the road-like trail.

<0.1 Bypass an access road to the left (north). Continue hiking east toward the boat dock shelter.

0.1 Hike past the boat dock shelter (N34 38.454'/W79 53.936') and follow the shoreline northeast.

0.2 Cross the boardwalk.

0.4 The boardwalk ends at the levee. Head right as you continue hiking southeast on the levee.

0.5 The trail leads across a spillway (N34 38.571'/W79 53.612'). On the south side, follow the narrow path to the base where the pups can safely splash around in the water.

0.6 The trail ends at the park road leading into the campground. Backtrack to the trailhead.

1.2 Arrive at the trailhead.

Taking a dip in Lake Juniper is a great way to start the Boardwalk Trail hike.

Resting up

Quality Inn, 885 Chesterfield Hwy., Cheraw, (843) 537-5625; pet fee required.
Days Inn, 820 Market St., Cheraw, (843) 537-5554; pet fee required.

Camping

Onsite.

Fueling up

Magnolia on Main, 224 E. Main St., Bennettsville, (843) 479-9495.
Pig-N-Vittles, 126 Main St., Chesterfield, (843) 623-5225.

Puppy Paws and Golden Years

Take them to the swim area—they'll love it!

Camden

16 Big Pine Tree Nature Trail– Goodale State Park

One hiking trail is found within N. R. Goodale State Park. It's about half the length of the Canoe/Kayak Trail that dips out into Adams Grist Mill Lake. Massive cypress trees tower over the water, adding an air of mystery to this rather barren park. Using the park map, it looks like you can see the lake from the Nature Trail. In reality, the trailhead is the only place you get a good view. The pathway is well maintained, and wildlife ranges from raccoons to rabbits, and turtles to turkeys.

Start: 650 Park Rd., Camden; northeast of the brick boathouse/park office and playground. A sign reads "Nature Trail."
Distance: 1.5-mile loop
Hiking time: About 50 minutes
Blaze color: Arrow markers
Difficulty: Easy
Trailhead elevation: 236 feet
Highest point: 236 feet
Best season: Year-round
Schedule: Mar 15–Nov 30 open daily from 9 a.m. to 6 p.m.; Dec 1–Mar 14, 9 a.m. to 6 p.m., open Friday–Sunday only
Trail surface: Hard-packed dirt, hard-packed sand
Other trail users: None
Canine compatibility: Leash required

Land status: South Carolina Department of Natural Resources
Fees: No fee
Maps: *DeLorme: South Carolina Atlas & Gazetteer:* Page 37, A9
Trail contacts: (803) 432-2772; www.south carolinaparks.com/goodale/introduction.aspx
Nearest town: Camden, Bishopville
Trail tips: Restrooms are near picnic shelter #2. Bring lots of water for you and the dogs.
Special considerations: Alligators do inhabit Adams Grist Mill Lake. Use caution near the banks. The park office is only open from 11 a.m. to noon during park hours, but the park ranger should be somewhere on the premises during park hours.

Finding the trailhead: From the junction of US 1 and SC 34 in Camden, drive north on US 1 for 1.7 miles to a right onto Old Stagecoach Road. Travel for 2.5 miles to a left onto Park Road (SR 331). Travel for 0.3 mile to the park on the right. Drive 0.3 mile into the park to the brick boathouse.

From the junction of US 1 and SC 341 in Bethune, drive south on US 1 for 14.0 miles to a left onto Park Road. Follow directions above.

Note: Old Stagecoach Road sneaks up on you when coming from the south (Camden).
Trailhead GPS: N34 17.148'/W80 31.452'

Massive cypress trees thrive within Goodale's Adams Grist Mill Lake.

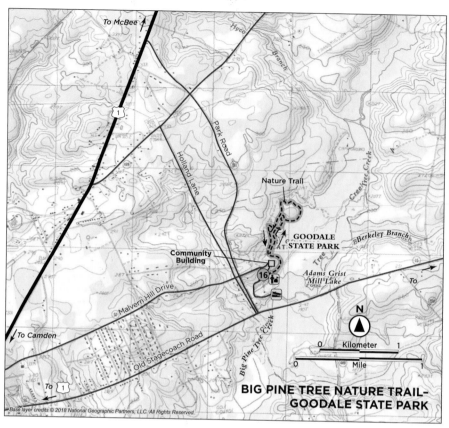

The Hike

Goodale State Park is best known for its 140-acre millpond. This marvelous man-made lake spans a good portion of the park and dates back to the Civil War. The park boasts a 3-mile paddle trail, and you can rent a canoe seasonally, or bring your own. This wonderful waterway leads out among stunning cypress trees growing right up from the water, and towering overhead. The enormous width of their trunks can be viewed from the shore, but by boat you can weave a path between them. Despite its proximity to I-20, this is an incredibly peaceful park. The community building sits up on a hill, and as the wide road-like path leads into the woods, you'll follow a contour around the base of that hill. Brush separates you from the lake, and a canopy of imma-ture oaks envelops the path. Numbered posts on the path act as interpretive identifi-ers. Unfortunately, there are no brochures to coincide with them. But if you pop into the office, they have a reference book for the posts. You could also take photos of the book with your phone, creating your own brochure. Beginning the counterclockwise loop, you'll hear the faint sounds of moving water, and gentle climbs and descents add character. When this lovely shaded path loops back toward the trailhead it widens, and you're likely to see footprints of deer, raccoons, or turkey. A variety of birds thrive here. Wading birds like great blue herons and great egrets can be found fishing in the

Left: Canoe rentals are available seasonally at Goodale State Park.
Right: This infant raccoon holds on for dear life while waiting for his mother's return.

shallows. With elegance and poise, each stands over 3 feet tall. Hawks, and owls with their keen eyesight, readily swoop in, and waterfowl like ducks and geese drift over the water as if floating on air. On land you may spy a brilliant red cardinal, or wily woodpecker up in the pines. It's a birder's paradise, and tranquil hike. All you'll hear are the birds singing, your puppies' panting, and the earth moving beneath your feet.

Miles and Directions

0.0   Hike east into the forest.

0.25 Come to a fork where the loop begins. Left is west. Go right (north).

0.45 Cross a footbridge; continue hiking northwest.

1.25 Come to the fork where the loop began. Backtrack to the trailhead.

1.5   Arrive at the trailhead.

Resting up

Comfort Inn, 220 Wall St., Camden, (803) 425-1010; pet fee required.
Econo Lodge Inn and Suites, 529 Hwy. 601 South, Lugoff, (803) 438-6990; pet fee required.

Camping

Sesquicentennial State Park, 9564 Two Notch Rd., Columbia, (803) 788-2706.
Lee State Park, 487 Loop Rd., Bishopville, (803) 428-5307.

Fueling up

Sam Kendall's, 1043 Broad St., Camden, (803) 424-2005.

Puppy Paws and Golden Years

Take them to the large grassy area near the boathouse/park office and Adams Grist Mill Lake.

Columbia

17 Sandhills Trail–Sesquicentennial State Park

Affectionately known as Sesqui, Sesquicentennial State Park is the jewel of the capital city. It's packed full of activities, and even has a dog park. Looping around the park's beautiful 30-acre lake, you'll find a fantastic forest, clear creek, marshy area, and a spillway keep you entertained. And there are plenty of swim spots for the pups.

Start: 9564 Two Notch Rd., Columbia; northeast corner of the gravel parking lot
Distance: 2.1-mile loop
Hiking time: About 1 hour, 5 minutes
Blaze color: White
Difficulty: Easy
Trailhead elevation: 266 feet
Highest point: 314 feet
Best season: Year-round
Schedule: 8 a.m. to 6 p.m. (extended hours during Daylight Saving Time)
Trail surface: Sidewalk, paved path, finely crushed gravel

Other trail users: Bicycles on a small section
Canine compatibility: Leash required
Land status: South Carolina Department of Natural Resources
Fees: Fee required
Maps: *DeLorme: South Carolina Atlas & Gazetteer:* Page 36, E4
Trail contacts: (803) 788-2706; www.south carolinaparks.com/sesqui/introduction.aspx
Nearest town: Columbia
Trail tips: Trailhead information sign at the trailhead. Restrooms and water near the boathouse.

Finding the trailhead: From I-77 in Columbia, get off at exit 17 and follow US 1 north for 2.3 miles to the park on the right. Drive 1.2 miles to the parking lot on the right just past the boathouse. **Trailhead GPS:** N34 05.236'/W80 54.357'

The Hike

Found within the capital city of Columbia, it's no surprise that Sesqui stays busy year-round. A variety of activities draw visitors from near and far, basketball, softball, volleyball, and horseshoes among them. Picnic shelters, playgrounds, and a campground add to the excitement. But perhaps the biggest draw is the park's centrally located lake. Fishing and boating are very popular, and you can rent a boat or bring your own. A splash pad is open in summertime, which is ideal, since there's no swimming allowed in the lake. Dogs aren't allowed at the splash pad, but there's a wonderful dog park. The dog park has shallow pools for the pups and is partly shaded by the pines (annual permit is required). Twelve miles of hiking and mountain bike trails run through the park, each connecting with the Sandhills Trail in one place or another. As you make the loop around the lake, it's a mixed bag of sidewalk, paved path, and crushed gravel.

Left: Boating on the pond is a popular pastime at Sesquicentennial State Park.
Right: The dogs will have plenty of shade hiking around Sesquicentennial's 30-acre lake.

Follow the white blazes to stay on track. You'll pass the boathouse, which was built by the Civilian Conservation Corps (CCC) in the 1930s. After appreciating the quality of their craftsmanship, you'll pass a picnic shelter and arrive at the small spillway. You may notice raccoon footprints in the sand, and ducks floating out in the water. When you pass a second picnic shelter, you begin to move away from the populated part of the park. Lily pads cover the water in a little cove, blossoming into white and yellow water lilies in summertime. As the trail leads into the forest, a thicket of brush stands between you and the water. But several footbridge crossings give the dogs ample opportunity to splash around in sandy-bottomed creeks. Benches are randomly placed, and the forest is primarily made up of longleaf pines. Hardwoods like oak, maple, and flowering dogwoods are also mixed in. The dogs will perk up at the sight of a grey squirrel, and if you're lucky, you may see a fox squirrel, or flying squirrel. Wildflowers are found along the length of the trail, and a brief stint through a marshy area adds diversity.

Miles and Directions

0.0 Follow the steps down into the woods and immediately come to a T. Left is north. Go right, following the sidewalk south.

0.1 Hike past the boathouse.

0.15 Hike south past a nice swim spot.

0.25 Hike past a picnic shelter.

0.35 Bypass the yellow-blazed Jackson Creek Nature Trail to the right (southwest). Follow the sidewalk southeast along the lake.

0.37 Take the side trail about 50 feet to see the spillway (N34 04.964'/W80 54.356'). Continue hiking east on the main trail.

0.4 Cross a footbridge, and come to a fork. Right (south) is the Jackson Creek Nature Trail. Go left (northeast) on the paved path.

0.5 Hike past another picnic shelter.

0.6 Cross a footbridge, and come to a fork. Bypass the trail that leads straight (south). Go left (east), following the Sandhills Trail.

0.9 Cross a footbridge; continue hiking north.

1.2 Cross a footbridge over a clear creek. Continue hiking northeast.

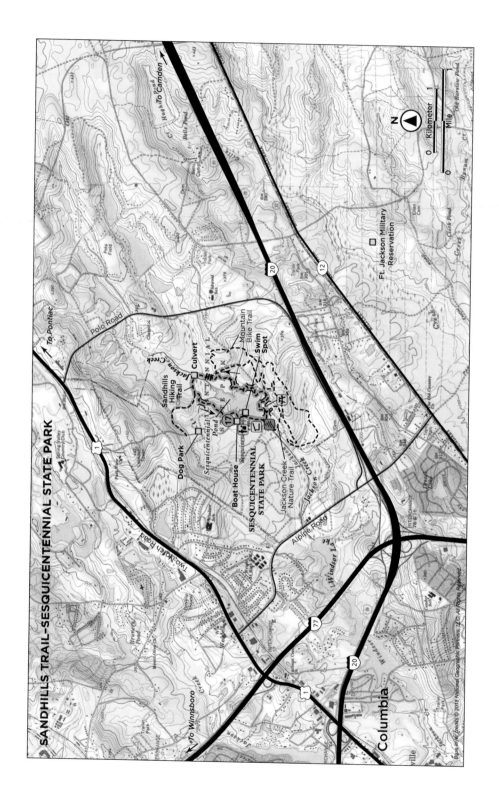

SANDHILLS TRAIL–SESQUICENTENNIAL STATE PARK

Sandhills Hiking Trail

Culvert

Jackson Creek

Mountain Bike Trail

Swim Spot

Dog Park

Sesquicentennial Pond

Boat House

SESQUICENTENNIAL STATE PARK

Jackson Creek Nature Trail

Jackson Creek

Alpine Road

Windsor Lk.

Columbia

Polo Road

Polo Field

To Pontiac

Spring Valley Country Club

Two Notch Road

To Winnsboro

Brewer Pond

Bella Pond

High To Camden

Ft. Jackson Military Reservation

Old Barnyard Pond

Clark Pond

N

0 Kilometer 1
0 Mile 1

The log cabin at Sesqui dates back to the mid-1700s.

1.37 Cross a boardwalk over a marshy area. Continue hiking north.

1.45 Come to a T. Go left (north), following white blazes, but you're now sharing the trail with the blue-blazed mountain bike trail.

1.6 Cross a creek on a culvert. Continue hiking west.

1.75 Come to a fork. The mountain bike trail goes straight (west). Go left (south), following white blazes.

1.85 Cross a footbridge over a creek. Continue hiking south.

2.1 The loop ends near the trailhead.

Resting up

Hampton Inn, 101 Woodcross Dr., Columbia, (803) 749-6999; no pet fee.
La Quinta Inn and Suites, 1538 Horseshoe Dr., Columbia, (803) 736-6400; no pet fee.

Camping

Onsite.

Fueling up

Travinia Italian Kitchen, 101 Sparkleberry Crossing Rd., Columbia, (803) 419-9313.
The Kraken Gastropub, 2910 Rosewood Dr., Columbia, (803) 955-7408.

Puppy Paws and Golden Years

Take them to the swim spot past the boathouse. It's only 0.3 mile round-trip. Or visit the park's dog park.

18 Boardwalk Trail–Congaree National Park

A long boardwalk makes a loop through the floodplain of Congaree National Park. You'll pass champion cypress trees stretching to the sky, while their knees blanket the ground around them. The forest offers lots of shade, and the cypress trees are joined by maple, oak, holly, and the occasional pine. Birdlife is abundant; bring binoculars.

Start: 100 National Park Rd., Hopkins; northwest corner of the visitor center
Distance: 2.6-mile loop
Hiking time: About 1 hour, 20 minutes
Blaze color: None
Difficulty: Easy
Trailhead elevation: 161 feet
Highest point: 168 feet
Best season: Year-round
Trail surface: Wooden boardwalk, hard-packed dirt
Other trail users: None
Canine compatibility: Leash required
Land status: National Park Service–Congaree National Park
Fees: No fee

Maps: DeLorme: North Carolina Atlas & Gazetteer. Page 45, A10
Trail contacts: (803) 776-4396; www.nps .gov/cong/planyourvisit/upload/COSW_Trail _Guide_Text_front_prf3.pdf
Nearest town: Gadsden, Columbia, St. Matthews
Trail tips: Trail maps and a self-guided brochure are available at the visitor center. Restrooms near the trailhead. Apply bug spray in summertime. There are no water stops, so bring plenty along, and take the pups for a bathroom break before you hike.
Special considerations: Alligators may be present. Do *not* let the dogs in, or near, any water.

Finding the trailhead: From I-77 in Columbia, get off at exit 5 and drive east on SC 48 for 8.1 miles to a right onto Old Bluff Road (SR 734). Travel for 4.3 miles to the park on your right. Follow the park road for 0.5 mile to a stop sign. Go straight, driving another 0.6 mile to the visitor center.
From the junction of SC 48 and SC 769 in Gadsden, drive west on SC 48 for 1.1 miles to a left onto Cedar Creek Road. Travel for 0.1 mile to a right onto Old Bluff Road (SR 734). Drive 2.6 miles to the park on your left. Follow directions above. **Trailhead GPS:** N33 49.779'/W80 49.424'

The Hike

Although the Boardwalk Trail is unblazed, it's easy to follow. You'll hike on an elevated boardwalk through the forested wilderness of Congaree National Park. Pick up a map and brochure at the visitor center (VC) to follow along with the numbered posts. The brochure offers a wealth of knowledge on the trees, plants, and area around them. When you reach the fork where the loop begins, stay straight to hike counterclockwise. The boardwalk is wheelchair accessible, but not very wide. If your dogs are unfriendly, you may want to skip this hike. Initially, the walkway is just a few feet off the ground, and there are no railings closing you in. This is a good introduction for the dogs, since it's less confining. You'll find yourself pausing in admiration of the trees around you. The trunks are enormous, and their height matches their width. Although you're hiking through a floodplain, the path isn't too buggy, even in summertime. The forest keeps you shaded, and benches are built into the boardwalk. At each corner of the square-shaped loop, other trails lead off of the Boardwalk Trail. Bypass them all, staying on the wooden walkway. You'll pass champion-sized trees that are outstanding. Post #3 for instance, is a bald cypress tree with a trunk that's easily 10 feet around. The sheer might, girth, and height are mind boggling. And the cypress knees form a forest of their own. You have to wonder how old these regal trees must be to reach such a substantial size. The solitude of the forest is uncanny, and the sights are just as spectacular. Near the southeastern corner, Weston Lake comes into view. A spur trail at the T gives you a better view, but do not let the dogs in or near the water. Alligators inhabit the area. Following the boardwalk back north, the path is fenced in with tall railings. Passing through the mixed forest of cypress, holly, and buckeye, the roots intertwine, making a natural patchwork tapestry on the ground before you. Birds chirp, owls hoot, and squirrels

Congaree National Park was named for a Native American tribe that once inhabited the area.

scamper about. When you notice specimen #11, you'll be blown away. It's enormous compared to the trees around it. Even more astonishing, it's a loblolly pine tree, a variety that is uncommon in damp areas. Finishing on the last leg of the loop, you'll bypass a few trails, before returning to the VC where you began.

Miles and Directions

0.0 Hike west on the boardwalk, and immediately come to a fork. Left (east) is the Bluff Trail. Bypass this, following the boardwalk south.

0.2 Come to a fork where the loop begins. Left is east. Go straight (south).

0.7 Come to a fork. The Weston Lake Loop goes straight (south). Go left (east), on the boardwalk.

Option: To extend the hike, follow the Weston Lake Loop Trail down to Cedar Creek.

1.0 Hike east, crossing the Sims Trail.

1.19 Bypass the Kingsnake, Weston Lake, and Oakridge Trails on the right. Continue straight (east).

1.2 Come to a T. Right (south) leads 100 feet to an overlook of Weston Lake. Hike north on the Boardwalk Trail.

1.85 Come to a T. Right (northeast) the Bluff Trail leads to the campground. Go left (southwest) on the boardwalk.

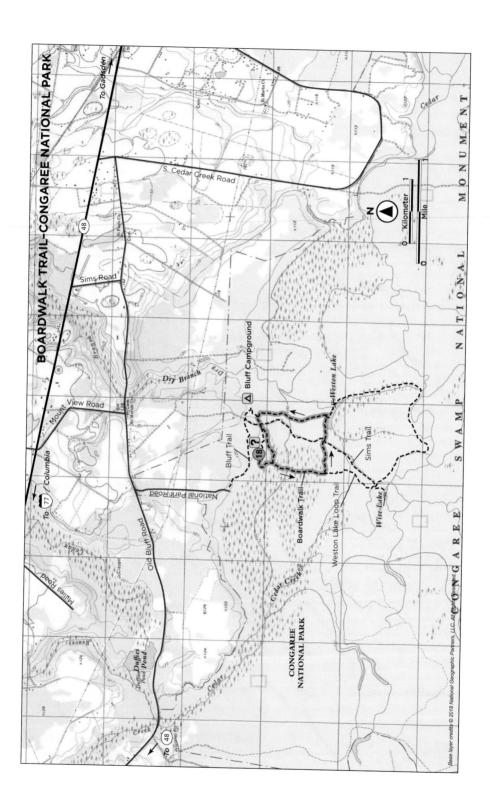

BOARDWALK TRAIL–CONGAREE NATIONAL PARK

You'll be stunned by the size of some of the trees in Congaree National Park.

1.9 Hike west across the gravel Sims Trail.

2.1 Bypass the dirt trail to the right (west) that also leads to the VC. Follow the boardwalk southwest.

2.4 Arrive at the fork where the loop began. Backtrack to the trailhead.

2.6 Arrive at the trailhead.

Resting up

Hampton Inn, 101 Woodcross Dr., Columbia, (803) 749-6999; no pet fee.
La Quinta Inn and Suites, 1538 Horseshoe Dr., Columbia, (803) 736-6400; no pet fee.

Camping

Poinsett State Park, 6660 Poinsett Park Rd., Wedgefield, (803) 494-8177.

Fueling up

The Kraken Gastropub, 2910 Rosewood Dr., Columbia, (803) 955-7408.
Travinia Italian Kitchen, 101 Sparkleberry Crossing Rd., Columbia, (803) 419-9313.

Puppy Paws and Golden Years

Take them on the Boardwalk Trail—just shorten the length based on your needs, making it an out-and-back hike.

Manning

19 Coquina Trail–Poinsett State Park

Poinsett State Park is wonderfully charming, which is surprising for such a sizable park. It encompasses 1,000 acres, but has a delightful, old-fashioned feel. Many of the structures were built by the Civilian Conservation Corps (CCC) in the 1930s, and even the Coquina Trail was cut by their hardworking hands. The trail loosely loops around the park's lake, bringing you high upon a hillside, and down through a marshy wetland. With this kind of diversity, it's easily a favorite.

Start: 6660 Poinsett Park Rd., Wedgefield; southwest of the park office, shared with the Knot Trail. Follow the water's edge west from the office.
Distance: 1.45-mile loop
Hiking time: About 50 minutes
Blaze color: Green
Difficulty: Moderate
Trailhead elevation: 112 feet
Highest point: 207 feet
Best season: Year-round
Schedule: 9 a.m. to dark
Trail surface: Hard-packed dirt
Other trail users: Mountain bikers allowed on part of the trail

Canine compatibility: Leash required
Land status: South Carolina Department of Natural Resources
Fees: No fee
Maps: *DeLorme: South Carolina Atlas & Gazetteer:* Page 46, A3
Trail contacts: (803) 494-8177; www.south carolinaparks.com/poinsett/introduction.aspx
Nearest town: Manning, Sumter
Trail tips: Restrooms, trash cans, picnic tables near the trailhead. Print a trail map from the park's website before arrival.
Special considerations: Alligators may be present in the lake. Please use caution.

Finding the trailhead: From the junction of SC 261 and SC 120 in Pinewood, drive north on SC 261 for 5.9 miles to a left onto Poinsett Park Road (SR 63). Travel for 1.7 miles to the entrance to the park. Drive 1.0 mile to the park office.

From the junction of SC 261 and SC 763 in Wedgefield, drive south on SC 261 for 6.1 miles to a right onto Poinsett Park Road. Follow directions above. **Trailhead GPS:** N33 48.275'/W80 32.944'

The Hike

Before hitting the trail, stop over to see the old mill site. A narrow waterfall enveloped by stone walls drops from one tier to the next as it rushes away from the lake. A working grist mill once stood here, but today all you see are remnants. This fabulous spillway was built by the CCC, as was the "tea room," which overlooks the lake and houses the park office. This historic structure is available for rent, and people host events such as weddings and reunions here.

A small waterfall swiftly flows past the old mill site at Poinsett.

Several trails intersect on this hike, so bring a map to help you navigate. You'll begin by crossing a levee, which offers splendid views of the 10-acre lake. Great blue herons and cunning kingfishers frequent the waterway, while hawks, woodpeckers, and warblers prefer the woodland. Within the first quarter-mile, you'll cross a footbridge, where the pups can splash around in the creek, which then leads upstream to a smooth stone spillway. The path is nicely shaded, which you appreciate as you climb and descend through the forest. This is one of the more rustic trails in the Piedmont, with a nice change in topography. As the green blazes guide your way, stay left at each fork. By doing so, you'll make a loop around Old Levi Mill Lake. At times you'll follow the water from high above, but when you reach the east end of the lake, the forest transforms into a damp wetland. Passing through a cypress swamp, a series of footbridges, planks, and boardwalks help keep your feet dry. Frogs croak with enthusiasm, and you may see them leap from the wooden walkway, or spy a turtle sunning himself. There's even a family of armadillo that have taken up residence here. With a creek, spillway, swamp, forest, and topography, you'll enjoy every step of the way.

Great blue herons are one of many bird species found at Poinsett State Park.

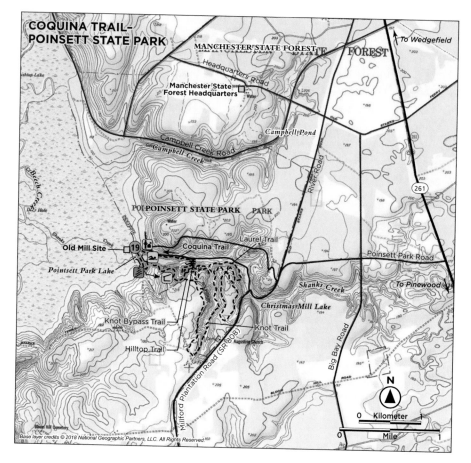

Miles and Directions

0.0 Hike south along the levee.

0.15 Cross a footbridge over Shanks Creek. Hike east and upstream.

0.17 Pass the spillway. Follow green blazes southeast.

0.25 Come to a fork. Go left (north) rapidly downhill.

0.35 Come to a T. Go left (east).

0.55 Hike past a shelter.

0.76 Past the halfway marker, come to a fork. Right (southeast) is the Knot Trail. Go left (northeast), hiking around the split rail fence.

0.85 Come to an intersection. The Knot/Hilltop Trail is right (east). Go straight (north).

1.0 Cross a footbridge.

1.02 Come to a T. Right is the purple-blazed Laurel Trail. Go left (west).

1.05 Hike across a series of boardwalks, footbridges, and wooden planks. Continue hiking west.

1.4 The trail exits the forest east of the boathouse and swim area. Continue hiking west toward the swim area.

1.45 Arrive near the trailhead.

Resting up

Quality Inn, 3031 Paxville Hwy., Manning, (803) 473-7550; pet fee required.
Howard Johnson, 2816 Paxville Hwy., Manning, (803) 473-5135; pet fee required.

Camping

Onsite.

Fueling up

None nearby.

Puppy Paws and Golden Years

Take them to the swim area or over to the old mill site.

Left: The dogs enjoy taking a dip before heading out on the Coquina Trail.
Right: This gorgeous guy kindly paused and posed for the picture.

20 Bike Trail–Santee State Park

Following the western shore of Lake Marion, the Santee Bike Trail leads from the park's Cypress View Campground to a picnic area. The trail is open to mountain bikes, but doesn't see much traffic, so they shouldn't interfere with the peaceful hike ahead. If you follow the entire 7.5-mile loop, a good portion is inland. For this reason, I've adapted this hike into an out-and-back, with the picnic area as your turn-around point.

Start: 251 State Park Rd., Santee; on the right (east) side of the road, before the right turn leading to the Cypress View Campground

Distance: 7.0 miles out and back from the trailhead to the picnic area

Hiking time: About 3.5 hours

Blaze color: Blue

Difficulty: Easy to moderate

Trailhead elevation: 78 feet

Highest point: 103 feet

Best season: Year-round

Schedule: 6 a.m. to 10 p.m.

Trail surface: Hard-packed dirt

Other trail users: Mountain bikers

Canine compatibility: Leash required

Land status: South Carolina Department of Natural Resources

Fees: Fee required

Maps: *DeLorme: South Carolina Atlas & Gazetteer:* Page 46, F4

Trail contacts: (803) 854-2408; www.south carolinaparks.com/santee/introduction.aspx

Nearest town: Santee, St. Matthews, Manning

Trail tips: Bring lots of drinking water.

Special considerations: Alligators do inhabit Lake Marion, and the park's Sinkhole Pond. Please use caution.

Finding the trailhead: From I-95 get off at exit 98. Drive west on SC 6 for 1.1 miles to a right onto State Park Road (SR 105). Travel for 2.3 miles to a stop sign. Continue straight across and drive 1.9 miles to the trailhead on the right.

From the junction of SC 6 and SC 267 near Elloree, drive east on SC 6 for 3.6 miles to a left onto State Park Road (SR 105). Follow directions above. **Trailhead GPS:** N33 32.854'/W80 29.896'

The Hike

Boaters and fishermen flock to the wide open waters of Lake Marion. The lake encompasses 110,000 acres, has over 300 miles of shoreline, and is the largest lake in the state. As you hike alongside this sprawling waterway, deer are abundant, and a variety of birds keep them company. As the path parallels the shoreline, a patch of forest stands between you and the water. Through the trees you may see osprey nesting up high or swallow-tail kites hovering overhead. The trail climbs ever so slightly on a slope that's barely noticeable. If you enjoy trail running, this is a great place for it. Most mountain bikers follow the loop counterclockwise, so you're likely to see them coming. Beyond the 1-mile marker, a bench sits by a stand of pine trees. Pause

The sunsets are simply stunning at Santee State Park.

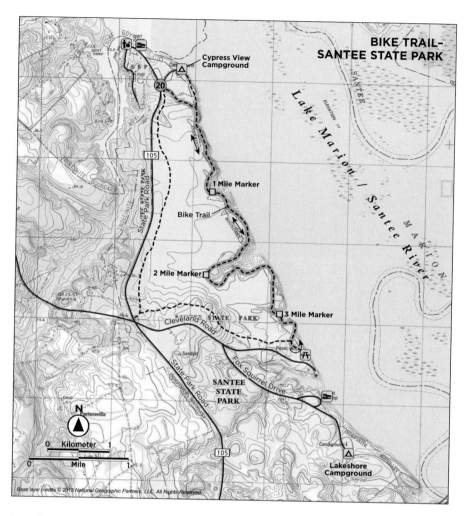

here for a moment and you may see the woodpeckers at work. Bring a camera or binoculars for a better view. Along with the stray sinkhole, the topography includes slight hills, dips, and climbs. After passing the 3-mile mark, you'll come very close to the lake, but the banks are steep, and not suitable for the pooches to access the water. Be patient. When you reach the open grassy picnic area, you can take a detour to the shore where the pups can play in the glorious water of Lake Marion.

Miles and Directions

0.0 Hike southwest into the woods and immediately come to a fork where the loop begins. Go left (southeast) toward the lake.

0.3 Come to a T. Left leads north to the Cypress View Campground (N33 32.963'/W80 29.742'). Go right (south).

1.0 Pass the 1.0-mile marker.

2.0 Pass the 2.0-mile marker.

The white-tailed deer is the state animal of South Carolina.

3.0 Pass the 3.0-mile marker.

3.4 Come to a fork. Right (west) is the continuation of the loop trail. Bypass this, continue straight (south) on the wide grassy trail. Follow the water's edge past the picnic shelters.

3.5 Hike past the posts sticking out of the ground and enter the picnic area (N33 31.105'/ W80 28.746'). Let the dogs play in the water, then backtrack to the trailhead.

7.0 Arrive at the trailhead.

Option: At 3.4 miles, follow the loop inland. This adds 0.5 mile to the total distance of the hike, but I recommend staying with the water. It's cooler for the dogs.

Resting up

Howard Johnson, 249 Britain St., Santee, (803) 854-3221; pet fee required.
Quality Inn, 8929 Bass Dr., Santee, (803) 854-2121; pet fee required. Must call ahead.

Camping

Onsite.

Fueling up

None nearby.

Puppy Paws and Golden Years

Drive directly to the picnic area mentioned at 3.5 miles in the Miles and Directions above. The pups can swim and explore the sights and scents left behind by picnickers.

21 Fit Trail/Interpretive Trail Loop–Lake Warren State Park

This peaceful hike begins along the Fit Trail. Pine trees offer shade, and you'll pass a variety of fitness stops where you can do exercises like leg lifts and body raises. The path is easy to follow, and the deeper you get into the forest, the more diverse it becomes. When you reach the Interpretive Trail, signs help identify a wide range of species, and an assortment of birds serenade you and your canine companions. Enjoy the solitude.

Start: 1079 Lake Warren Rd., Hampton; The trailhead is northeast of the office. Follow the tree line due east for less than 0.1 mile and the Fit Trail begins near the first fitness station.
Distance: 1.2-mile loop
Hiking time: About 45 minutes
Blaze color: Arrows reading "trail"
Difficulty: Easy
Trailhead elevation: 91 feet
Highest point: 105 feet
Best season: Year-round
Schedule: 9 a.m. to dark
Trail surface: Wide grassy path, hard-packed dirt with rooty sections
Other trail users: None
Canine compatibility: Leash required

Land status: South Carolina Department of Natural Resources
Fees: No fee, but donation box located near the park entrance
Maps: *DeLorme: South Carolina Atlas & Gazetteer*: Page 58, A2
Trail contacts: (803) 943-5051; www.south carolinaparks.com/lakewarren/introduction .aspx
Nearest town: Hampton
Trail tips: Restrooms, trash cans, and recycling bins near the trailhead
Special considerations: Alligators inhabit the park pond and lake. Do *not* let the dogs in, or near the water.

Finding the trailhead: From the junction of US 601 and US 278 in Hampton, drive south on US 601 for 3.7 miles to a right onto Lake Warren Road (SR 510). Travel for 1.1 miles to the park on the left. Drive 0.2 mile to the office on the left.

From the junction of SC 363 and US 321 in Luray, drive northeast on SC 363 for 3.1 miles to a right onto Lake Warren Road. Travel for 1.3 miles to the park on the right. Follow directions above.
Trailhead GPS: N32 49.870'/W81 09.881'

The Hike

This peaceful park covers over 400 acres and surrounds the spectacular Lake George Warren. At 200 acres, the lake takes up nearly half the park. A fishing pier juts well out in the water, with a picturesque gazebo at the end. But that's not all this lovely

Left: Bees help pollinate a variety of flowering plants.
Right: Look for passion flower blossoms along the Fit Trail from summer through autumn.

landscape has to offer. The developed portion of the park includes picnic shelters, playgrounds, and a community building. Although the park is best known for the large lake, it also houses a small 2-acre pond. The lake and pond support a variety of life, including armadillo, alligators, deer, raccoon, squirrel, opossum, and fox. Hawks, osprey, and even bald eagles have been seen soaring overhead, while herons and egrets wade along the banks. The two trails featured here form a figure-eight-style loop. You'll begin along the wide grassy Fit Trail, where frequent fitness stops encourage you to do sit-ups and push-ups and such. Pine trees line the path and keep you shaded most of the day. After about a quarter-mile, the wide path narrows and all you hear are birds chirping, and the occasional woodpecker in the tall pines. When you reach the Interpretive Trail the forest immediately thickens, and markers help you identify a variety of trees. Pine, maple, beech, and oak enhance the scenery, and an assortment of ferns line the understory. There are hills, and topography, which is unexpected this far south in the state. Placards will educate you on things like animal tracks, birds, ferns, and nature in general. Looping around the park's pond, the scent of magnolia fills the air. Toads and bullfrogs bellow out loud, and the ground becomes a rooty, moss-covered corridor. Alligator alert—use caution near the pond. Returning to the trailhead, you'll have hiked through three types of forest: pineland, upland hardwoods, and wetland. Enjoy them all!

Miles and Directions

0.0 Follow the wide, grassy Fit Trail south.

0.2 Bypass a side trail to right (southwest). Continue (southeast) on the Fit Trail.

0.5 Come to a T. Left (north) leads 0.1 mile back to the trailhead on the Fit Trail. Go right (south) on the Interpretive Trail.

Option: Shorten the hike to 0.6 mile by returning to the trailhead from here on the Fit Trail.

0.8 Hike past an old plow.

0.9 Come to a T. Right (west) leads 100 feet to an overlook of the pond (N32 49.918'/W81 09.838'). Go left (east).

1.0 Cross a footbridge; continue hiking north.

1.1 Come to a fork. Left (west) passes an outdoor amphitheater and goes to the trailhead. Go right (northwest) toward the picnic area.

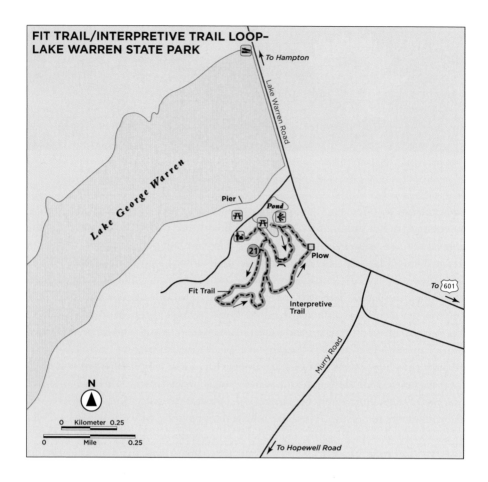

FIT TRAIL/INTERPRETIVE TRAIL LOOP– LAKE WARREN STATE PARK

To Hampton

Lake Warren Road

Lake George Warren

Pier

Pond

21

Plow

Fit Trail

Interpretive Trail

Murry Road

To 601

N

0   Kilometer   0.25

0   Mile   0.25

To Hopewell Road

1.15 Hike through the picnic area. Trail bends left.

1.2 Arrive at the trailhead.

Resting up

Best Western, 3536 Point South Dr., Yemassee, (843) 726-8101; pet fee required, must call ahead.

Knights Inn, 420 Campground Rd., Yemassee, (843) 726-8488; pet fee required.

Camping

Primitive, group camping onsite.

Point South KOA, 14 Campground Rd., Yemassee, (843) 726-5733.

Fueling up

None nearby.

Dogs are allowed on the pier at Lake Warren State Park.

Puppy Paws and Golden Years

Let them play in the large grassy field near the office.

Barnwell

22 Dogwood Interpretive Trail–Barnwell State Park

This lovely interpretive trail begins and ends near the park's swimming area. The dogs are allowed in the water, just not in the swim area. Grab a brochure from the office and follow along with numbered posts. As you educate yourself on the natural features, you're also taking a tour of the park. As you loop around the lake, you'll pass the community building, cabins, and campground. Near the trail's end, a quaint creek and splendid spillway form the finale.

Start: 223 State Park Rd., Blackville; right (north) of the swim area
Distance: 1.3-mile loop
Hiking time: About 45 minutes
Blaze color: None
Difficulty: Easy
Trailhead elevation: 215 feet
Highest point: 267 feet
Best season: Year-round
Schedule: 9 a.m. to 6 p.m. (extended to 9 p.m. Fri, Sat, and Sun during Daylight Saving Time)
Trail surface: Hard-packed dirt

Other trail users: None
Canine compatibility: Leash required
Land status: South Carolina Department of Natural Resources
Fees: No fee
Maps: *DeLorme: South Carolina Atlas & Gazetteer:* Page 52, A4
Trail contacts: (803) 284-2212; www.south carolinaparks.com/barnwell/introduction.aspx
Nearest town: Blackville, Barnwell, Denmark
Trail tips: Restrooms near the park office
Special considerations: Alligators may be present in the park lakes. Please use caution.

Finding the trailhead: From the junction of SC 3 and SC 70 in Barnwell, drive north on SC 3 for 7.0 miles to the park on your left. Follow the park road for 0.2 mile to the park office.

From the junction of SC 3 and US 78 in Blackville, drive south on SC 3 for 1.7 miles to a stop sign. Turn left, and follow SC 3 for another 0.9 mile to the park on your right. Follow directions above. **Trailhead GPS:** N33 19.881'/W81 18.282'

The Hike

It's important to note that the official park map is oriented incorrectly. North on their map is actually facing east. Refer to the accurate map that I've provided instead. This peaceful park boasts three small ponds on the property. You'll be looping around the largest of them all, the 16-acre "lower pond." The hike begins and ends at the swimming area, and the playful pups can go in the water, just not in the official swim area. Use caution with the dogs and the water; alligators do inhabit the park. The easy to follow path leads along the shoreline, and numbered posts coincide with a

The Dogwood Trail loops around a lovely lake.

brochure you can get from the park office. You'll hike past the popular community building, which can be rented out. A number of local events are hosted here, from dances to family reunions. Next you pass by the cozy cabins and you begin to realize you're getting a full tour of the park. What soon follows is the campground, picnic shelters, fishing pier, spillway, and back to the swim area. Be on the lookout for wildlife and waterfowl, especially near the north end of the pond. The forest keeps you shaded for most of the hike, and you can test your knowledge with flip-down boards identifying a variety of trees. On the western shore, a side trip to the fishing pier is worth a peek. The view is fantastic, and there's a natural spring nearby. The hounds will gulp down the fresh, clean water flowing through a pipe, and then out toward the pond. Crossing your third boardwalk, the flora is astonishing. Huge poplars tower overhead, with switch cane, magnolia, and an array of ferns accompanying them. Benches at the south end of the pond offer stunning views. You'll finish your stroll by

A turtle suns himself along the boardwalk at Barnwell.

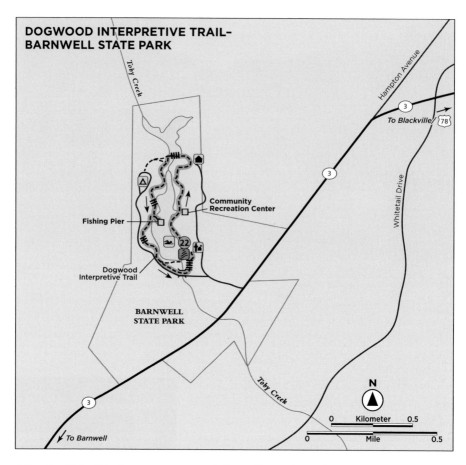

**DOGWOOD INTERPRETIVE TRAIL–
BARNWELL STATE PARK**

Toby Creek

Hampton Avenue

To Blackville 78

Community
Recreation Center

Whitetail Drive

Fishing Pier

Dogwood
Interpretive Trail

**BARNWELL
STATE PARK**

To Barnwell

Toby Creek

N

0   Kilometer   0.5

0   Mile   0.5

following Toby Creek upstream toward the spillway. The spillway is a wonderful man-made waterfall that was constructed in the 1930s by the Civilian Conservation Corps (CCC). The CCC was part of President Franklin Roosevelt's New Deal, creating shovel-ready jobs following the Great Depression. The steady sound of moving water is a fabulous finale.

Miles and Directions

0.0   Hike north into the forest between two split rail fences.

0.1   Hike past the Community Recreation Center (N33 19.969'/W81 18.324').

0.4   Come to a fork. Left leads northwest. Stay right, following the nature trail north.

0.45   Hike past the cabins. Cross a boardwalk.

0.5   Come to a fork. Straight leads to the campground. Go left (southwest) and climb some steps. At the top of the steps reach a second fork. Right leads to the campground. Stay left following the split rail fence to an opening back to the trail.

0.75   Cross a boardwalk. Continue hiking south.

0.8   Hike past the picnic shelters. A side trail leads left about 150 feet to the fishing pier (N33 19.956'/W81 18.375'). After the side trip, continue hiking south.

The spillway is a highlight of the hike at Barnwell State Park.

0.95 Cross a boardwalk.

1.1 Hike southeast past the levee toward the steps leading up to the park road.

1.2 Climb the steps. Go left (southeast) on the park road across the bridge.

1.25 Go left (north) on the long boardwalk, following Toby Creek upstream.

1.3 The trail leads past the spillway (N33 19.822'/W81 18.246') and ends near the swim area.

Resting up

Days Inn, 10747 Dunbarton Blvd., Barnwell, (803) 541-5000; pet fee required.

Camping

Onsite.

Fueling up

None nearby.

Puppy Paws and Golden Years

Take them over to the spillway, or out to the levee.

Contrary to popular belief, dogs are not completely color blind.

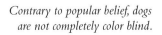

Aiken

23 Hopeland Gardens Trail–Hopeland Gardens

Soft clay dirt and bare brick walkways form a maze of paths leading in all directions through the park. Brilliant blossoms, flowing fountains, magnificent live oaks, and peaceful ponds await your exploration. Because so many conduits crisscross the property, I recommend you explore at will. If you walk every path in the park, you'll cover a total of 1.5 miles. While you get swept away in the beauty, the dogs enjoy the fragrant scents. The residents of Aiken are fortunate to have such a wonderful, well-kept park within easy reach.

Start: 135 Dupree Place, Aiken; The main entrance is at the northeast end of the parking lot.
Distance: 1.5 miles
Hiking time: About 40 minutes
Blaze color: None
Difficulty: Easy
Trailhead elevation: 508 feet
Highest point: 526 feet
Best season: Year-round
Schedule: Open daily 10 a.m. to sunset
Trail surface: Soft clay dirt, brick walkways
Other trail users: None

Canine compatibility: Leash required
Land status: City of Aiken Parks and Recreation
Fees: No fee
Maps: *DeLorme: North Carolina Atlas & Gazetteer:* Page 43, E9
Trail contacts: (803) 642-7650; www .visitaikensc.com/whattodo/detail/ hopelands_gardens
Nearest town: Aiken
Trail tips: Trail maps and garden brochures are near the main entry gate. Bring enough drinking water for you both.

Finding the trailhead: From the junction of SC 19 (Whiskey Road) and US 78/US 1 in Aiken, drive south on SC 19 for 0.8 mile to a right onto Dupree Place. Drive 0.1 mile to the parking lot on the left.

From the junction of SC 19 (Whiskey Road) and SC 118 (Pine Log Road) in Aiken, drive north on SC 19 for 1.8 miles to a left onto Dupree Place. Follow directions above. **Trailhead GPS:** N33 32.935'/W81 43.393'

The Hike

Lampposts line the sidewalks, and painted horses decorate the lovely town of Aiken. But perhaps their greatest treasure is the hallowed grounds of Hopeland Gardens. When you first enter the park, it seems small. But as you explore the gardens and walk from one area to the next, you realize there are actually 1.5 miles of "trails" streaming across a 24-acre parcel of property. There are ponds, fountains, and magnificent

Hopeland Gardens is also home to the Aiken Thoroughbred Racing Hall of Fame and Museum.

live oak trees. A variety of flowers bloom year-round, and signs identify many of the different species. A red brick walkway circles around the perimeter, while narrow clay paths crisscross throughout the park. Dogwood, holly, hibiscus, and magnolia all offer shade, and although you can hear the traffic whizzing by, it's not intrusive. The beautiful breeze, the trees, and the birds singing in these glorious gardens override any distraction. Turtles beg for food as you cross footbridges. They seem to come on cue to the sound of footsteps on the wooden trestles. Koi fish frolic near the small spillway, and rainbow eucalyptus adds to the colorful array of the flora. They have statues of dogs and horses, which is apropos. Hopeland also houses the Aiken Thoroughbred Racing Hall of Fame and Museum. This barn-like building has memorabilia, photo displays, and pays tribute to the many champions that have trained in the area. The park is also home to the "Dollhouse," a pint-size structure used by the Aiken Garden Club. Dogs aren't allowed inside any of the buildings, but with so much beauty around you, you'll want to remain outdoors. The town of Aiken is surrounded by horse country. You'll find horse racing, polo ponies, horse carriages, fox hunts, and even a steeplechase. With this kind of enthusiasm, you'd think you were in Kentucky, prepping for the Derby, Preakness, or Belmont Stakes. Either way, their Hopeland Gardens earns a triple crown rating from me.

Miles and Directions

0.0 A maze of pathways weave throughout the gardens. Explore at will. Walking every path on the property covers 1.5 miles.

Clockwise from top: Benches and blossoms, ponds and pathways all add to the beauty at Hopeland Gardens.
Bandit took an accidental dip in the fountain at Hopeland Gardens.
Turtles beg for food as soon as they see you coming.
Magnificent magnolia trees offer shade and beauty to Hopeland Gardens.

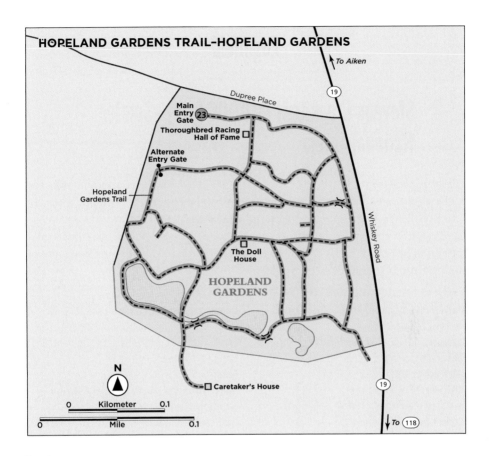

Resting up

Quality Inn and Suites, 3608 Richland Ave. West, Aiken, (803) 641-1100; pet fee required.

Clarion Inn and Suites, 155 Colony Pkwy., Aiken, (803) 648-0999; pet fee required.

Camping

Aiken State Park, 1145 State Park Rd., Windsor, (803) 649-2857.

Fueling up

Apizza Di Napoli, 740 Silver Bluff Rd., Aiken, (803) 226-0700.
Malia's, 120 Laurens St. Southwest, Aiken, (803) 643-3086.

Puppy Paws and Golden Years

Suitable for all dogs, just temper the distance to suit the needs of your pups.

Edgefield

24 Stevens Creek Trail (MODOC Trail)–Sumter National Forest

This trail caters to mountain bikers, but it's quite enjoyable for you and the dogs too. And except for weekends, it doesn't see much traffic. The trail topography gives you a nice challenge as it climbs and falls, and climbs and falls. The map is a bit deceiving though. It appears as though you closely follow the creek, but in reality a good amount of brush separates you from the water. So bring plenty of water along for you and your canine compadres.

Start: On the north side of SC 23, just west of the Stevens Creek bridge
Distance: 4.0 miles out and back
Hiking time: About 2 hours
Blaze color: Red
Difficulty: Moderate
Trailhead elevation: 246 feet
Highest point: 298 feet
Best season: Year-round
Schedule: Open daily from sunrise to sunset
Trail surface: Hard-packed dirt
Other trail users: Mountain bikers

Canine compatibility: Voice control; Keep them on leash until well into the woods.
Land status: South Carolina Department of Natural Resources
Fees: No fee
Maps: *DeLorme: South Carolina Atlas & Gazetteer:* Page 42, B4
Trail contacts: (803) 637-5396; www.fs.usda .gov/recarea/scnfs/recreation/bicycling/ recarea/?recid=47193&actid=24
Nearest town: Edgefield, McCormick
Trail tips: Bring a hiking stick, and lots of drinking water for you and the dogs.

Finding the trailhead: From the junction of SC 23 and SC 230 in Edgefield, drive west on SC 23 for 8.1 miles to the trailhead on the right (just after crossing the bridge over Stevens Creek).

From the junction of SC 23 and US 221 in Modoc, drive east on SC 23 for 1.2 miles to the trailhead on the left (just before crossing the bridge over Stevens Creek). **Trailhead GPS:** N33 43.774'/W82 11.051'

The Hike

This popular mountain biking destination is often referred to as MODOC, for the nearby town. If you want to steer clear of the majority of mountain bikers, avoid the weekends. Also, use caution unloading your eager pups. The trailhead is very close to the road. You'll begin by following a rugged, rocky path downhill into the forest. Crossing a small tributary gives the pups one of few freshwater encounters.

Left: Puppies big and small will enjoy hiking along the singletrack trail at Stevens Creek.
Center: The dogs enjoy splashing across this rocky creek crossing.
Right: Sometimes you have to stop and smell the flowers.

Keep your eyes peeled; turtles, snakes, turkey, and deer all flourish here. Hunting season runs from September to January, so if you hike then, wear blaze orange. And dress the dogs in the flashy color as well. The path is easy to follow, since it's well trodden by bicycles. When you cross the shallow, rocky bed of Key Branch, give the dogs lots of time to play. This is their primary water stop. The natural topography leads you over rolling hills that climb and fall over the length of the trail. This adds a bit of a challenge to the hike, so bring lots of water for you and your four-legged friends. Even though you're not hiking creekside, the forest is fabulous. It's heavily wooded, hilly, and there's an abundance of wildlife. Raccoons, fox, deer, coyote, squirrels, and bear all inhabit the area. Wildflowers add a splash of color in spring and summer, and birds fill the air with song. The trees keep you shaded and cool from overhead, and ferns cover the forest floor, creating a corridor for you and the dogs to hike through. When you reach 2 miles deep, a narrow path leads left up to an alternative trailhead. This is a good turnaround point,

Camping at nearby Hamilton Branch State Park is some of the best in the state.

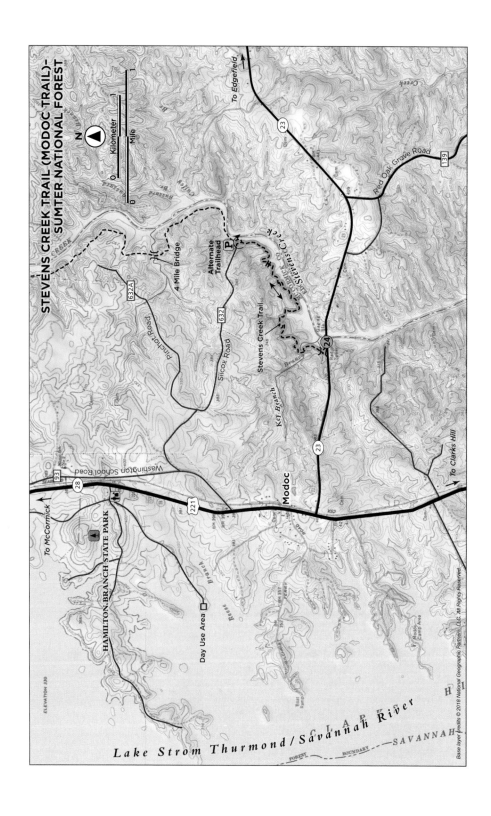

STEVENS CREEK TRAIL (MODOC TRAIL)–SUMTER NATIONAL FOREST

To Edgefield

23

Red Oak Grove Road

139

4 Mile Bridge

Alternate Trailhead

P

632A

632

Pinchot Road

Silcox Road

Stevens Creek Trail

Lake Stevens Cr

24

Key Branch

Bread

23

Modoc

To Clarks Hill

93

28

Washington School Road

221

HAMILTON BRANCH STATE PARK

To McCormick

Branch

Rease

Day Use Area

ELEVATION 330

Lake Strom Thurmond / Savannah River

SAVANNAH

FOREST BOUNDARY

N

Kilometer

Mile

0   1

making this a 4-mile outing. Although you're in the Piedmont, this one has a mountain feel to it. If you have extra time, visit nearby Hamilton Branch State Park. The park rests on a pristine peninsula that juts out into Lake Strom Thurmond, and has one of the best campgrounds in the state. Sunsets are stupendous, and the dogs can swim and play in the crystal-clear water.

Miles and Directions

0.0   Hike west downhill into the woods.

0.05   Cross a footbridge over a tiny tributary. Continue hiking north.

0.3   Rock-hop across Key Branch.

1.6   Cross some wooden planks over a dried up tributary.

1.7   Hike across a rocky area. The trail bends right (south).

2.0   Come to a fork. Left (northwest) is a narrow path leading to an alternate trailhead on Silcox Road (FR 632). Right (northeast), the Stevens Creek Trail continues for another 3.5 miles. Backtrack to the trailhead.

Option: To extend the hike, stay right at the fork and continue following Stevens Creek Trail generally north.

4.0   Arrive at the trailhead.

This little guy was not shy as he hiked along the path too.

Resting up

La Quinta Inn, 3020 Washington Rd., Augusta, GA, (706) 733-2660; no pet fee.
Quality Inn and Suites, 3608 Richland Ave. West, Aiken, (803) 641-1100; pet fee required.

Camping

Hamilton Branch State Park, 111 Campground Rd., Plum Branch, (864) 333-2223.

Fueling up

Blue Sky Kitchen, 990 Broad St., Augusta, GA, (706) 821-3988.
Mellow Mushroom, 1167 Broad St., Augusta, GA, (706) 828-5578.

Puppy Paws and Golden Years

Take them over to the day use area of Hamilton Branch State Park. The park is surrounded by the clear green water of Lake Strom Thurmond.

McCormick

25 Wild Mint Nature Trail–Baker Creek State Park

This quaint state park rests peacefully on a peninsula along the banks of Baker Creek and Lake Thurmond. The nature trail quickly leads to a fantastic sandy beach where the dogs can romp around in and out of the water. Pay close attention to the Miles and Directions, since this hike can be a bit hard to follow. In general, you'll start along the waterline, before looping inland. Keep your eyes peeled; a variety of birds and wildlife make their home here.

Start: 863 Baker Creek Rd., McCormick; near the entrance to Campground # 2, across the street (east) from the restrooms. A sign reads "Nature Trail."
Distance: 0.9 mile
Hiking time: About 30 minutes
Blaze color: White
Difficulty: Easy to moderate
Trailhead elevation: 346 feet
Highest point: 381 feet
Best season: Open Mar 1–Sep 30
Schedule: 6 a.m. to 6 p.m. (extended to 9 p.m. during Daylight Saving Time)
Trail surface: Hard-packed dirt

Other trail users: None
Canine compatibility: Leash required
Land status: South Carolina Department of Natural Resources
Fees: Fee required; self-pay station, bring singles
Maps: *DeLorme: South Carolina Atlas & Gazetteer:* Page 33, H7
Trail contacts: (864) 443-2457; www.south carolinaparks.com/bakercreek/introduction .aspx
Nearest town: McCormick, Greenwood
Trail tips: Restrooms and a trail map near the trailhead.

Finding the trailhead: From the junction of US 378 and US 221 in McCormick, drive west on US 378 for 3.7 miles to a right onto Hugenot Parkway (SR 467). Travel for 1.1 miles to a left onto Baker Creek Road at the entrance to the park. Follow signs to Campground #2. Park by the restrooms near the entrance to Campground #2.

From the SC/GA state line and US 378, drive east on US 378 for 2.9 miles to a left onto Huge-not Parkway and follow the directions above. **Trailhead GPS:** N33 52.815/W82 21.881'

The Hike

This waterfront park draws a number of aquatic enthusiasts. Boaters and fishermen flock to this wonderful waterway, and the park makes it easy to access, with two boat ramps onsite. Even campers can cruise their boats right up to the edge of some of the sites. Swimming is allowed, and guests freely float on tubes out in the water, or sun themselves on the banks. Land lovers will find a basketball hoop on one side

The long-range views of Lake Strom Thurmond are outstanding.

of the park, and a sand volleyball court on the other. There are picnic shelters and playgrounds, or you can relax on the lovely deck overlooking the water. If you prefer action, miles of mountain bike trails traverse the park. You can use these mountain bike trails on foot if you want a longer hike. But to avoid the two-wheeled traffic, stick to the Wild Mint Nature Trail, which is dedicated solely to hiking. Pine trees are predominant here, but you'll also find some young hardwoods mixed in. The forest supports a variety of wildlife. Deer are abundant, and turkey, woodpeckers, waterfowl, and an array of other birds fill the air with song. As you begin to hike, the lake imme-

diately comes into view, and you quickly arrive at a fantastic sandy "beach." This is a perfect place for the dogs to get some extra energy out as they run, dig, splash, and swim. The first part of the loop follows the shoreline, but sometimes from up above. Steep climbs and descents add a taste of topography, and you both enjoy the challenge it presents. The views are fantastic, and a gentle breeze helps to keep you cool. As the trail dips inland, you'll cross the park road two times, so keep the dogs on leash. Shade is intermittent, so bring lots of water to keep your happy hounds hydrated. As you return to the trailhead, you'll pass the swim area again. Make sure you have a towel in the car so the pups can play in the water again. They'll still be damp when you reach the car, no matter how many times they shake. This park is open seasonally. To hike year-round, visit their sister park, Hickory Knob (see Beaver Run Trail).

Osprey are easily identifiable by the sleek stripe on the side of their head.

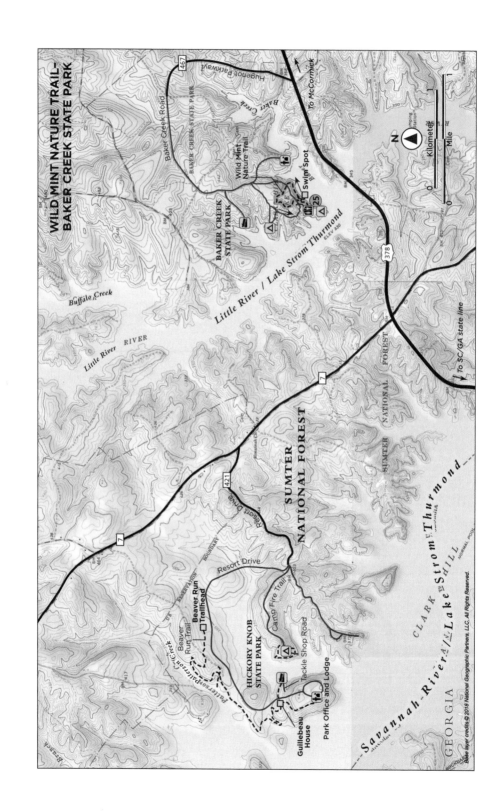

WILD MINT NATURE TRAIL–BAKER CREEK STATE PARK

This pair of ponies is well fed.

Miles and Directions

0.0 Hike east, steeply down to the lake.

100' Stop at the sandy "beach." Continue hiking northeast.

0.1 Cross a footbridge and come to a fork where the loop begins. Go right (southeast).

0.12 Cross a footbridge; hike southeast, steeply uphill.

0.33 Cross the road. Hike northwest into the forest.

0.75 Cross the road. Hike south toward the lake.

0.8 Come to the fork where the loop began. Backtrack to the trailhead.

0.9 Arrive at the trailhead.

Resting up

Quality Inn, 719 Bypass 25 Northeast, Greenwood, (864) 229-5329; pet fee required.
Baymont Inn and Suites, 109 Enterprise Ct., Greenwood, (864) 942-0002; pet fee required.

Camping

Onsite March 1 to September 30.
Hickory Knob State Resort Park, 1591 Resort Dr., McCormick, (864) 391-2450.

Fueling up

None nearby.

Puppy Paws and Golden Years

Take them to the swim area about 100 feet into the hike.

26 Beaver Run Trail–Hickory Knob State Resort

Spanning the eastern edge of this active resort, the trail starts across from the club-house and ends near the park's lodge. Pine trees offer shade, and depending on lake levels, you may pass a pair of swim spots. Although the park is populated, you'll feel as though you're deep in the forest. When the lake comes into view, a gentle breeze blows, and you and the dogs enjoy a breath of fresh air.

Start: 1591 Resort Dr., McCormick; northwest corner of the parking lot, marked with a purple blaze on a post
Distance: 5.0 miles out and back
Hiking time: About 2 hours, 30 minutes
Blaze color: White
Difficulty: Easy
Trailhead elevation: 388 feet
Highest point: 414 feet
Best season: Year-round
Schedule: Open 24 hours a day
Trail surface: Hard-packed dirt
Other trail users: Mountain bikers

Canine compatibility: Leash required
Land status: South Carolina Department of Natural Resources
Fees: No fee
Maps: *DeLorme: South Carolina Atlas & Gazetteer:* Page 33, H6
Trail contacts: (864) 391-2450; www.south carolinaparks.com/hickoryknob/introduction .aspx
Nearest town: McCormick, Greenwood
Trail tips: Bring lots of drinking water for you and the dogs. Swim spots depend on lake levels.

Finding the trailhead: From the junction of US 378 and US 221 in McCormick, drive west on US 378 for 5.8 miles to a right turn onto SR 7. Travel for 1.6 miles to a left onto Resort Drive (SR 421). Drive 2.2 miles to a right onto a dirt road across the street from the golf pro shop. Before this road leads into the skeet/archery area, park to the left.

From the junction of SC 81 and SC 28 near McCormick, drive north on SC 81 for 1.7 miles to a left onto SR 7. Travel for 5.2 miles to a right onto Resort Drive (SR 421). Follow directions above.
Trailhead GPS: N33 53.517'/W82 25.320'

The Hike

The abundance of activities at Hickory Knob is absolutely astonishing! They have a swimming pool, eighteen-hole golf course, basketball, volleyball, tennis, campground, cabins, a lodge, boat ramp, fishing, archery, mountain bike trails, hiking, and even a skeet shooting range. Without exaggeration, there's something for everyone. This park is top of the line, and with all these activities, has earned the designation of state "resort" park. Although the park is populated, when you hit the trail, you'll leave the droves of people behind, and feel like it's just you and the dogs off in the forest. The narrow path is open to mountain bikers, but they prefer the longer Lakeview Loop Trail. Following a long, slow, steady descent, the trail zigzags through the forest for about a half-mile before the lake comes into view. A patch of woods separates you from the water, but the wind

Left: A variety of activities are available at Hickory Knob.
Right: An eighteen-hole golf course is one of the many amenities at Hickory Knob State Park.

instantly picks up. It's like night and day from the forest to the shoreline. Shade, a breeze, birds singing, and waterfront views are all enjoyed here. The trail loosely shadows the main park road, so abide by the park's leash law. You may hear an occasional car pass by, but in general, it's quite peaceful. And you're more focused on the shoreline than any traffic in the distance. You'll cross two dirt access roads along the way. Both lead to the water's edge. Pending water levels, you'll find a nice swim spot for the dogs, or they'll end up with awfully muddy paws. In times of drought, take them for a dip near the boat ramp. The trail is shaded, and by 2.0 miles loops around the Guillebeau House. This vintage structure was built circa 1770. It stands today as one of the park's lodging options, and can be rented nightly or weekly. The white-blazed path remains under the cover of the forest until it comes to an end near the end of the park road. Deer, skunks, opossum, and raccoons are among the mammals you may encounter here. Birdlife is also abundant, which is no wonder, since the park rests on the shores of Lake Strom Thurmond (Clarks Hill Lake). This reservoir encompasses a full 71,000 acres, and forms part of the border between South Carolina and Georgia. The sunsets are exceptional.

Miles and Directions

0.0 Hike west into the forest.

0.9 Hike across a dirt access road.

1.6 Hike across a dirt access road. This may make a good swim spot, pending lake levels.(N33 53.081'/W82 26.065'). Continue hiking south.

1.9 The trail is routed left (east) jutting back inland. Follow the white blazes. This is the only tricky spot on the trail.

2.0 The trail loops around the Guillebeau House (N33 53.001'/W82 25.939'). Continue hiking south.

Option: If the lake levels were low and you want to take the dogs for a dip, hike down to the boat ramp (N33 52.972'/W82 25.725') from here. It's 0.1 mile down Tackle Shop Road.

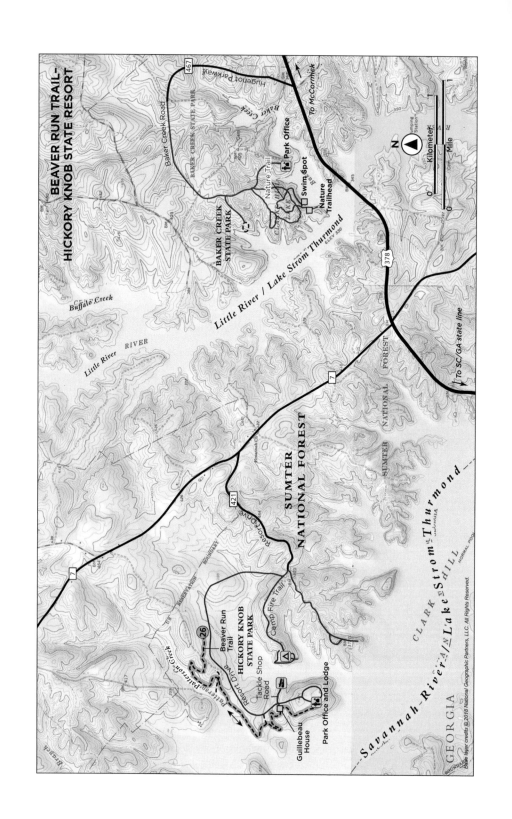

Left: Are we there yet?
Right: Goats can be domesticated too.

2.5 The trail ends at the park road near the park office and lodge (N33 52.730'/W82 25.850'). Backtrack to the trailhead.

5.0 Arrive at the trailhead.

Resting up

Quality Inn, 719 Bypass 25 Northeast, Greenwood, (864) 229-5329; pet fee required. America's Best Value Inn, 1215 NE CR 72 Bypass, Greenwood, (864) 223-2838; pet fee required.

Camping

Onsite.

Fueling up

None nearby.

Puppy Paws and Golden Years

Take them for a dip near the boat dock or boat ramp. Or visit Baker Creek State Park, where you can bring them to the swim "beach" (see Wild Mint Nature Trail hike).

Calhoun Falls

27 Mariner Nature Trail–Calhoun Falls State Park

Visitors flock to Calhoun Falls State Park for the pristine waters of Richard B. Russell Lake. The park houses a marina, tackle shop, boat ramp, fishing pier, and swim area. On top of that, you can rent a boat slip, or simply cruise your craft right up to your campsite. As you'll see on the hike, you can also enjoy the crystal-clear water from dry land as well. This short and shady hike brings you across several footbridges, and the dogs enjoy refreshing dip after dip.

Start: 46 Maintenance Shop Rd., Calhoun Falls; East of the park office you'll see a small footbridge. This is the trailhead.
Distance: 0.5 mile out and back
Hiking time: About 20 minutes
Blaze color: Blue
Difficulty: Easy
Trailhead elevation: 483 feet
Highest point: 532 feet
Best season: Year-round
Schedule: 6 a.m. to 6 p.m. (extended to 9 p.m. during Daylight Saving Time)
Trail surface: Hard-packed dirt
Other trail users: None
Canine compatibility: Leash required

Land status: South Carolina Department of Natural Resources
Fees: Fee required
Maps: *DeLorme: South Carolina Atlas & Gazetteer:* Page 32, D4
Trail contacts: (864) 447-8267; www.south carolinaparks.com/calhounfalls/introduction .aspx
Nearest town: Calhoun Falls, Abbeville
Trail tips: Bring a towel for the dogs; there are plenty of swim spots for them, and the trail is short. They may still be damp by the time you return to the trailhead.
Special considerations: Alligators may inhabit Richard B. Russell Lake. Use caution.

Finding the trailhead: From the junction of SC 81 and SC 72 in Calhoun Falls, drive north on SC 81 for 1.0 mile to a left onto Calhoun Falls State Park Road. Travel for 0.9 mile to the park at the end of the road. Follow the park road for 1.7 miles to a right toward the park office. Drive 0.3 mile to the parking at the bottom of the hill.

From the junction of SC 81 and SC 71 near Lowndesville, drive south on SC 81 for 7.9 miles to a right onto Calhoun Falls State Park Road. Follow directions above. **Trailhead GPS:** N34 06.031'/ W82 37.181'

The Hike

Calhoun Falls State Park is brimming with activities. The park sits on a cloverleaf-style peninsula jutting into the fabulous waters of Richard B. Russell Lake. The lake is massive and forms part of the border between South Carolina and Georgia. It encompasses nearly 27,000 acres and has 540 miles of shoreline. But what's so extraordinary

A beautiful mare roams the pasture.

about this reservoir is that it has very limited development. If you explore by boat, you'll find this untainted treasure is absolutely stunning! People are drawn to the magical clear green water, and the park provides easy access with a boat ramp, seasonal swim beach, and two fishing piers. They also have a full-service marina, in-water fueling station, tackle shop, fish cleaning station, and boat slips for long-term lease. If that wasn't enough, you can also rent a boat slip nightly or pull your boat right up to your campsite, anchoring in the flawless water of Lake Russell with your dog as your first mate. You couldn't ask for more from a waterfront park, yet they give you more. The park also has tennis, basketball, picnic shelters, and playgrounds, so you can enjoy it by land as much as you do by water. Also, the neighboring McCalla State Natural Area has miles of equestrian trails that are open to hikers. But right here on the Calhoun Falls property, you'll find a fantastic little hiking trail. The Mariner Trail offers several swim spots for the dogs and keeps you shaded for most of the hike. The swim spots are spectacular. Brilliant green water meets the orange clay coast, and the contrast of color is captivating. The dogs can take a cooling dip or chase a stick out into the lake. As you follow the shoreline, the views are phenomenal. Although it's a short hike, you'll cross several footbridges. Beyond the seventh and final footbridge, the trail climbs, and moves away from the water. At 0.25 mile, the Mariner Trail comes to an abrupt stop at a T with the Cart Trail. Left leads to the campground. If you're camping here, you could do this hike backwards. To the right, the Cart Trail leads back toward the park office. You could make a loop, but I prefer returning on the Mariner Trail, since it stays with the water. The breeze is lovely, the views are unmatched, and the canine kids get to swim again. Ahoy mates.

Miles and Directions

0.0   Cross a footbridge and follow the shoreline northeast.

150'   Cross a footbridge and come to a clay beach (N34 06.043'/W82 37.210'). Continue hiking near the shoreline.

0.07   Cross a footbridge and head down some steps.

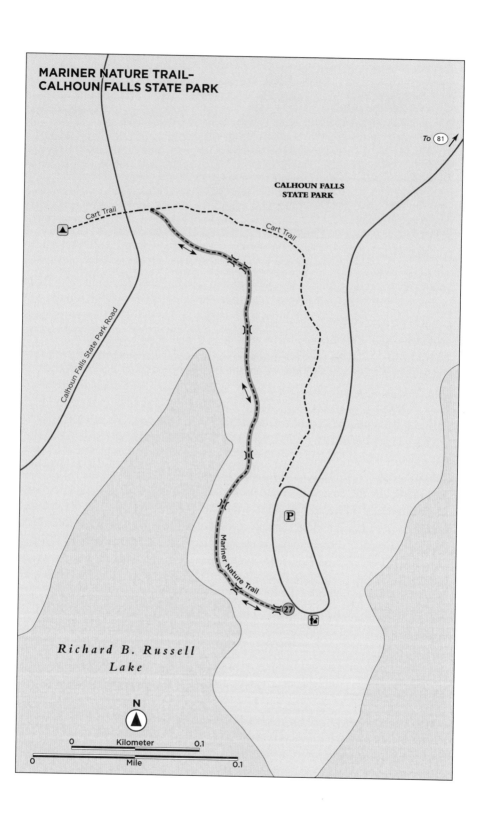

MARINER NATURE TRAIL–
CALHOUN FALLS STATE PARK

To 81

CALHOUN FALLS
STATE PARK

Cart Trail

Cart Trail

Calhoun Falls State Park Road

P

Mariner Nature Trail

27

Richard B. Russell
Lake

N

| 0 | Kilometer | 0.1 |
| 0 | Mile | 0.1 |

John Deere, a household name in the midlands.

0.1 Cross a footbridge and pass another swim spot.

0.16 Cross a footbridge; continue hiking north.

0.19 Cross a footbridge.

0.2 Cross your final footbridge over a gully. Continue hiking west.

0.25 The trail ends at a T with the Cart Trail. Backtrack to the trailhead.

Option: Follow the Cart Trail back to the park road. It ends less than 0.1 mile from the park office.

0.5 Arrive at the trailhead.

Resting up

Magnuson Hotel, 970 Elbert St., Elberton, GA, (706) 283-8811; pet fee required. Quality Inn, 719 Bypass US 25, Greenwood, (864) 229-5329; pet fee required.

Camping

Onsite.

Fueling up

None nearby.

Puppy Paws and Golden Years

Dogs both young and old will be able to hike 150 feet in to the second footbridge. Just after crossing it, there's a beautiful clay sandy beach where the pups can cool off and enjoy relaxing in the refreshing water of Lake Russell.

Greenwood

28 Greenwood Lake Nature Trail–Lake Greenwood State Park

This short but lovely loop trail skirts along the banks of Lake Greenwood before making its return inland. Local fishermen use the narrow paths leading off to the lake to cast their lines. You can use these same paths to access swim spots for the dogs. On the latter interior half of the hike, you'll enjoy shade from the tall longleaf pine trees as they shoot straight toward the sky. From osprey to owls, and coots to cardinals, you'll find a variety of birds inhabit the park both on the shore and in the forest. Bring your binoculars.

Start: 302 State Park Rd., Ninety Six; The trailhead is in Campground #1, on the west side of the Recreation Building.
Distance: 0.7-mile loop
Hiking time: About 20 minutes
Blaze color: Blue
Difficulty: Easy to moderate
Trailhead elevation: 509 feet
Highest point: 515 feet
Best season: Year-round
Schedule: 6 a.m. to 6 p.m. (extended to 10 p.m. during Daylight Saving Time)
Trail surface: Hard-packed dirt
Other trail users: None

Canine compatibility: Leash required
Land status: South Carolina Department of Natural Resources
Fees: Fee required
Maps: *DeLorme: South Carolina Atlas & Gazetteer:* Page 34, C1
Trail contacts: (864) 543-3535; www.south carolinaparks.com/lakegreenwood/introduction.aspx
Nearest town: Ninety Six, Greenwood, Newberry
Trail tips: Restroom and water spigots inside the loop for Campground #1

Finding the trailhead: From the junction of SC 702 and SC 246 near Ninety Six, drive east on SC 702 for 5.3 miles to the park on the left. Drive 0.7 mile to the park office. Go left, following signs to Campground #1. Park at the Recreation Building on your left near the entrance to Campground #1.

From the junction of SC 702 and SC 34 near Ninety Six, drive west on SC 702 for 1.9 miles to the park on the right. Follow directions above. **Trailhead GPS:** N34 11.811'/W81 57.146'

The Hike

As you enter Lake Greenwood State Park, your first introduction is a colorful array of flowers. The state park service and the Garden Club of South Carolina have done a fantastic job planting and maintaining a variety of floral displays for your viewing

Clockwise from top left: She found a friend. Pasture grass is an important part of a healthy horse diet. Barns abound across the Piedmont.

and fragrant pleasure. An abundance of wisteria dangles from the trees, coming into full bloom in early spring, while tulips, iris, and daffodils sprout up from the ground offering a rainbow of color. Be on the lookout while you hike as well, since a variety of wildflowers are also found along the nature trail. As you begin this hike, the trail skirts around the edge of the campground, and the sounds of campers can be heard in the background: children riding their bikes, pots and pans clanging as people make a morning meal, and families laughing as they bond together with nature. After crossing what looks like an old logging road, the path leads you out toward a little cove on the south side of the lake. A number of narrow footpaths left by fishermen lead right to the water's edge. You can use these same routes to take the dogs out for a refreshing dip. The trail briefly bends inland, but you soon find yourself once again following the shoreline along a neighboring cove. Osprey squawk, owls hoot, cardinals tweet, and warblers serenade you with their sweet-sounding songs. At about the halfway mark, the trail leaves the view of the lake, and heads inland again. As you explore the interior of this pleasant peninsula, you'll find an abundance of longleaf pine trees shooting straight toward the sky. Within the pines keep an eye out for woodpeckers blending in with the bark. Listen for their laugh as they fly from tree to tree, or the sound of their drumming as they perch and persistently peck on the pines. The undergrowth holds a large number of immature oak saplings, which one day may stand as tall as the pines beside them. After crossing a tiny footbridge, the trail begins to climb. It's amazing

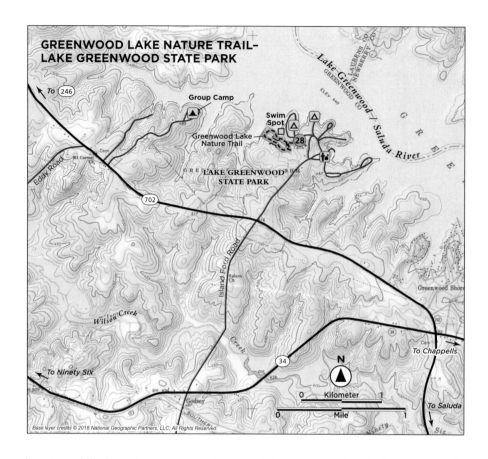

how incredibly busy the campground is, especially on the weekends. But when you're out on the trail, you'll find a wonderful respite of peace and quiet. As you continue your exploration of the area, you'll find the forest quickly transforms into poplars. Their bright yellow and orange blossoms dot the ground on which you walk. Make sure you take a moment to look up and appreciate these natural beauties. When you return to the fork where the loop began, you may want to follow it around a second time, just for fun. Lake Greenwood State Park dates back to the 1930s, and is one of many that was built by the Civilian Conservation Corps (CCC). Some of the structures that were built by these hardworking men are still standing on the property today. A museum honoring their memory is found within the park's Drummond Center. Dogs are not allowed inside, so you'll have to save that for another day.

Miles and Directions

0.0   Hike south along the west side of the Recreation Building. An obvious footpath leads into the woods.

0.1   Hike across an access road. The trail makes a steep dip and climb across a small gully. After the gully, go right (north) toward the lake.

0.15 Take any of the small footpaths to the water's edge so the dogs can swim.

All that's missing is your puppy's paw prints.

0.4 Cross a footbridge. Continue hiking east as you climb.

0.6 Come to a fork near the gully at 0.1 mile. Follow the gully to the first fork, and backtrack to the trailhead.

0.7 Arrive at the trailhead.

Resting up

Quality Inn, 719 Bypass 25 Northeast, Greenwood, (864) 229-5329; pet fee required. America's Best Value Inn, 1215 NE Bypass Highway 72, Greenwood, (864) 223-2838; pet fee required.

Camping

Onsite.

Fueling up

Frayed Knot Bar and Grill, 1701 Dreher Island Rd., Chapin, (803) 945-1792.

Puppy Paws and Golden Years

Take them to the swim spot at 0.15 mile along the trail.

Newberry

29 Little Gap Trail–Dreher Island State Park

A beautiful lake, hilly terrain, and lots of swimming spots for the dogs puts this one among my favorites. And although you'll find this park tends to be busy, once you get out on the trail the only presence around you will be that of peace and quiet. Ahh, take a deep breath and take it all in. You'll enjoy shade from the forest, a nice change in topography, and the wagging tails of your happy pups.

Start: 3677 State Park Rd., Prosperity; As soon as you enter the parking lot, the trailhead is on the right before reaching shelter #7. Southwest corner of the parking lot.
Distance: 2.45 miles out and back
Hiking time: About 1 hour, 15 minutes
Blaze color: White blazes with arrows
Difficulty: Easy to moderate
Trailhead elevation: 413 feet
Highest point: 445 feet
Best season: Year-round
Schedule: Dawn to dusk
Trail surface: Hard-packed dirt
Other trail users: None

Canine compatibility: Leash required
Land status: South Carolina Department of Natural Resources
Fees: Fee required
Maps: DeLorme: South Carolina Atlas & Gazetteer: Page 35, E8
Trail contacts: (803) 364-4152; www.south carolinaparks.com/dreherisland/introduction .aspx
Nearest town: Newberry, Columbia
Trail tips: A detailed map and trash can are near the trailhead. Restrooms are at the southeast corner of the parking lot.

Finding the trailhead: From I-26 southbound, get off at exit 91 and go left following Columbia Avenue for 2.0 miles. Cross the railroad tracks and go right on US 76. Travel for 0.2 mile and go left on St. Peters Church Road (SR 29). Drive 3.5 miles to a left onto Dreher Island Road (SR 231). Travel for 2.9 miles to a left onto State Park Road (SR 571). Travel for 2.6 miles to the park at the end of the road. Follow State Park to a left onto Red Maple Drive. Drive up the hill less than 0.1 mile and park near Shelter #7.

From SC 391 (Main Street) and US 76 in Prosperity, drive south on SC 391 for 0.6 mile to where SC 391 heads right and becomes Broad Street. At this intersection, follow Main Street straight ahead. After 0.8 mile, Main Street becomes Macedonia Church Road. Travel for 8.0 miles (from Broad Street) to a left onto Dreher Island Road. Follow directions above. **Trailhead GPS:** N34 04.927'/W81 24.137'

The Hike

Sitting out on three islands in the middle of Lake Murray, Dreher Island State Park is a very popular fishing and boating destination, to say the least. They have 12 miles of

Cypress trees add to the scenery along the shores of Lake Murray.

shoreline, three busy boat ramps, and an in-water fuel dock to accommodate this active aquatic community. People swim offshore, pull water skiers and tubes, hang out on pontoon boats, jump wakes with their personal watercraft, and cast their fishing lines while their bait wells stir. Amid all this action, there's a little known secret at the south end of the park: the Little Gap Trail. This wonderful trail leads you out to explore the only undeveloped lobe of land in the park. It's a refreshing getaway from the people and endless activity going on within the park. This hike brings you closer to the simplicity of just plain old Mother Nature. As you hike through a forest of tall pine trees, the ground is carpeted with pine needles, and the shady path skirts along the edge of the island. With the lake in view, you'll hike along a contour. The trail is a bit off camber, which is harder on you, but the dogs don't even seem to notice. The terrain is surprisingly hilly for being in the middle of the state, and on a lake to boot. You'll climb up and down steep stretches of trail. The park map shows the trail far more inland than it actually is. The trail follows the shoreline, and the only signs of humanity are the blazes on the trees and the boaters anchored in the little coves. You'll appreciate the occasional white quartz jutting up curiously out of the earth, and several swim holes are ideal for the playful pups. The dogs will love frolicking about in the water, as small waves ebb and flow on the shore. Along with the blazes, you may notice other markers that are part of the Eagle Scout Orienteering Course. If you enjoy navigating, you may want to grab a map and compass and try your hand at it. A steady breeze keeps you cool, and the views of Lake Murray are constant. When you reach a large sign greeting boaters to the state park, a bench accompanies it. This is a fantastic place to sit and take it all in. The long-range views are exceptional. Unfortunately, this isn't a very good swim spot for the canine kids. You're up on a small bluff, and the waves have washed away the earthen shore, forming a wall of eroded earth. Instead, sit, stay, take a break, have a snack, and enjoy the fabulous breeze that comes with the view of wide-open water. When you're ready to continue hiking, the trail loops around on a

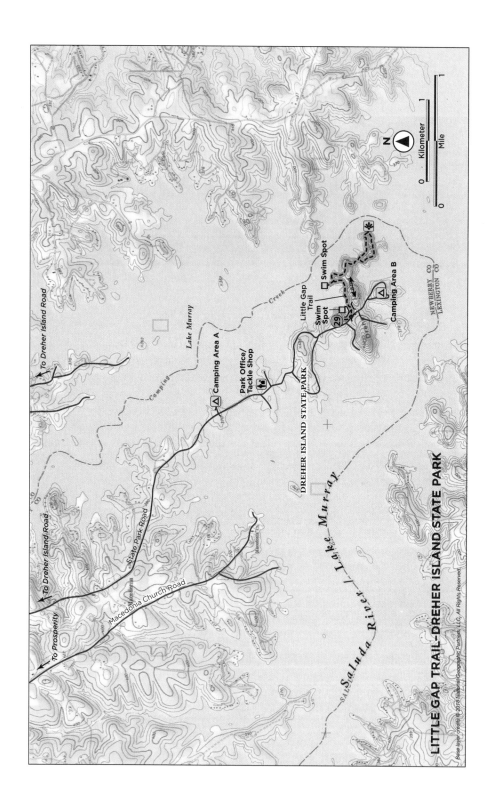

LITTLE GAP TRAIL-DREHER ISLAND STATE PARK

small ridgeline. The strong scent of pine trees fills the air, but you'll also find oak, maple, poplar, sweet gum and holly complement the pines. As you explore this untainted portion of the park, take it all in, and enjoy the solitude while you can.

Miles and Directions

0.0 Hike south into the forest.

0.15 Cross a footbridge. To the left is a great swim area.

0.17 Cross a footbridge. Continue hiking northeast.

0.5 Come to a fork. Left leads north to another perfect swim hole and sandbar. Right (east) is the continuation of the Little Gap Trail. Go left to the swim hole.

0.57 Arrive at the sandbar swimming hole. Return to the fork.

0.65 Arrive back at the fork. Follow the Little Gap Trail east.

0.95 Come to power lines. Go left, following the power lines southeast for 100 feet. Cut back into the forest.

1.0 Come to a fork where the loop begins. Go right (southwest).

1.35 Come to a bench and a large sign for the state park. Continue hiking northwest on the loop.

1.6 Arrive at the fork where the loop began. Backtrack to the trailhead.

2.45 Arrive at the trailhead.

Resting up

Econo Lodge Inn and Suites, 1147 Wilson Rd., Newberry, (803) 276-1600; pet fee required.
Days Inn, 50 Thomas Griffin Rd., Newberry, (803) 276-2294; pet fee required.

Camping

Onsite.

Fueling up

Frayed Knot Bar and Grill, 1701 Dreher Island Rd., Chapin, (803) 945-1792.
Tonella's Pizza Kitchen, 1349 Dutch Fork Rd., Ballentine, (803) 749-7901.

Puppy Paws and Golden Years

Take them to the first swim hole at 0.15 mile.

Top: Mikey takes a dip near a sandbar in Lake Murray.
Bottom: The Little Gap Trail is surprisingly hilly.

Winnsboro

30 Desportes Nature Trail–Lake Wateree State Park

The first thing you should know about this hike is that the general park map is wrong. Be sure to refer to the park's trail map, or the map that I've provided. The trail makes a double lollipop-style loop, reaching out to both sides of the southern part of the island. Birdlife is abundant, and you may hear the loud honking cry of a heron, or the chirping peeps of a brilliant red cardinal. Other than the sounds of nature, the only thing you may hear along this peaceful hike is a boat buzzing by in the distance.

Start: 881 State Park Rd., Winnsboro; southwest corner of the parking lot
Distance: 2.2 miles out and back
Hiking time: About 1 hour and 10 minutes
Blaze color: None
Difficulty: Easy
Trailhead elevation: 231 feet
Highest point: 303 feet
Best season: Year-round
Schedule: 6 a.m. to 6 p.m. (extended to 10 p.m. during Daylight Saving Time)
Trail surface: Hard-packed dirt
Other trail users: Mountain bikers

Canine compatibility: Leash required
Land status: South Carolina Department of Natural Resources
Fees: Fee required
Maps: *DeLorme: South Carolina Atlas & Gazetteer:* Page 27, G9
Trail contacts: (803) 482-6401; www.south carolinaparks.com/lakewateree/introduction .aspx
Nearest town: Winnsboro, Lancaster
Trail tips: Restrooms are located at the park office/tackle shop.

Finding the trailhead: From I-77 get off at exit 41 and drive east on Old River Road (SR 41) for 2.6 miles to a left onto US 21. Follow US 21 north for 2.1 miles to a right onto River Road (SR 101). Travel for 5.1 miles to the park on the left. Follow the park road for 0.5 mile to a stop sign. Continue driving another 0.7 mile to the large parking lot for the park office/tackle shop.

From the junction of US 21 and SC 200 near Mitford, drive south on US 21 for 7.5 miles to a left onto River Road (SR 101). Follow directions above.

Note: As you follow the park road, bypass the alternate trailhead on the south side of the park road between the campground and the tackle shop. **Trailhead GPS:** N34 25.955'/W80 51.578'

The Hike

This wide, hard-packed dirt trail leads you on a wonderful excursion out to the south end of the island. That's right, I said island. The main body of this popular state park actually sits out on an island within Lake Wateree. The lake is quite sizable and covers nearly 14,000 acres. Around the park you'll find farmland with rolling hills, cattle, and

Stay for sunset; you won't be disappointed.

horses. But amid this country living, you'll also find a very popular boating and fishing community. The park itself caters to boaters, with a boat ramp, tackle shop, and even a fueling dock. Fishing tournaments are hosted annually on the lake, and bass is the big catch of the day. Anglers also have great success snagging crappie, catfish, and perch. The park participates in a tackle loaner program, so you can borrow a rod, reel, and tackle box. All you need to bring is the bait and your state fishing license. As for the trail, you must know that the general park map is incorrect. They do have a fantastic representation of the trail on their "trail map" though. So either refer to that, or to the map I've provided. In general, the trail splits in the middle, and forms a double lollipop-style loop. One loop is on the west end, and the other leads to the east side of the island. The hike is extremely tranquil, leading you out to the uncharted parts of the park. The trail makes its split near the half-mile mark, and I prefer to head west first. The hike is also described as such in the Miles and Directions. As you head west, the hike follows a marshy cove leading out toward Dutchman Creek. You'll see deer prints in the path, and the dogs' ears perk up as they pick up on the scent. If you hope to catch a sighting, hike early in the morning, or late afternoon. Great blue herons and great white egrets frequent this area as well. You may hear the loud honking cry of a heron as it soars across the water with its wings spread wide, or an osprey crying out from above as it hovers over the water looking for a meal. When

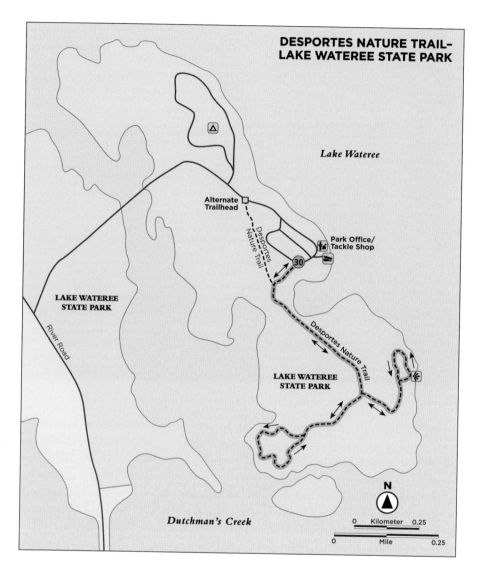

DESPORTES NATURE TRAIL–
LAKE WATEREE STATE PARK

Lake Wateree

Alternate
Trailhead

Desportes
Nature Trail

Park Office/
Tackle Shop

30

LAKE WATEREE
STATE PARK

River Road

Desportes Nature Trail

LAKE WATEREE
STATE PARK

Dutchman's Creek

N

| 0 | Kilometer | 0.25 |
| 0 | Mile | 0.25 |

you reach the western loop, you'll find the area is in disarray. Downed trees scattered here and there are reminders of storms that have passed through. Returning to the fork, you'll enjoy a chorus of birds singing in the background. Then, when you head to the eastern side of the island, you'll pass a wooden bench that was kindly donated by local Boy Scout Troop #737. This is a nice place to sit and enjoy the view from afar. Beyond the bench, the trail leads to another small loop, but this one is on the edge of Lake Wateree. A short spur trail off the loop gives you amazing views of the lake. A picnic table rests along the shoreline, and it's a perfect place to stop and have a snack, or simply take in the stunning scenery. The only negative here is that you're up on a little bluff with a steep bank, so it's not easy for the dogs to hop in and out of the water. Other than that, without a doubt, this is the prettiest place on the hike. Also, you always have the option to take the dogs for a dip at the swim area before and after you hike.

Miles and Directions

0.0 Hike southwest into the woods.

0.1 Come to a T. Right leads north to an alternate trailhead. Go left, following the Nature Trail south.

0.45 Come to a fork where the trail splits in two. Left (southeast) leads to the eastern loop. Go right (southwest) toward the western loop.

0.65 Come to a fork where the lollipop loop begins. Go either way; they both lead back to this fork.

1.0 Arrive back at the fork where the loop began. Hike northeast back toward the fork at 0.45.

1.2 Arrive back at the fork. Go right (southeast) toward the eastern loop.

1.3 Hike past a notable bench.

1.4 Come to a fork where the eastern lollipop loop begins. Go right (east).

1.43 A spur trail heads right 50 feet to an overlook (N34 25.738'/W80 51.289'). Return to the loop continuing north.

1.55 The loop ends at the fork where it began. Go right (south), backtracking to the split at 0.45.

1.75 Arrive at the fork where the trail split (at 0.45). Go right (north), backtracking to the trailhead.

2.2 Arrive at the trailhead.

This family of furry Chihuahuas rinses off after a day in the park.

Resting up

America's Best Value Inn, 1894 US 321 Bypass South, Winnsboro, (803) 635-1447; pet fee required.
Days Inn, 3217 Lancaster Hwy., Richburg, (803) 789-5555; pet fee required.

Camping

Onsite.

Fueling up

Dutchman Creek Marina & Restaurant, 5546 River Rd., Winnsboro, (803) 482-3067.

Puppy Paws and Golden Years

Take them to the park's picnic area, or out on the trail—just shorten the distance to suit your needs.

Top left: Since dogs only sweat through their pads, panting is how they keep cool.
Bottom left: You never know what the pups might sniff out in the forest.
Right: Alley is ready and waiting.

Lancaster

31 Nature Trail/Canal Trail–Landsford Canal State Park

The hiking trails at Landsford Canal State Park give you the best of both worlds: raw natural beauty, and the structural remains of days gone by. You'll first find yourself hiking alongside the wide and rocky Catawba River. While the river is stunning year-round, in springtime it comes to life as an abundance of spider lilies paint the river white with their showy blossoms. The trail then heads slightly inland, where you'll trace the steps where the Landsford Canal actually ran. This canal was cut nearly 200 years ago to bypass the river rapids, quite an amazing feat.

Start: 2051 Park Dr., Catawba; northeast end of the parking lot
Distance: 3.15 miles out and back
Hiking time: About 1 hour, 40 minutes
Blaze color: None
Difficulty: Easy
Trailhead elevation: 475 feet
Highest point: 480 feet
Best season: Year-round
Schedule: Open from daylight to dark
Trail surface: Wide crushed gravel, hard-packed dirt
Other trail users: None

Canine compatibility: Leash required
Land status: South Carolina Department of Natural Resources
Fees: Fee required
Maps: *DeLorme: South Carolina Atlas & Gazetteer:* Page 27, A9
Trail contacts: (803) 789-5800; www.south carolinaparks.com/landsfordcanal/ introduction.aspx
Nearest town: Lancaster, Rock Hill
Trail tips: Trail map, restrooms, and water fountain near the trailhead

Finding the trailhead: From the junction of US 21 and SC 223 (Wyles Mill Road) in Landsford, drive north on US 21 for 2.6 miles to a right onto Landsford Road (SR 327). Travel for 1.6 miles to the park on the left. Follow the park road for 0.9 mile to the end.

From the junction of US 21 and SC 5 near Rock Hill, drive south on US 21 for 5.8 miles to a left onto Landsford Road (SR 327). Follow directions above. **Trailhead GPS:** N34 47.475'/W80 52.885'

The Hike

When you arrive at Landsford Canal, a picnic shelter, playground, and rustic log cabin are all that stand between you and the river. And when you catch your first glance of the waterway, your jaw will drop at the sight of it. The river is absolutely gorgeous, and wide, and free-flowing, and quite honestly indescribable. Following the sidewalk path, you'll pass the rustic log cabin, and a wooden Indian greets you from the porch. The dogs can take a dip before you head out on the hike, and you'll notice the locals

Left: Rocks strewn across the wide waterway add to the ambiance of the Catawba River.
Right: You'll come across a number of unique structures as you hike along the Landsford Canal.

use this as a swim spot too. When the sidewalk ends, you'll follow a wide, gravel path alongside the Catawba River. Staying left at each fork keeps you on the Nature Trail. As you continue to admire the river, downed trees add character, and the scenery is spectacular. You may see raccoon paw prints in the mud along the banks, or a brown water snake sunning himself on the rocks. Meanwhile, the repetitive chirps of the birds blend in the background. The gravel path is well trodden, so it's been ground into dirt. This makes it easier on the puppy's paws, but if your dog has sensitive feet bring booties just in case. Several benches, swim spots, and footbridges welcome you as you continue following the Nature Trail south. The astonishingly wide river will mesmerize you. To put it into perspective, the Catawba is wider than a football field. While the dogs enjoy popping in and out of the water, you'll enjoy the view. And when you reach the spider lily overlook, you're in for a real treat. Thousands of tall white spider lilies burst into full bloom out in the river. If you visit in late spring, you're likely to capture a spectacular show, as the blossoms paint the river white with flowers, creating quite a contrast with the tannic brown color of the water. Returning to the last fork brings you to the Canal Trail. Here, you'll lose the gravel, and the trail transitions into a surface of hard-packed dirt. Although you've left the river's edge, there's still a nice assortment of birds and wildflowers. The trail is shaded most of the way, and placards give you an understanding of the construction and purpose of the Landsford Canal. As you hike between the narrow stone walls, it's as though you're crossing through a mossy, gilded gateway. The farther along the trail you go, the more evident the canal becomes. The trail ends at the Upper Locks, where a stone bridge forms a beautiful backdrop. Returning to the trailhead, stay left on the loop so you can see the rest of the Canal Trail. On this northern stretch of the trail you'll find there's water in the canal. But it's not stagnant, and it's not buggy. Still, I would reserve any swimming for the dogs to the river. Poplar trees stand tall overhead, while birds, crickets, frogs, turtles, and snakes all keep you company. If you think about it, the construction of this canal was an amazing feat. Without the help of heavy machinery, hundreds of workers dug the canal and built the locks, culverts, weir, and walls whose remains you see here today. The ingenuity and arduous work that went into this project is remarkable. Footnote: As a general rule, if you stay left at every intersection, you'll make it out to the Upper Locks and back to the trailhead, while seeing everything of note in between.

Miles and Directions

0.0 Follow the sidewalk east toward the river. When the sidewalk ends, follow the wide gravel path south alongside the river.

0.15 Come to a fork. Right (southwest) is the Canal Trail. Go left (southeast), following the river on the Nature Trail.

0.16 Cross a footbridge; continue hiking southeast.

0.3 Come to a good swim spot for the dogs.

0.4 Come to a bench near another swim spot. Continue hiking south.

0.6 Come to another bench with a swim spot. Continue hiking southwest.

0.7 Cross a footbridge, and come to a fork. Right (north), the Canal Trail leads back toward the trailhead. Go left (south) and the Nature and Canal Trails merge.

0.95 Come to fork. Right (west) is the Canal Trail. Go left (southeast) toward the Spider Lily Overlook and immediately cross a footbridge.

0.97 The Nature Trail ends at the Spider Lily Overlook (N34 46.808'/W80 52.652'). Backtrack to the fork.

1.0 Arrive back at the fork. Go left (south) on the Canal Trail.

1.01 Cross a footbridge near a culvert. Continue hiking south.

Left: Keep your eyes peeled; the prothonotary warbler is one of many bird species living along the canal.
Right: If you're lucky, you may spy a bald eagle high along the riverbanks of the Catawba.

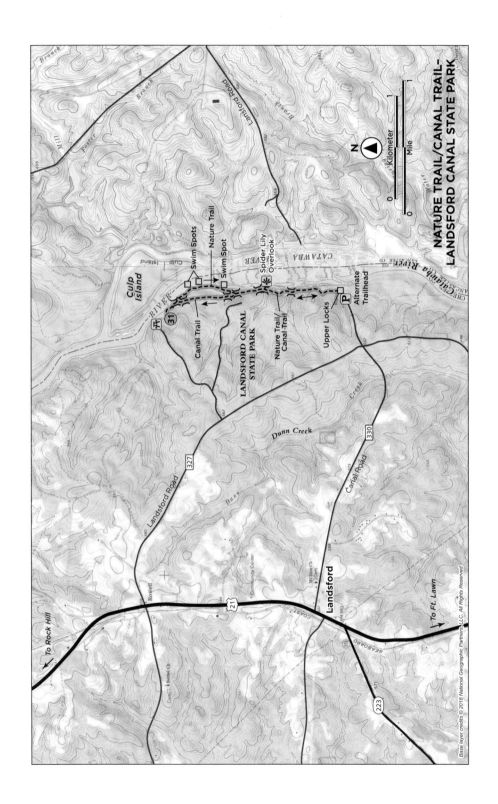

NATURE TRAIL/CANAL TRAIL–
LANDSFORD CANAL STATE PARK

Lansford Road

Mill Branch

Foster Branch

Branch

Culp
Island

Culp Island

RIVER

CATAWBA

CHESTER/CATAWBA RIVER CO.

LANCASTER CO.

Swim Spots

Nature Trail

Swim Spot

Spider Lily
Overlook

Nature Trail/
Canal Trail

Upper Locks

Alternate
Trailhead

Canal Trail

31

LANDSFORD CANAL
STATE PARK

Dunn Creek

Dunn

Creek

Landsford Road

327

Canal Road

330

Rowell

Community Center

Mt Zion Ch
& Cem

Cem
Bethel Ch

Landsford

SEABOARD

COAST

21

223

To Rock Hill

To Ft. Lawn

N

Kilometer

Mile

0   1

Base layer credits © 2018 National Geographic Partners, LLC. All Rights Reserved

Enjoy the journey.

1.25 Cross a footbridge. Hike past the old Davies Mill. Continue hiking south.

1.6 The trail ends at the Upper Locks (N34 46.321'/W80 52.673'). Backtrack to the fork at 1.0 mile.

2.2 Arrive back at the fork you came to at 1.0 mile. Go left (north) and backtrack to the fork at 0.7 mile.

2.45 Arrive at the fork you came to at 0.7 mile. Go left (west) following the Canal Trail back toward the trailhead.

2.55 Cross a footbridge; continue hiking north.

2.9 Cross a footbridge; continue hiking north.

2.95 Hike north past the Guardlock (N34 47.408'/W80 52.771').

3.0 Arrive at the first fork you came to at 0.15 mile. Go left (northwest) toward the trailhead.

3.15 Arrive at the trailhead.

Resting up

Quality Inn, 114 Commerce Blvd., Lancaster, (803) 283–1188; pet fee required.
Days Inn, 3217 Lancaster Hwy., Richburg, (803) 789-5555; pet fee required.

Camping

Andrew Jackson State Park, 196 Andrew Jackson Park Rd., Lancaster, (803) 285-3344.

Fueling up

McHale's Irish Pub, 122 E. Main St., Rock Hill, (803) 329-8580.
Michael's Rock Hill Grille, 1039 Charlotte Ave., Rock Hill, (803) 985-3663.

Puppy Paws and Golden Years

Take them to the picnic area and stroll along the Nature Trail as far as they're able.

32 Garden of the Waxhaws Trail–Andrew Jackson State Park

This easy and enjoyable hike begins by crossing a grass-covered levee, and then circles around the park's 18-acre lake. Without a doubt, the stunning views of the lake are certainly a highlight. But keep your eyes peeled, since the trail is also home to the endangered Schweinitz's sunflower, which blooms in autumn. This species of sunflower has a smaller center, but is just as stunning as its common siblings of superior stature. You'll also encounter a variety of birds, and/or wildlife such as deer and raccoons.

Start: 196 Andrew Jackson Park Rd., Lancaster; to the left (west) of the small fishing pier
Distance: 1.03-mile loop
Hiking time: About 30 minutes
Blaze color: None
Difficulty: Easy
Trailhead elevation: 564 feet
Highest point: 579 feet
Best season: Year-round
Schedule: Nov1–Mar 31, 8 a.m. to 6 p.m.; Apr 1–Oct 31, 9 a.m. to 9 p.m.
Trail surface: Wide grassy path, hard-packed dirt

Other trail users: None
Canine compatibility: Leash required
Land status: South Carolina Department of Natural Resources
Fees: Fee required
Maps: *DeLorme: South Carolina Atlas & Gazetteer:* Page 21, H10
Trail contacts: (803) 285-3344; www.south carolinaparks.com/andrewjackson/introduction.aspx
Nearest town: Lancaster, Rock Hill
Trail tips: A map and trash can are near the trailhead.

Finding the trailhead: From the junction of US 521 and SC 5 near Rock Hill, drive north on US 521 for 0.5 mile to the park on your right. Follow the park road for 0.2 mile and take the first left. Drive 0.1 mile down the hill and take the first left again onto the dirt road. Travel 0.1 mile to the parking area at the end of the road.

From the junction of US 521 and SC 75 West, drive south on US 521 for 1.5 miles to the park on the left. Follow directions above. **Trailhead GPS:** N34 50.614'/W80 48.423'

The Hike

This splendid and easy to follow hike begins near a small fishing pier that briefly juts out into the water. A wide grass levee crosses the southern end of the park's lake, and over the distance of the hike, you'll circle it in its entirety. From the levee, you'll enjoy fantastic, long-range views of the waterway. Johnboats rest along the shore, waiting for someone to row them out into the great green yonder. Out in the middle of the lake, a beautiful little island is perched and ready for exploration. You can rent a johnboat by the hour or by the day. Or, you can launch your own watercraft. But gasoline motors are not permitted. Also, there's no boat ramp, so you'll have to carry your craft to the water's edge for launching. If you can tune out the white noise of US 521 in the background, this is a super peaceful park. After crossing the levee the trail heads north into the forest. Signs here and there help you identify some of the trees and plants in the area. As you continue along the western shore, the trail narrows from the wide grassy path to a narrow, shaded, pine mulch–covered path. The occasional bench is perfectly placed within small openings in the forest. This gives you a number of spots to sit and take in the serenity of the lake. You can

The nature trail is open to foot traffic only.

fish from the pier or the shore, and you may see locals with their lines cast near these openings in the forest. Bream and bass are the predominant catch of the day, and it's catch and release only. A state fishing license is required. A pleasant breeze blows off the water, which is especially nice in the warmer months. At the north end of the lake, the trail follows a muddy creek and a long boardwalk leads you over a wet area. Keep your eyes peeled! I was fortunate enough to spy a spotted fawn hiking in the high brush from this boardwalk. The dogs quickly spooked it away, but it was a delightful treat to see such precious new life along the trail. As you make your way back toward the trailhead on the eastern shore, the wide, well-trodden dirt path returns. The big, square, chunky bark of the slash pines stands out among the conifers, and you'll also enjoy the shade of oak, holly, and cedar. About three-quarters of the way around, you'll pass between the lake and the campground. As you do, you'll find a perfect clay sandy "beach." Although there's no swimming allowed in the lake, the dogs can wade out into the water as long as you keep them on a leash. Tails will wag, and the dogs will perk up as they splash around in the crisp cool water, especially in the warmer months of spring and summer. Spring and summer also bring a stunning array of wildflowers to greet you. The sweet scent of honeysuckle and yellow jessamine fills the air, while a magical assortment of brilliant purple hues is found amid the spiderwort, phlox, and heal-all. In autumn you'll get a special treat, as the endangered Schweinitz's sunflower blooms along the trail. Bring a camera to capture the beauty of them all. Beyond the clay beach, an oddly placed tiny footbridge acts as a gateway back into the forest. You'll enjoy one last bit of shade before returning to the trailhead.

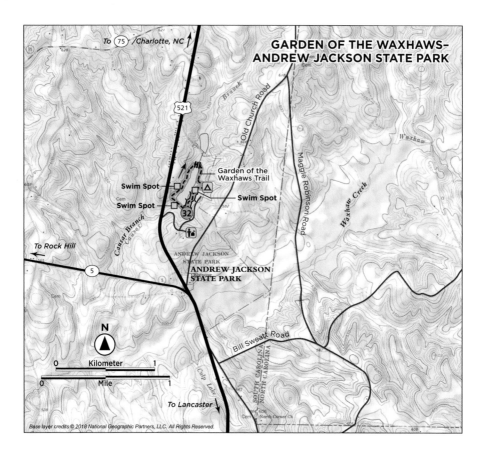

Miles and Directions

0.0 Hike northwest on the wide grassy path across a levee.

0.15 The levee ends; follow the trail to the right (northeast).

0.25 Come to a bench and swim spot.

0.5 Cross a boardwalk.

0.85 Come to a sandy beach/swim spot near the campground (N34 50.736'/W80 48.358').

0.88 Cross a footbridge.

1.0 Hike past the boat docks and cross a footbridge.

1.03 Arrive at the trailhead.

Resting up

Wingate by Wyndham, 760 Galleria Blvd., Rock Hill, (803) 324-9000; pet fee required.

Baymont Inn and Suites, 1106 N. Anderson Rd., Rock Hill, (803) 329-1330; pet fee required.

Serenity greets you as you hike around the lake at Andrew Jackson State Park.

Camping

Onsite.

Fueling up

McHale's Irish Pub, 122 E. Main St., Rock Hill, (803) 329-8580.
Michael's Rock Hill Grille, 1039 Charlotte Ave., Rock Hill, (803) 985-3663.

Puppy Paws and Golden Years

Hike counterclockwise and take them to the sandy beach by the campground. It's 0.3 mile round-trip.

Chester

33 Caney Fork Falls Trail–Chester State Park

The perfect amount of well-spaced swim spots, a diverse forest, bird variety, and outstanding views of the lake put this hike among my favorites—not to mention how wonderfully peaceful Chester State Park is. Along the trail, you don't hear a soul, except when you pass below the park's campground. At 1.2 miles, the path comes to an abrupt end at a small spillway forming the headwaters of Caney Fork Creek. Water levels dictate how much water flows over or under the smooth cement wall.

Start: 759 State Park Dr., Chester; northwest corner of the parking lot

Distance: 2.4 miles out and back

Hiking time: About 1 hour, 15 minutes

Blaze color: None

Difficulty: Easy

Trailhead elevation: 419 feet

Highest point: 445 feet

Best season: Year-round

Schedule: 9 a.m. to 6 p.m. (extended to 9 p.m. during Daylight Saving Time)

Trail surface: Hard-packed dirt

Other trail users: None

Canine compatibility: Leash required

Land status: South Carolina Department of Natural Resources

Fees: Fee required

Maps: *DeLorme: South Carolina Atlas & Gazetteer:* Page 26, C5

Trail contacts: (803) 385-2680; www.south carolinaparks.com/chester/introduction.aspx

Nearest town: Chester

Trail tips: Restrooms are located south of the trailhead off of the loop road.

Finding the trailhead: From the junction of SC 72 and US 321, drive south on SC 72 for 1.4 miles to a left onto State Park Drive. Travel for 1.0 mile to the large parking area near Shelter #2. From here, follow the gravel road to the right leading down toward the nature trail and boathouse. Park at the end of this gravel road.

From the junction of SC 72 and SC 215 near Carlisle, drive north on SC 72 for 11.0 miles to a right onto State Park Drive. Follow directions above. **Trailhead GPS:** N34 40.614'/W81 14.352'

The Hike

Although you're very close to town, when you visit Chester State Park you'll find it's incredibly peaceful. A beautiful large lake sits in the middle of the property and covers nearly a third of the total acreage. You'll find the trail stays near the shore of this fabulous lake over the full length of the hike, and that it's truly a trail for all seasons. In springtime, a variety of wildflowers welcomes you. The scent of these flowers, along with pine and cedar, fill the air in spring and summer. But come autumn, it's not the wonderful aroma that draws your attention. Instead, it's a magical mixture of color

Left: If you stay and camp at Chester State Park, you'll enjoy sunsets over the park's large lake. Right: The swim spots and long-range views are fantastic along the Caney Fork Falls Trail.

that lines the banks. The pine trees are accompanied by an assortment of deciduous hardwoods. Maple, oak, and hickory light up the lake with an amazing array of color. The view transforms and the reflection of bright red, yellow, orange, and even purple leaves is outstanding. When winter arrives, the underbrush thins and the views just keep on coming. The trail begins by passing the boathouse, where johnboats patiently wait for someone to paddle them out. The boats are available for rent and are actually very stable.

As you follow the shore, you'll find some brush separates you from the banks, and you'll see several narrow footpaths leading to the water's edge. These are the footsteps of local fishermen, hoping to make their big catch of the day. The lake is stocked regularly, and a variety of bass, bream, catfish, and crappie are the common bites. As the land juts out into the lake, you'll find a bench and a small clay sandy "beach." This is perfect for the dogs to pop in and out of the water while you sit and watch them play. Beyond the "beach," maple and red cedars add to the scenery, and you'll soon pass the campground and a little fishing pier. Although it's posted as "no swimming," the dogs can dip their paws once again in the refreshing cool water. Bypass any footpaths to the right. They lead up to the campground and act as a means of travel for campers to visit the water's edge. Once again the trees grab your attention. You can't help but notice

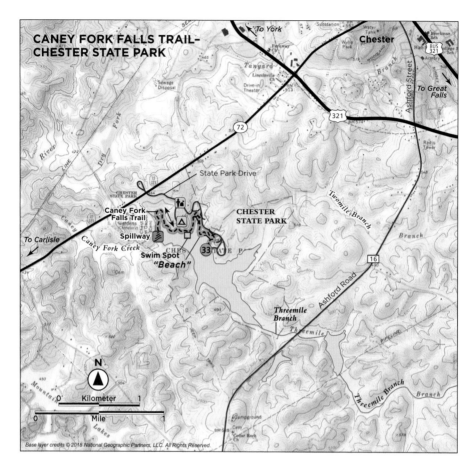

CANEY FORK FALLS TRAIL–
CHESTER STATE PARK

how immense the slash pines are. The trunks are wide, spanning several feet. And they stand tall and straight, towering above you with branches reaching outward. The pine needles form a soft bed upon the ground beneath your feet, and when the trail ends it leads you to a small stone spillway. The spillway was built in the 1930s by the Civilian Conservation Corps (CCC) and stands strong and sturdy to this day. This hike is easily a favorite for a number of reasons. It's well shaded by a diverse forest. There's a wonderful variety of wildflowers and birdlife. You can see the water the entire way, including stellar long-range views. There are plenty of well-spaced swim spots for the furry ones in the family. And, it's peaceful! What's not to like? As an added bonus, the park has this listed as 1.3 miles out and back. I am very pleased to announce that they are incorrect. It's actually 1.2 miles one way! Which is fantastic, because you get to enjoy twice the time on this terrific trail. To reach the base of Caney Fork Falls, you'll have to bushwhack downstream. I recommend doing that another day when you don't have the dogs in tow.

Left: Bracket fungi grows like a shelf on the side of live and downed trees.
Right: Creeping phlox is one of many wildflowers found in and around Paris Mountain State Park.

Miles and Directions

0.0 Hike north past the boathouse and into a little cove.

0.1 Cross a footbridge. Continue hiking west.

0.3 Come to a bench near a perfect clay, sandy "beach" (N34 40.719'/W81 14.493'). Continue following the shoreline north.

0.4 Cross a footbridge.

0.45 Cross a footbridge, continue hiking west.

0.5 Bypass the grassy road to the right (northwest). Hike straight, following the grassy road-like path south.

0.6 Come to a doggy swim spot near the campground.

1.2 The trail ends at the spillway (N34 40.722'/W81 14.833'). Backtrack to the trailhead.

2.4 Arrive at the trailhead.

Resting up

Days Inn, 3217 Lancaster Hwy., Richburg, (803) 789-5555; pet fee required.
Quality Inn and Suites, 3041 Lancaster Hwy., Richburg, (803) 789-7100; pet fee required.

Camping

Onsite.

Fueling up

None nearby.

Puppy Paws and Golden Years

Let them play on the grassy banks near the boathouse. If they're able, hike to the "beach" at 0.3 mile.

34 Nature Trail/River Trail Loop–Rose Hill Plantation State Historic Site

This hike is surprisingly challenging, but certainly worth every ounce of effort, and easily a favorite. As you arrive onsite you're greeted by the gallant Gist Mansion. The home site stands tall, and glorious gardens grace the grounds surrounding this pristine plantation house. The entire property is crisp and clean, so you expect a simple stroll. But what you find is a rustic forest hike leading down to the tannic Tyger River. Here, you'll find a soft, swift current. But the water is shallow, and sandbars help make this a fantastic swim hole for both you and your furry friends.

Start: 2677 Sardis Rd., Union; southeast of the picnic area

Distance: 1.2 miles out and back

Hiking time: About 50 minutes

Blaze color: Yellow

Difficulty: Moderate

Trailhead elevation: 557 feet

Highest point: 557 feet

Best season: Year-round

Schedule: 9 a.m. to 6 p.m.

Trail surface: Hard-packed dirt

Other trail users: None

Canine compatibility: Leash required while in state park. The River Trail leads you across the state park boundary as you near the Tyger River. Voice control beyond the park boundary.

Land status: South Carolina Department of Natural Resources; Sumter National Forest– Enoree Ranger District

Fees: Fee required

Maps: *DeLorme: South Carolina Atlas & Gazetteer:* Page 25, D10

Trail contacts: (864) 427-5966; www.south carolinaparks.com/rosehill/introduction.aspx. Sumter National Forest: (803) 276-4810

Nearest town: Union, Whitmire, Clinton

Trail tips: Restrooms and water fountain near the trailhead. Bring a hiking stick.

Special considerations: If water levels are up, the current may be too swift for the dogs to swim in the river. Use your discretion.

Finding the trailhead: From junction of SC 49 and SC 56 in Cross Anchor, drive east on SC 49 for 4.9 miles to a right onto Old Buncombe Road (SR 18). Travel for 0.1 mile to a stop sign in front of the Cross Keys House. Continue straight for another 5.1 miles to a left onto Sardis Road (SR 16). Travel for 2.1 miles to a T. Turn right and continue following Sardis Road for 0.2 mile to the park on the right. Follow the park road for 0.2 mile, pass the Gist Mansion, and park near the picnic area on the left.

From the junction of US 176 and SC 49 in Union, drive south on US 176 for 1.0 mile to a right onto Sardis Road. Travel for 8.1 miles to the park on the left. Follow directions above. **Trailhead GPS:** N34 36.320'/W81 39.745'

The Hike

If you visit the Rose Hill Plantation without dogs in tow, I highly recommend that you take a visit to the restroom before you hike. You've never heard me say that before, and I may never say it again. But in this case, the bathhouse was an old servants' quarters. With a fireplace, chimney, and historical information, it's an interesting diversion before you hit the trail. Unfortunately, dogs aren't allowed inside the bathrooms, or the plantation house for that matter. So if you have your canine kids with you, you'll have to come back another day to see this elegant edifice. The park offers guided tours daily, but the days fluctuate throughout the year. Begin the hike by following the Nature Trail into the forest. The lovely, wide path leads slightly downhill, and a bed of pine needles covers the ground. All you'll hear as you follow this pleasant path is the sound of the birds singing, and the wind tickling the leaves. The trees keep you well shaded, and by 0.1 mile you'll come to a T. Left is the Nature Trail, and you'll return to the trailhead that way after taking a detour down the River Trail. For now, head right and you're now following the River Trail. The transition is amazing. On the Nature Trail, the path was covered in pine needles from the tall sweet-scented conifers that shaded the path. But now, on the River Trail, you'll find the forest has transformed. You're now treading on a rugged, hard-packed dirt trail. The rooty traits of the hardwood trees begin

to stand out. And the deeper you go into the forest, the steeper and steeper the trail becomes as you make a rapid descent. You'll want to bring a hiking stick along for this one. After hiking downhill for about a quarter-mile, you'll reach the forest floor. Here you'll find lush green ground cover lines the pathway. As you approach the half-mile mark, and just before reaching the river, you cross over into the Sumter National Forest. The beauty of this is that you're no longer on state park property, so you can let the dogs run free as long as they're under voice control. You can see the excitement in their eyes and their tails wagging with enthusiasm as you let them off leash. The playful pups are now free to run, play, swim, chase sticks, and simply enjoy their freedom. The river has a soft, swift current about it, but it's shallow, with sandbars out in the middle. You may want to join the

The Gist Mansion stands proudly up on a hill at the Rose Hill Plantation.

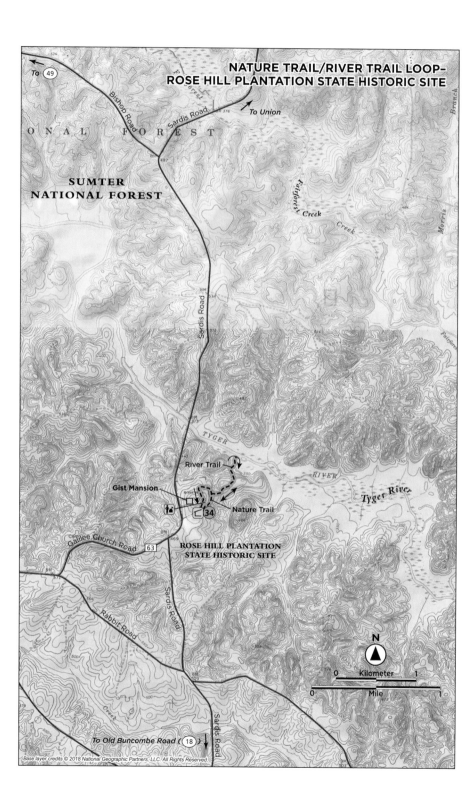

To 49

To Union

Bishop Road

Sardis Road

O N A L   F O R E S T

**SUMTER
NATIONAL FOREST**

Fairforest Creek

Creek

Morris

Branch

Sardis Road

T Y G E R

RIVER

River Trail

Gist Mansion

Tyger River

34

Nature Trail

Galilee Church Road   63

**ROSE HILL PLANTATION
STATE HISTORIC SITE**

Rabbit Road

Sardis Road

Sardis Road

N

To Old Buncombe Road   18

Kilometer 0 ──── 1

Mile 0 ──── 1

Step back in time at the Rose Hill Plantation.

dogs and wade out into the water as well. Although it appears brown on the surface, the water is actually crystal clear. And refreshing! As you return to the T, you realize just how steeply you dropped on the way out to the river. Continuing to follow the Nature Trail leads you on a loop around the east side of the property. At the time of this writing, the Nature Trail ended at a large open lawn on the northeast side of the mansion. You would then cut across the lawn to return to the trailhead. The park has plans to reroute this trail, swinging it farther around to end near the gardens. Please check in with the park prior to hiking to see if this change has been made effective yet.

Miles and Directions

0.0 Follow the nature trail east into the forest.

0.1 Come to a T. Left (north) is the continuation of the Nature Trail. Go right (southeast) on the River Trail.

Option: To shorten the hike to 0.4 mile, bypass the River Trail.

0.48 Come to a clearing. It looks as though you should continue straight ahead, but instead, go right (east) on the River Trail.

0.5 Cross the state park boundary into Sumter National Forest (N34 36.656'/W81 39.482'). Arrive at the Tyger River. Backtrack to the T at 0.1 mile.

0.9 Arrive at the T with the Nature Trail. Go right (north).

1.1 The Nature Trail ends at the lawn northeast of the Gist Mansion. Stay left, shortcutting (south) across the grass toward the picnic shelter.

1.2 Arrive at the picnic shelter near the trailhead.

Resting up

Quality Inn, 315 N. Duncan Bypass, Union, (864) 427–5060; pet fee required.
Days Inn, 101 Toshes Creek Circle, Union, (864) 427–0308; pet fee required.

Left: Bandit needs a towel.
Right: Mikey takes a dip along the River Trail.

Camping

Sedalia Campground, (803) 276-4810 primitive camping only.
Chester State Park, 759 State Park Dr., Chester, (803) 385-2680.

Fueling up

None nearby.

Puppy Paws and Golden Years

Take them for a stroll around the gardens. Or if they're able, just follow the 0.4-mile Nature Trail, bypassing the River Trail.

The rose gardens at Rose Hill Plantation are enchanting.

Clinton

35 British Camp Trail–Musgrove Mill State Historic Site

Picnic areas, a pond, river frontage, and a fabulous forest make Musgrove Mill a marvelous place to visit—not to mention its deep roots in history. As you follow the British Camp Trail down to the banks of the Enoree River, placards placed along the pathway give you insight into the Revolutionary War battle that commenced here. The river provides spectacular scenery, and the swim holes are unmatched. After the hike, be sure to visit the northern portion of the park. Here, you'll find a 0.1-mile walkway leads to the small but scenic Horseshoe Falls.

Start: 398 State Park Rd., Clinton; southeast of the park office on the east side of the road
Distance: 1.0-mile loop
Hiking time: About 35 minutes
Blaze color: Red
Difficulty: Moderate
Trailhead elevation: 483 feet
Highest point: 500 feet
Best season: Year-round
Schedule: 9 a.m. to 6 p.m.
Trail surface: Hard-packed dirt
Other trail users: None
Canine compatibility: Leash required
Land status: South Carolina Department of Natural Resources

Fees: No fee
Maps: *DeLorme: South Carolina Atlas & Gazetteer:* Page 25, D8
Trail contacts: (864) 938-0100; www.south carolinaparks.com/musgrovemill/introduction .aspx
Nearest town: Clinton, Laurens, Union, Woodruff
Trail tips: Restrooms, soda machine that sells water near the trailhead. Apply bug spray in the summertime.
Special considerations: Use caution with the dogs in the river. Pending water levels, the current can be swift. There are water moccasins in the pond. Don't let the dogs swim there.

Finding the trailhead: From SC 56 and SC 49 in Cross Anchor, drive south on SC 56 for 3.9 miles to the park on the right. Follow State Park Road for 0.4 mile to the parking lot on the left past the park office.

From I-26 near Clinton (from the south), get off at exit 52. Drive north on SC 56 for 5.8 miles to the park on the left. Follow directions above.

Note: When coming from the north on SC 56, you'll pass the first entrance to the park at 1.8 miles. This leads to the Horseshoe Falls Trailhead. Continue another 2.1 miles to the second entrance to the park. **Trailhead GPS:** N34 35.540'/W81 51.138'

The Hike

Two interpretive trails are found within the Musgrove Mill State Historic Site. On the north side of the river, the Battlefield Trail leads you through the area where the

Left: Dixie takes a dip in the swimming hole.
Right: The dogs enjoy a little leash-free time splashing around at the Enoree River.

battle of Musgrove Mill actually occurred, while on the south side of the river is the British Camp Trail. This hike leads through the Musgrove property, and then follows the river. It's here, on this south side of the river, that Mr. Musgrove fed and housed the British soldiers. They kept camp here, giving rise to the trail's name. His daughter Mary Musgrove was said to be a spy, listening in around the camp, and then reporting back to the Patriots. The Patriots were outnumbered two to one, but still managed to win this short but bloody battle. Placards along the path give you added information on the battle, the area, the ford where the soldiers crossed the river, and the old mill site. You'll appreciate the many steps placed in the trail to ease the rapid descent as you head into the forest. A giant sinkhole adds to the topography, and you wonder if it was here when the British occupied the area. You'll hike past a monument that was erected in honor of Ms. Musgrove, and then cross a lovely open grassy meadow. This is the only part of the hike that's not shaded. When you return to the forest, the trail brings you alongside the Enoree River. As you follow the river upstream, birds serenade you, and tall grass lines the sides of the pathway. The birds are soon drowned out by the sounds of a shoal flowing freely in the middle of the rocky river. A narrow path leads out to the water's edge. Here you'll notice the remnants of an old bridge that once led across the wide waterway. This area is fantastic for you and the pups to explore. Large flat rocks reach well out in the water, and you can keep your feet dry while you take a closer look at the foundation and footings of the old bridge known as Musgrove's Ford. This crossing was used by the Loyalists to gain access to and from their "British Camp" site. Return to the trail and hike upstream, and you'll immediately come to some steps that again lead to the water's edge. This spot is a perfect swim hole, with water deep enough for both you and the dogs to take a dip. You can also access this swimming hole from a parking lot on the north side of the river, so don't be surprised if you see people out in the middle of the river. When you're ready to move on, the rugged trail leads you away from the water and soon transforms into a wide mulch path. Passing the park's pond, birds, crickets, and

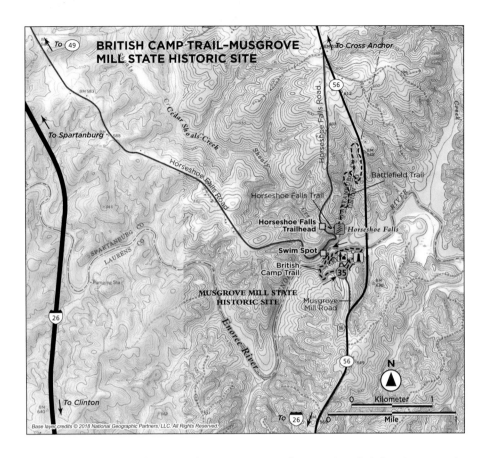

frogs create a chorus of song, and you may see turtles popping their heads up to take in a breath. Just beyond the pond, the trail emerges from the forest on the park road, across the parking lot from where you began. Returning to the car as you cross the grassy island in the parking lot, make sure you pause and appreciate the incredibly tall poplar trees. Looking up, these trees completely dwarf you. It feels as though you've been shrunk and are now walking around in wonderland. The park hosts an annual Living History Festival in springtime. Hundreds participate, dressing in period attire, and reliving a time that forged our country. For more information about the festival, contact the park directly.

Miles and Directions

0.0 Hike south into the forest.

100' Cross a footbridge. The trail bends left (north).

0.16 Hike past the Mary Musgrove Monument. Continue hiking east across a grassy meadow.

0.56 Come to a fork. Go right (north) on the steps to the swimming hole.

0.57 Return to the trail and hike south.

0.58 Cross a footbridge. Continue hiking southwest.

Large boulders form the fantastic Horseshoe Falls at Musgrove Mill.

0.9 Hike past the pond. Continue hiking east.

0.94 The trail ends at the park road. Shortcut across the parking lot to the trailhead.

1.0 Arrive at the trailhead.

Resting up

Comfort Suites, 12865 Hwy. 56 North, Clinton, (844) 296-8198; pet fee required.
Days Inn, 12374 Hwy. 56 North, Clinton, (855) 499-0001; pet fee required.

Camping

Sedalia Campground, (803) 276-4810; primitive camping only.
Chester State Park, 759 State Park Dr., Chester, (803) 385-2680.

Fueling up

None nearby.

Puppy Paws and Golden Years

Take them to visit Horseshoe Falls, regardless of their age!

Spartanburg

36 Nature Trail–Croft State Park

A lush forest, fantastic swim holes, and a creek that's absolutely gorgeous put this one among my favorites. Rocks are perfectly placed in the water to create a sound that is simply divine. You could sit and stare at the sandy-bottomed creek for hours at a time. The first portion of the hike is an easy stroll, but as you move away from the water, the trail climbs, giving you and the dogs a nice workout. An abundance of birds serenade you, and the forest is quite diverse, which is a wonderful combination for a walk in the woods.

Start: 450 Croft State Park Rd., Spartanburg; The trailhead is on the south side of Croft State Park Road, 0.3 mile past the park office.
Distance: 1.65-mile loop
Hiking time: About 50 minutes
Blaze color: Blue
Difficulty: Moderate
Trailhead elevation: 594 feet
Highest point: 634 feet
Best season: Year-round
Schedule: 7 a.m. to 6 p.m. (extended to 8 p.m. on Fri); 7 a.m. to 9 p.m. during Daylight Saving Time
Trail surface: Hard-packed dirt
Other trail users: None

Canine compatibility: Leash required
Land status: South Carolina Department of Natural Resources
Fees: Fee required
Maps: *DeLorme: South Carolina Atlas & Gazetteer:* Page 19, G8
Trail contacts: (864) 585-1283; www.south carolinaparks.com/croft/introduction.aspx
Nearest town: Spartanburg
Trail tips: Restrooms are located in the picnic area, so stop on the way in to the trailhead if you need to use the facilities before you hike. Bring a hiking stick for the climbs, and plenty of drinking water for you and the dogs.

Finding the trailhead: From the junction of SC 56 and SC 295 in Spartanburg, drive south on SC 56 for 2.2 miles to a left onto Dairy Ridge Road. Travel for 0.25 mile to a right onto Croft State Park Road. Drive 0.1 mile, pay the fee. Continue another 3.0 miles to a stop sign near the park office. Continue straight ahead for 0.3 mile to the trailhead on the right.

From the junction of SC 56 and SC 215 near Pauline, drive north on SC 56 for 3.5 miles to a right onto Dairy Ridge Road. Follow directions above. **Trailhead GPS:** N34 51.654'/W81 50.184'

The Hike

As you drive through Croft State Park, you can't help but notice that they cater to the equestrian community. You'll pass stables and show rings, and they even offer equestrian camping. But amid all this equine activity you'll find a lovely little nature

Enjoying the hike back from the "beach" at Croft State Park.

trail tucked away in the woods. The wide, well-maintained path immediately leads you into the forest, and although you may hear gunfire in the distance, it's quite peaceful. The gunfire stems from a firing range that sits at the south end of the property. The trail is shaded and tranquil, and occasionally you'll see a sign identifying different tree and plant species for you. You'll soon reach the fork where the long loop begins, and the hike is described in a counterclockwise fashion, simply because I prefer to let the dogs in the water early on. Less than 0.1 mile into the loop you'll come to a bench. Don't even bother to sit. Instead, follow the spur trail out to the creek. A stunning swim hole awaits below a shoal in the sandy-bottomed creekbed. The creek is absolutely gorgeous! You could spend all day staring at the moving water while the sound hypnotizes you. After spending as long as you like here, the trail follows the creek downstream.

The rocks are so perfectly placed in this creek. It's as though Mother Nature hand laid each one in place to create a chorus of sound that outshines any symphony. It's simply divine. The trail briefly climbs and gives you a different perspective. You're now following the creek from high above, but you can still hear the splendid sound of it. Just after crossing your third footbridge, the trail brings you back down to the creek. Once again a side path leads out to Fairforest Creek. And once again, the creek is simply magnificent. A second fabulous swim hole is waiting for you and the dogs to splash around. Beyond this swim hole, the trail leads away from the water and stays in the forest for the remainder of the hike. With that being said, don't rush the dogs away from their playtime. As the sound of the creek fades, a variety of birds now serenade you. You can't help but notice how lush and green the area is, and the occasional wildflower adds a splash of color to the mix. At 0.8 mile, you'll pass the old Foster's Mill Site. All that remains are some stone remnants, and you probably wouldn't have noticed if it wasn't marked. But it's neat to think that many years ago a flourishing mill once stood here. Beyond the mill, the trail climbs, giving you a bit of a workout. Overall, this is a marvelous hike. You get a workout in, and the creek is absolutely gorgeous. An old mill site adds character, and there's a variety of trees. Inhabiting

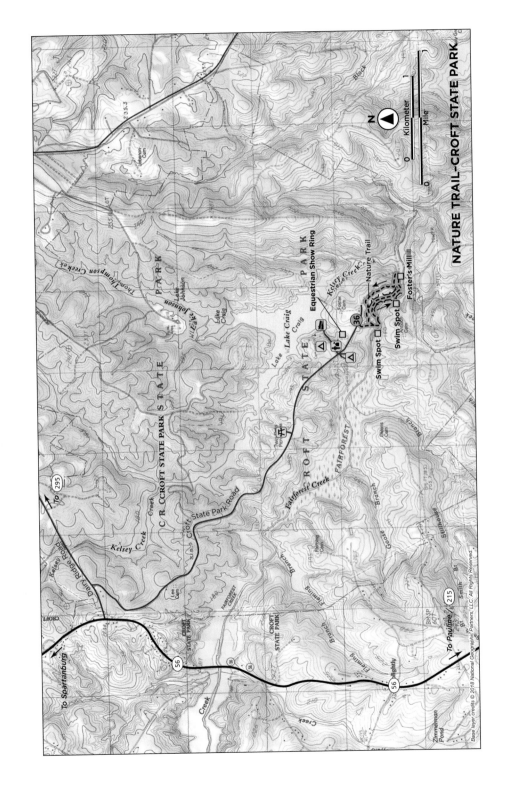

NATURE TRAIL–CROFT STATE PARK

Left: Saddle up: Croft State Park has miles of equestrian trails.
Right: Croft State Park caters to the equestrian community.

those trees you'll find an abundance of birds, and wildflowers enhance the scenery. Last, but certainly not least, there are two outstanding swim holes! Spartanburg is fortunate to have such a fine facility within easy reach. People come to horseback ride, mountain bike, road bike, hike, picnic, camp, and swim. The park is incredibly large, covering a full 7,000 acres. It houses two lakes, two creeks, and an amazing trail system that spans over 50 miles of terrain. Who could ask for more?

Miles and Directions

0.0   Hike southwest into the forest.

0.15 Come to a fork where the loop begins. Go right (south).

0.2   Come to a bench. Follow the side path 100 feet to the swim spot. Return to the trail, continue hiking west.

0.3   Hike past a bench. The trail bends left (north).

0.45 Cross back-to-back footbridges. Continue hiking southwest.

0.6   Cross a footbridge. Follow the side trail to a swim spot. Return to the main trail, continue hiking south.

0.65 Cross a footbridge. Continue hiking southeast.

0.8   Pass the Foster's Mill site (N34 51.366'/W81 49.845'). The trail bends left (north) and climbs.

1.1   Hike north past a bench.

1.5   Come to the fork where the loop began. Backtrack to the trailhead.

1.65 Arrive at the trailhead.

Resting up

Comfort Inn and Suites, 154 Candlenut Ln., Spartanburg, (864) 814-2001; pet fee required.
Red Roof Inn, 6765 Pottery Rd., Spartanburg, (864) 587-0129; no pet fee.

Camping

Onsite.

Fueling up

Wild Ace Pizza and Pub, 148 W. Main St., Spartanburg, (864) 764-1480.
Mellow Mushroom, 464 E. Main St., Spartanburg, (864) 582-5495.

Puppy Paws and Golden Years

Take them to the park's picnic area or boat ramp for a dip. If they are able, hike to the first swim spot at 0.2 mile.

Left: The dogs love laying on the soft, sandy bottom of Fairforest Creek.
Right: Wood along the trail is often used to control runoff and prevent erosion.

Blacksburg

37 Living History Farm Trail–Kings Mountain State Park

What a delightful hike. This marvelous trail leads you along a quaint creek, past a splendid spillway, and then ends at a charming replica of a 19th-century farm. The hike is generally easy, with a few quick climbs, and when you reach the farm you can't help but be impressed. There are live chickens, peach trees growing, gardens, a barn, and even a cotton gin. Please make sure you keep the dogs on a leash at all times. We wouldn't want them banned for disturbing the denizens of this lovely living history farm.

Start: 1277 Park Rd., Blacksburg; southwest corner of the parking lot, to the right of the brown building
Distance: 1.7 miles out and back
Hiking time: About 50 minutes
Blaze color: Yellow
Difficulty: Easy, with a few quick climbs
Trailhead elevation: 820 feet
Highest point: 861 feet
Best season: Year-round
Schedule: 8 a.m. to 6 p.m. (7 a.m. to 9 p.m. during Daylight Saving Time)
Trail surface: Hard-packed dirt

Other trail users: None
Canine compatibility: Leash required
Land status: South Carolina Department of Natural Resources
Fees: Fee required
Maps: *DeLorme: South Carolina Atlas & Gazetteer:* Page 20, C4
Trail contacts: (803) 222-3209; www.south carolinaparks.com/kingsmountain/ introduction.aspx
Nearest town: York, Gaffney
Trail tips: Trail information sign at the trailhead

Finding the trailhead: From the junction of SC 161 and SC 55 in Bethany, drive north on SC 161 for 3.2 miles to a left onto Park Road. Travel for 0.9 mile to a right turn, following signs toward the campground. Travel for 0.8 mile to a parking lot on the left where a sign points toward "trailhead."

From I-85 in North Carolina, get off at NC exit 2. Drive south on Highway 216/Park Road for 6.9 miles to a left turn, following signs toward the campground. Travel for 0.8 mile to a parking lot on the left where a sign points toward "trailhead."

Note: When you are coming from I-85, you'll pass through Kings Mountain National Military Park. **Trailhead GPS:** N35 08.940'/W81 20.724'

The Hike

Although the trail to the living farm is only 0.85 mile, you can extend it by exploring this charming historic farm at will. Among other things, the farm features a chicken coop, a barn, a mill, and even a cotton gin. In November each year, the farm comes to life. They host a fall festival, with music, folk tales, and demonstrations that take

This scarecrow seems to be working; not a crow in sight.

you back in time. You'll enjoy a keen insight into what life may have been like back in the 1800s: for starters, no smartphones, if you can imagine that. To reach the farm, you'll hike past the big brown bathhouse on your way to the shores of Lake Crawford. The lake is one of two on the property, and a clear creek runs between them. A number of structures here were built by the Civilian Conservation Corps (CCC) as part of Franklin Roosevelt's New Deal in the 1930s, among them the bathhouse, and the Lake Crawford Dam. The trail leads you right below the base of this stately, stone spillway and you can see the handiwork of these hardworking men first hand. At the base of the dam, a narrow creek is formed. You can either rock-hop across, or walk on the wooden footbridge. The dogs prefer the rock-hop so they can give you a little splash on your way across. Beyond the creek crossing, stay with the yellow blazes, and you soon move away from the water. Rolling hill topography greets you, and the forest keeps you shaded year-round. A second water crossing takes you over a trickling stream, and the dogs enjoy getting their paws wet once more. The trail soon flattens out, and you'll hike along an old logging road. The logging road brings you out to the main park road before heading back into the forest. Make sure you keep the dogs on a leash, and cross with caution. The trail quickly puts you right back in the forest where you'll remain for another quarter-mile. When you come to a second park road, this is the official end of the trail. But obviously you came this far to see the farm. To do so, cross the road, and you'll see the "privy" building in front of you. If you need to top off your water, the "privy" or restrooms do have running water. Beyond the privy, briefly follow the wide gravel path to where it ends at the Living Farm. The farm covers quite a bit of ground and is absolutely wonderful. Rustic old buildings,

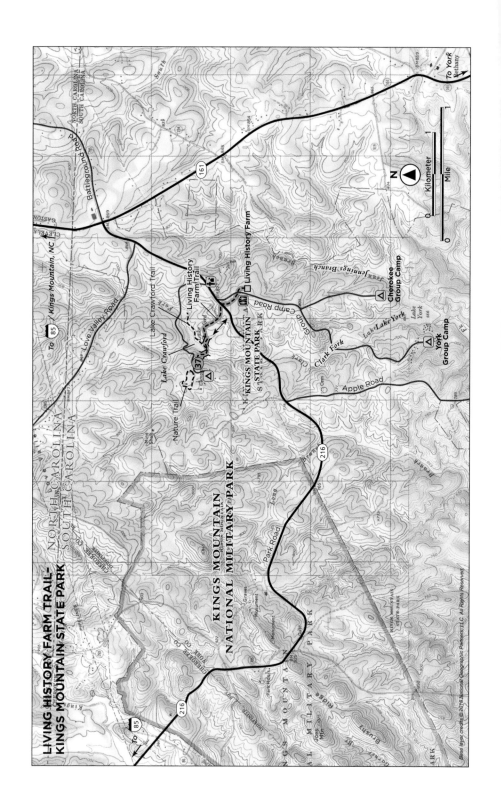

LIVING HISTORY FARM TRAIL–
KINGS MOUNTAIN STATE PARK

Left: Taking a break beside the cotton gin at Kings Mountain State Park.
Right: These big boys enjoy camping as much as I do.

gardens, and split rail fences all add to the scenery. Explore at will. The park itself covers nearly 7,000 acres. To the west it butts up to Kings Mountain National Military Park, and to the east you'll find sprawling farmland with goats, cows, pigs, and ponies. It feels quite remote, despite the close proximity to several towns including the park's namesake, Kings Mountain, North Carolina. If you'd like to stay and discover more of what this vast park has to offer, the campground is fantastic. And they also have a group camp, and equestrian camping. Picnicking, playgrounds, basketball, and volleyball are among the activities. Plus with two lakes on the property, you can paddle or fish. An astounding 15 miles of bridle trails and 20 miles of hiking trails are an added bonus, and to top it all off, of course, the fabulous living farm is exceptional.

Miles and Directions

0.0 Stay right of the brown building and hike down the steps toward Lake Crawford.

0.1 Cross a footbridge at the base of a spillway. The trail bends left, following the shoreline east.

0.15 Come to a fork. Left (north) is the orange-blazed Lake Crawford Trail. Stay right, following the yellow-blazed Farm Trail east.

0.25 Cross a footbridge.

0.6 Carefully cross the park road. Continue hiking south.

Among the exhibits on the living history farm you'll find this rustic chicken coop.

0.65 Cross under power lines. Continue hiking south.

0.8 The Farm Trail ends at Group Camp Road. Carefully cross the road and follow the wide gravel path past the privy.

0.85 Arrive at the Living Farm. Explore at will. Backtrack to the trailhead.

1.7 Arrive at the trailhead.

Resting up

Deluxe Inn, 1568 Alexander Love Hwy., York, (803) 684-2525; pet fee required. Quality Inn, 722 York Rd., Kings Mountain, NC, (843) 686-5700; pet fee required.

Camping

Onsite.

Fueling up

Wing Bonz, 20 N. Congress St., York, (803) 684-9434.

Puppy Paws and Golden Years

Hike out to the spillway and back for a 0.2-mile stroll. Also, you can drive directly to the Living History Farm.

◀ *The sweet and juicy peach is the official fruit of South Carolina.*

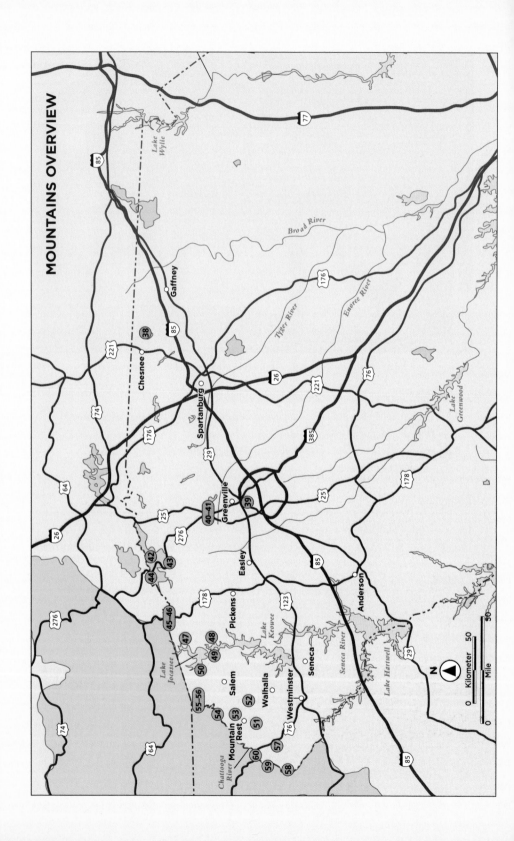

MOUNTAINS OVERVIEW

The Upcountry–Mountains

A h the glorious mountains, off in the distance peering back at you. With one layer on top of another, creating such a stunning landscape, it will leave you speechless. These mountains give rise to waterfalls galore, and surround some of the prettiest lakes in the east. Take a visit to historic sites like Cowpens National Battlefield and the Stumphouse Tunnel, or admire the handiwork laid to ground by the Civilian Conservation Corps back in the 1930s. Hike around a clear mountain lake or follow a creek upstream to any number of wonderful waterfalls. Whether it was man-made or built by Mother Nature, you're

King Creek Falls is one of many marvelous waterfalls in the upcountry.

A chimney is all that's left of this old home site (Wildcat Falls Trail).

sure to be impressed. And either way, you and your four-legged friends are in for a treat. Geographically, this is the smallest region in the state, but it really packs a punch. As a matter of fact, I've included twenty-three spectacular hikes from this region alone. Enjoy stunning views from the overlook at Caesars Head State Park, and then head out into the Mountain Bridge Wilderness. See the front face of Table Rock from the CCC Lakeside Trail, and then view the back of it from the top of Bald Rock. Whether you glide down the sliding rock of Long Shoals, or take a picnic at Pigpen Falls, you and the pups will love every minute. Spend a day at the "beach" along the banks of the Chattooga and Chauga Rivers, or hop in Lake Jocassee from the shores of Devils Fork. Whether you pull off the side of the road and hike at a wayside park, or delve deep into the Sumter National Forest, it's all outstanding. And the opportunities are endless when you start your adventure right here in the mountains of South Carolina. The FalconGuide *Hiking Waterfalls in Georgia and South Carolina* makes a great companion guide when exploring the upcountry.

Gaffney

38 Cowpens Battlefield Trail—Cowpens National Battlefield

As the trail leads you across this battlefield locale, you'll find you're standing where a strategic battle once took place, a battle that helped the Patriots turn the tables on the Brits in the South. Although this park is heavily used by locals, there's a reverent respect, a silence in the air that's only overshadowed by the sound of the birds chirping in the background. If you close your eyes and use your imagination, you can picture the history that happened here, a history that helped forge the freedom we Americans still enjoy to this day.

Start: 4001 Chesnee Hwy., Gaffney; behind the visitor center (east side)
Distance: 1.2-mile loop
Hiking time: About 45 minutes
Blaze color: None
Difficulty: Easy
Trailhead elevation: 976 feet
Highest point: 991 feet
Best season: Year-round
Schedule: Open daily 9 a.m. to 5 p.m.
Trail surface: Paved path, wide dirt "road"; the Park Service is planning on placing a rubber overlay on a portion of the paved path.
Other trail users: None on the Battlefield Trail; you may encounter bikes or equestrians on the paved path leading from the after-hours lot.
Canine compatibility: Leash required

Land status: National Park Service—Cowpens National Battlefield
Fees: No fee
Maps: *DeLorme: North Carolina Atlas & Gazetteer.* Page 19, C8
Trail contacts: (864) 461-2828; www.npplan .com/parks-by-state/south-carolina-national -parks/park-at-a-glance-cowpens-national -battlefield
Nearest town: Gaffney, Chesnee, Spartanburg
Trail tips: Restrooms and trail maps are available at the visitor center. There isn't much shade, so hike early in the day, or late afternoon. Bring lots of water for you and the dogs.
Special considerations: Starting at the after-hours entrance adds 1.5 miles to the hike.

Finding the trailhead: From I-85 east of Spartanburg, get off at exit 83 and drive north on SC 110 for 7.3 miles. Turn right onto SC 11 and travel for 0.2 mile to the entrance to Cowpens National Battlefield on the right. Follow the park road for 0.4 mile to the visitor center.
Note: The main gate closes at 5 p.m. There's an after-hours parking lot and entrance with an alternative trailhead. To reach it, drive east on SC 11 from the main gate for 1.2 miles to a right on Hayes Road. The parking lot is immediately on the left (N35 07.879'/W81 47.849').
Trailhead GPS: N35 07.869'/W81 47.872'

The Hike

At the far north end of the state, nearly bordering on North Carolina, you'll find the Cowpens National Battlefield site. People come to hike, bike, and run on the trails and loop road that circles around them. The famous Battle of Cowpens took place in the late 1700s and was a turning point of the Revolutionary War in the South. As you hike the loop trail across the battlefield locale, you're standing where a strategic battle once took place that helped the Patriots turn the tables on the Brits. Close your eyes and let your imagination drift back to a time when those who fought here fought for you, for the freedom and liberty we so cherish to this day. As you explore the park, you'll find subtle rolling hills, and lots of pretty trees scattered across the property. The trees offer some shade, but it's sparse, so bring plenty of drinking water for you and the dogs. Placards along the path educate you on the details of the battle and areas surrounding it. You'll learn where and how the armies staged and then met face to face on the battlefield. As the crickets chirp in the background, you can picture sitting behind one of these berms waiting for the call to arms. Unlike today's style of warfare, this was hand-to-hand combat. Fortunately, only twelve men lost their lives that day back in 1781. But it was an integral part of history, pointing America in the direction of independence. As you follow in the footsteps of our forefathers, a portion of the hike leads you along the Green River Road, which has a history all of its own. If your pups have sensitive paws, the gravel "road" is lined with grass, so they can keep their pads protected without the need of booties. You'll notice there are several alternate parking areas, and you can access the

The National Park Service has done a wonderful job preserving the 19th-century Robert Scruggs House at Cowpens.

Left: As you hike at Cowpens, you'll follow the Green River "Road" as part of the Battlefield Trail. Right: Exhibits along the Battlefield Trail give you insight into the historic battle that occurred here.

trail from any of them. The main gate and visitor center are open from 9 a.m. to 5 p.m. But if you visit after hours, you won't be turned away. Simply head over to the after-hours parking lot and enter the property from there. This will add a total of 1.5 miles to the hike. If you take this route, you'll pass the park's Robert Scruggs home site. The old one-room cottage lies 0.35 mile east of the loop trail off the Green River Road. The cabin is not significant because it survived the battle of Cowpens; it wasn't built until 1828, 50 years after the battle. It remains on the property to give you a perspective on how different life was during the formative years of our country. This humble homestead sheltered an entire family for many years. Wow, how times have changed.

Miles and Directions

0.0 From the visitor center, hike east toward the Green River Road.

0.1 Come to a T at the Green River Road. Go right, following the gravel "road" southeast.

0.2 Bypass a trail to the left. It leads to Parking Area #2. Continue hiking southeast on the gravel road.

0.55 Come to a fork. Left leads north to Parking Area #1. Straight is where the Green River Road leads to the after-hours parking lot. Go right (south) on the paved Battlefield Trail.

1.0 Hike past the Washington Light Infantry Monument (N35 08.104'/W81 48.894'). Continue hiking northwest.

1.2 Arrive at the visitor center.

Option: Add 1.5 miles to the hike by starting at the alternate trailhead in the after-hours parking lot (N35 07.869'/W81 47.872').

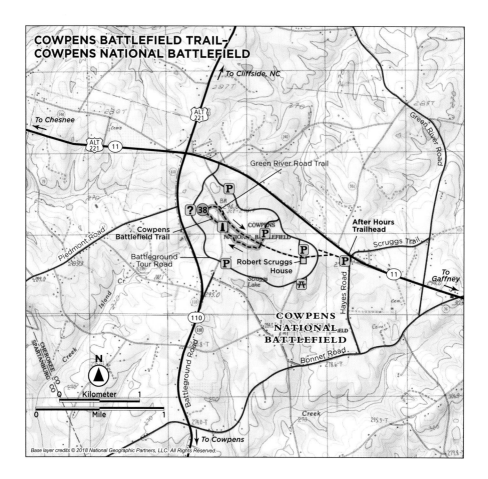

Resting up

Quality Inn, 143 Corona Dr., Gaffney, (864) 487-4200; pet fee required.
Sleep Inn, 834 Winslow Ave., Gaffney, (864) 487-5337; pet fee required.

Camping

Croft State Park, 450 Croft State Park Rd., Spartanburg, (864) 585-1283.

Fueling up

Daddy Joe's Beach House BBQ, 1400 W. Floyd Baker Blvd., Gaffney, (864) 487-7427.
Wild Ace Pizza and Pub, 148 W. Main St., Spartanburg, (864) 764-1480.

Puppy Paws and Golden Years

Hike this trail as an out-and-back. Adapt the length to suit your needs.

Stop and see the famous "peachoid" water tower in Gaffney. ▶

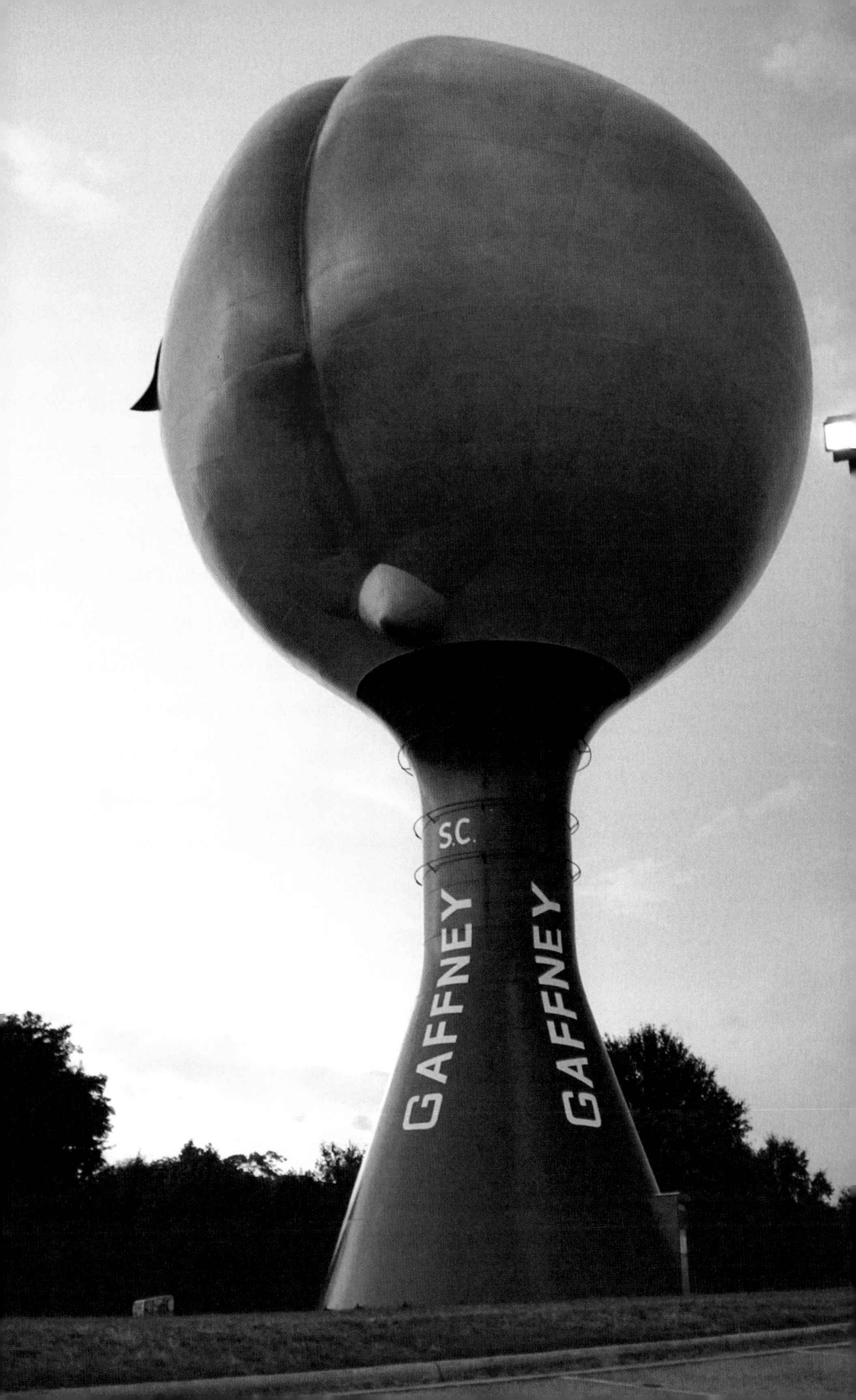

S.C.
GAFFNEY
GAFFNEY

Greenville

39 Swamp Rabbit Trail–Falls Park on the Reedy

This paved path begins in one of Greenville's most scenic parks. For starters, the park is home to Reedy River Falls. The waterfall and river are a fabulous focal point, and the town's spectacular Liberty Bridge crosses right over the top of the falls. But these are just perks to the hike. This stretch of the Swamp Rabbit Trail leads you through several local parks, while following the Reedy River over the length of the hike.

Start: Begin at the main entrance to Falls Park on the Reedy off of Main Street, at the northwest end of the park.
Distance: 2.8 miles out and back
Hiking time: About 1 hour, 20 minutes
Blaze color: None
Difficulty: Easy
Trailhead elevation: 955 feet
Highest point: 955 feet
Best season: Year-round
Trail surface: Paved path
Other trail users: Bicyclists

Canine compatibility: Leash required
Land status: Greenville County Parks and Recreation
Fees: No fee
Maps: *DeLorme: North Carolina Atlas & Gazetteer:* Page 18, H1
Trail contacts: (864) 288-6470; www.green villerec.com/ghs-swamp-rabbit-trail/
Nearest town: Greenville
Trail tips: There are two water fountains on this portion of the trail.

Finding the trailhead: From the junction of US 276 (Laurens Road) and SC 291 in Greenville, drive north on US 276 for 1.1 miles to a left onto E. Washington Street. Travel for 0.6 mile and veer left at the stoplight. You'll now be following E. McBee Avenue for 0.5 mile to a left onto Main Street. Travel for 0.3 mile to the entrance to the park on the left.
Note: Parking in this area is street side. **Trailhead GPS:** N34 50.703'/W82 24.117'

The Hike

The town of Greenville has done a fantastic job creating a number of green spaces across the city. And the Swamp Rabbit Trail is one of those greenways. The paved path covers a full 20 miles of ground as it weaves through town. Not only does this trail lead from one park to the next, to the next, but they have included multiple access points, so you are not committed to hiking or biking the full distance of the trail. On top of that, there are several water fountains along the way, so you can stay hydrated while you hike. It really is fantastic. Since 20 miles is a bit long to hike with your four-legged friends, I opted to highlight a 1.4-mile stretch of the trail. When you arrive at the park, you'll instantly see why I opted to begin the hike here. Although you are

The rocky Reedy River Falls sits in the heart of Greenville.

off of Main Street, in the heart of town, you'll not believe your eyes when you take a gander at Reedy River Falls. Layers of smooth stone form the riverbed where the water effortlessly flows over. An array of brown, beige, and tan-colored rocks create the waterfall, and it drops seamlessly from one tier down to the next. Geese and ducks rest peacefully near the banks, sometimes begging for a scrap, and there's a suspension bridge, the Liberty Bridge, crossing right over the falls. The bridge has a modern look to it, creating quite a contrast from the falls. As you begin to follow the river downstream, wildflowers fill the air with fragrance, and the park with color. It's a wonderful place to sit and read a book, or bring a picnic lunch. As you continue to follow the river southeast, the paved path parallels Furman College Way, and then leads you underneath US 29. Just past US 29, you'll cross a footbridge over the river. Although this bridge isn't nearly as spectacular as the Liberty Bridge, it too brings you over the top of another amazing waterfall. The trail now leads you through Cancer Survivors Park. Shortly after crossing under Cleveland Street, you'll enter Airplane Park, and find the aptly named park actually has an original U-2 aircraft on display. After passing the plane, you'll cross the river again on another well-built bridge. The path now crosses under McDaniel Avenue, and continues to follow the river downstream. You're now hiking through Cleveland Park, which is much bigger than the last two parks. Again you'll cross a footbridge, and the path leads toward a parking lot in the park. A water fountain sits on the north side of Cleveland Park Drive, southwest of the parking lot. If you don't need to top off your water, turn back at the footbridge.

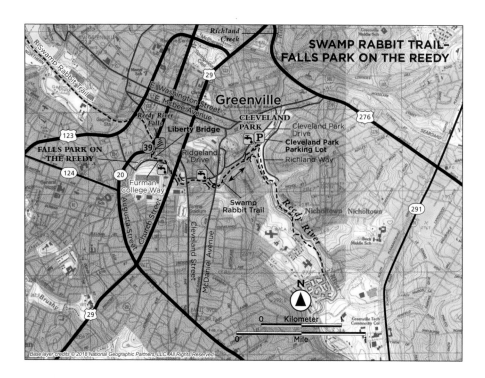

As you backtrack to the trailhead, you get to enjoy the splendor of this river all over again.

Miles and Directions

0.0 Hike down the steps into Falls Park on the Reedy River. Do not cross the Liberty Bridge; instead follow the path down to the river.

0.1 The trail crosses over a tributary and bends left. Follow the river downstream (southeast).

0.34 Hike under US 29 (Church Street). Continue hiking southeast.

0.4 Cross a footbridge. Continue hiking south through Cancer Survivors Park.

0.5 Hike under Cleveland Street.

0.75 Just after passing the airplane in Airplane Park, cross a footbridge over the river. Stay left, following the path along the river's edge.

0.85 Hike under McDaniel Avenue.

1.25 Come to a fork. Straight is a spur trail that ends in 0.25 mile. Go left (north) and cross the footbridge. The trail bends right (east), leading toward the road.

1.4 The trail comes to a fork where it meets Cleveland Park Drive. Right is the continuation of the Swamp Rabbit Trail. Across the street near the parking lot there is a water fountain. Backtrack to the trailhead.

2.8 Arrive back at the trailhead.

Option: To extend the hike, continue following the Swamp Rabbit Trail downstream.

Resting up

La Quinta Inn and Suites, 65 W. Orchard Park Dr., Greenville, (868) 233-8018; pet fee required.
Aloft, 5 N. Lauren St., Greenville, (864) 297-6100; no pet fee.

Camping

Paris Mountain State Park, 2401 State Park Rd., Greenville, (864) 244-5565.

Fueling up

Passerelle Bistro, 601 S. Main St., Greenville, (864) 509-0142.
Brazwells, 631 S. Main St., Greenville, (864) 568-5053.

Puppy Paws and Golden Years

Take them for a stroll around Falls Park on the Reedy. The park is fabulous, and the falls are spectacular.

The Liberty Bridge crosses over the top of the falls at Falls Park on the Reedy.

40 Lake Placid Trail–Paris Mountain State Park

Miles of hiking and biking trails crisscross the expanse of Paris Mountain State Park. The Lake Placid Trail is by far the easiest of them all. The smooth, wide, and fairly flat trail leads you on a lovely loop around Lake Placid. You'll take in the scenery while the dogs hop in for a dip. Then as you reach the eastern end of the lake, a splendid spillway greets you. Geese gather at the brink, peeking over while you cross a footbridge at the base. The park is within easy reach of Greenville, and well worth a visit.

Start: 2401 State Park Rd., Greenville; The trailhead is at picnic shelter #1.
Distance: 0.75-mile loop
Hiking time: About 20 minutes
Blaze color: Green
Difficulty: Easy
Trailhead elevation: 1,033 feet
Highest point: 1,033 feet
Best season: Year-round
Schedule: 8 a.m. to 9 p.m.; winter hours 8 a.m. to 6 p.m. (extended to 9 p.m. on Tues) Winter hours are in effect between the time changes that occur in fall and spring, and vary each year.
Trail surface: Hard-packed dirt
Other trail users: None

Canine compatibility: Leash required
Land status: South Carolina Department of Natural Resources
Fees: Fee required
Maps: *DeLorme: South Carolina Atlas & Gazetteer:* Page 18, F1
Trail contacts: (864) 244-5565; www.south carolinaparks.com/parismountain/ introduction.aspx
Nearest town: Greenville
Trail tips: There are no restrooms near the trailhead, but you'll hike past them at 0.2 mile.
Special considerations: When hiking near the spillway, the trail is near State Park Road. Keep the dogs on leash.

Finding the trailhead: From the junction of SC 253 and SC 290 in Sandy Flat, drive southwest on SC 253 for 2.9 miles to a hard right onto State Park Road (SR 344). Travel for 0.8 mile to the park on the left. From the gate, drive 0.1 mile to picnic shelter #1 on the right.

From the junction of SC 253 and US 25 in Greenville, drive northeast on SC 253 for 2.1 miles to a left onto State Park Road (SR 344). Follow directions above. **Trailhead GPS:** N34 55.635'/ W82 22.007'

The Hike

This splendid hike loops around Lake Placid at the far south end of the park. Lake Placid covers 8 acres of land and is one of four lakes inside the boundaries of this large park. The trail drops down below picnic shelter #1, and immediately leads you across a footbridge. Beyond the bridge the trail brings you through a lovely picnic area. Families gather to spend a day together in the park. Picnic tables are spread out over the area, and this part of the park is likely to be populated, especially on weekends. Although it's a busy area, this is a nice spot for the dogs to wade out into the water.

Left: A shallow pool forms at the base of this man-made spillway in Paris Mountain State Park. Right: And they're off.

Moving beyond the picnic area, you'll cross a second footbridge. This one takes you right out over the lake. The dogs might need a little coaxing here, because the boards of the bridge have some extra space between them. This can be visually intimidating for some more timid pups. Looping around onto the north shore of the lake, when you reach your first bench, you'll find another good swim spot for the dogs. They can again wade out into the water, while you sit and watch them splash about. This side of the lake is less occupied, so you enjoy a bit of peace and quiet. The path is smooth, wide, and fairly flat. You'll pass a second, and then third bench, where another fantastic swim spot presents itself. The dogs simply love this trail, and the playtime it affords them. As you near the end of the loop, you'll reach a tall, stone spillway. Following the steps down to the base of this man-made waterfall is the hardest part of this hike. Geese gather at the brink, and you can see them, one by one, peeking over the top at you. It's actually quite cute, and they continue their curiosity the entire time you're here. A footbridge crossing at the base of the "falls" gives the dogs one last chance to take a dip in the crystal-clear creek that is formed here. From here, you'll loop back a tenth of a mile and return to the trailhead. This hike is like night and day in comparison with the other featured trail in this park: Sulphur Springs Trail. You'll find this to be an easy, flat stroll through the forest, while the other is a long challenging trek covering over 4 miles of rugged terrain. Both are fantastic hikes, each with its own unique qualities. Despite its proximity to Greenville, this park is very peaceful, with no hint that you

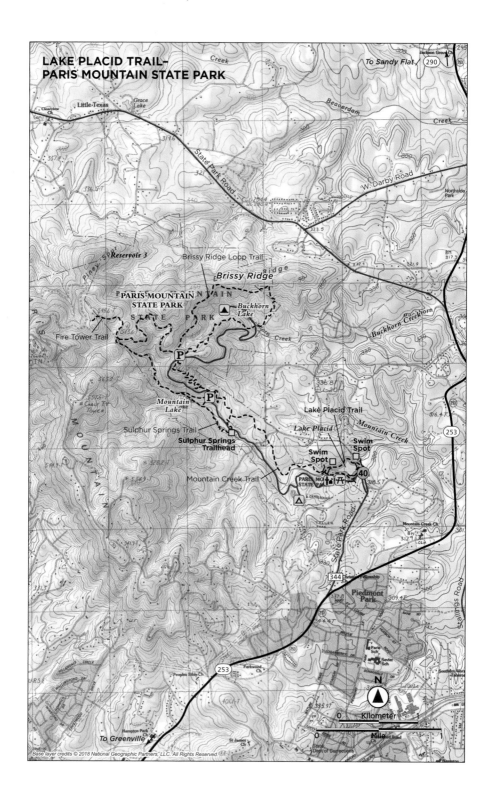

LAKE PLACID TRAIL–
PARIS MOUNTAIN STATE PARK

To Sandy Flat

Little·Texas
Grace Lake
Creek
Beaverdam
Creek

State Park Road
W. Darby Road
Northside Park

Reservoir 3
Piney S

Brissy Ridge Loop Trail
Brissy Ridge
Buckhorn Creek

PARIS MOUNTAIN
STATE PARK
Buckhorn
Lake

Fire Tower Trail

P

P

Mountain
Lake

P

Lake Placid Trail
Lake Placid
Mountain Creek

Sulphur Springs Trail
Swim
Spot

Sulphur Springs
Trailhead

Swim
Spot

40

PARIS MOUNTAIN
STATE PARK

Mountain Creek Trail

Mountains Creek Ch

Cable To
Tower
MOUNTAIN

State Park Road

344

Piedmont
Park

Stallings Road

253

Peoples Bible Ch

Parkwood
Ch

N

Kilometer

Mile

To Greenville

St James
Ch

are just outside a sprawling urban area. As you hike here, you leave it all behind. All you hear are the birds singing, wind blowing, and the occasional plane flying overhead. Wildlife ranges from raccoons and skunks to deer, and the variety of birds is astounding. During this short hike you'll see and hear an assortment of species, from great blue herons wading on the shore to beautiful little bluebirds whizzing by with a speed that's uncanny. Numbered posts along the path assist you in identifying some of the trees and plants. Stop at the Park Center building, and pick up a copy of the brochure to follow along as you hike. While you're there, take a tour of the fantastic exhibits they have on display. You'll gain a valuable insight into the history of this exceptional state park.

Miles and Directions

0.0 From picnic shelter #1, head down toward the lake and then go left (west) toward the footbridge.

150' Cross the footbridge. Continue hiking generally west following the shoreline.

0.2 Hike through the picnic area. This area doubles as a good swim spot for the dogs. Continue hiking west.

0.3 Cross a footbridge over the lake.

0.35 Come to a T. Left (southwest) is the Mountain Creek Trail. Go right (northeast) looping around the lake.

Option: Extend the hike by following the Mountain Creek Trail out and back.

0.4 Hike past a bench. This is a good swim spot.

0.6 Hike past a bench. This is an even better swim spot. Continue hiking east.

0.65 Cross a footbridge at the base of a spillway (N34 55.715'/W82 21.990'). Continue hiking generally south.

0.75 Arrive at the trailhead.

Left: He might be cute, but he packs a pungent punch.
Right: Goslings are able to fly within 2 to 3 months.

You can hike, bike, or paddle at Paris Mountain.

Resting up

La Quinta Inn and Suites, 65 W. Orchard Park Dr., Greenville, (868) 233-8018; pet fee required.
Aloft, 5 N Laurens St., Greenville, (864) 297-6100; no pet fee.

Camping

Onsite.

Fueling up

Karrie's Deli and Pub, 5000 Old Buncombe Rd., Greenville, (864) 235-3033.
Corona Mexican Restaurant, 2112 W. Hampton Blvd., Greenville, (864) 292-3719.

Puppy Paws and Golden Years

Hike the trail backwards and take them 0.1 mile to the spillway.

41 Sulphur Springs Trail–Paris Mountain State Park

For a trail that's not located very deep within the mountain region of the state, this is by far one of the most challenging hikes in this book. The first half-mile is easy, but beyond the spillway you begin to steeply climb a rocky path as you head up the mountain. Whether you have two legs or four, you'll be getting your workout in for the day. Luckily, there are plenty of creek crossings for the dogs to stay cool, and for you to take a break as you watch them splash about.

Start: 2401 State Park Rd., Greenville; west end of the parking lot, west of shelter #6
Distance: 4.1-mile loop
Hiking time: About 2 hours, 40 minutes
Blaze color: White
Difficulty: Strenuous
Trailhead elevation: 1,033 feet
Highest point: 1,581 feet
Best season: Year-round
Schedule: 8 a.m. to 9 p.m.; winter hours 8 a.m. to 6 p.m. (extended to 9 p.m. on Tues) Winter hours are in effect between the time changes that occur in fall and spring, and vary each year.
Trail surface: Hard-packed dirt, with rocky and rooty sections

Other trail users: Mountain bikers on a portion of the trail
Canine compatibility: Leash required
Land status: South Carolina Department of Natural Resources
Fees: Fee required
Maps: *DeLorme: South Carolina Atlas & Gazetteer:* Page 18, F1
Trail contacts: (864) 244-5565; www.south carolinaparks.com/parismountain/introduction .aspx
Nearest town: Greenville
Trail tips: Trail map, restrooms, and picnic shelters near the trailhead. Bring a hiking stick and lots of drinking water for you and the dogs.

Finding the trailhead: From the junction of SC 253 and SC 290 in Sandy Flat, drive southwest on SC 253 for 2.9 miles to a hard right onto State Park Road (SR 344). Travel for 0.8 mile to the park on the left. From the gate, drive 0.3 mile to a stop sign. Continue straight for 0.5 mile to a second stop sign. Again continue straight for another 0.8 mile to picnic shelters #5 and #6.

From the junction of SC 253 and US 25 in Greenville, drive northeast on SC 253 for 2.1 miles to a left onto State Park Road (SR 344). Follow directions above. **Trailhead GPS:** N34 55.920'/ W82 23.034'

The Hike

Whether you have two legs or four, you're about to get a good workout in. Although the first half-mile is a flat, easy, well-trodden path, I assure you, as you move past the stone spillway, the trail progresses on to become a challenge. The spillway is a nice swim spot, and the dogs can easily wade out into the crystal-clear water. Be sure you take advantage of these swim spots on the first half of the hike, because the latter half is mostly dry. As you move beyond the spillway, the trail briefly brings you

Left: This tower was an unexpected treat along the Sulphur Springs Trail.
Right: Holly, a pit bull mix, takes a water break while crossing the creek.

alongside the park's Mountain Lake. Above the lake, you'll follow a shallow, swiftly moving creek, and the trail transforms into a rocky, rooty path. When you reach the rock-hop at 0.8 mile, the dogs will have another chance to splash around before the path begins to climb steeply. Pretty cascades and steep rockslides form the creek, but a dense thicket of rhododendron and mountain laurel separates you from the water. With dogged determination, you'll climb, climb, climb alongside the waterway, and at last come to another rock-hop below a pretty cascade. While the dogs dip their paws, you may want to sit in one of the pools yourself to catch your breath. As you move away from the creek, you'll come to a T. Left leads out to the fire tower, but you want to go right (east) to remain on the Sulphur Springs Trail. For the remainder of the hike, mountain bikes are allowed on the trail, except for Saturdays, when bikes are banned from all trails in the park. As you begin to make your way back toward the trailhead, you'll find the trail has transformed into a wide, flat fire road. You'll begin a long, slow, steady descent following a contour. The descent is much easier than the steep climb you just made, and you'll appreciate the mountain views around you. Although there's no water, you'll enjoy a gentle breeze. It's along this second half of the hike that you come to realize how big this park really is. You'll hike across an alternate parking lot, where the Brissy Ridge Trail begins, and then cross the park road. After crossing the park road, the trail tapers, returning to a traditional narrow path. As the rocky route continues downhill, it seems to get steeper, with switchbacks to ease the descent. Along this stretch of trail, you may encounter a mountain biker, or trail runner. Technically, mountain bikers are supposed to yield to hikers. But when you're hiking with the dogs, have some courtesy, and yield to other trail users whether they're on foot, bike, or horse. A little trail etiquette can go a long way. And perhaps they'll pay it forward in the future. The trail skirts by another alternate parking lot, and you'll soon cross a footbridge over a tiny tributary. This is a welcome water break for the panting pups, since you haven't seen any freshwater in over 2 miles. That being said, make sure you bring lots of drinking water for both you and the dogs. Amazingly so, the trail continues to lead you downhill, and you come to realize just how much you climbed on the way in. By the time you return to the trailhead, you'll have covered an elevation gain and loss of about 1,100 feet.

Miles and Directions

0.0 Hike west into the woods following the creek.

0.05 Pass a swim spot for the dogs. Continue hiking west.

0.08 Cross a footbridge. Continue hiking north.

0.1 Cross a boardwalk. Continue hiking generally north.

0.3 Cross a footbridge. Continue hiking upstream.

0.38 Come to a gazebo. Bypass the connector trail to the right (north). Stay left; continue hiking west.

0.45 A set of stone steps leads down to a swim spot.

0.55 Come to a beautiful spillway (N34 56.168'/W82 23.428'). Pass the dam; hike west alongside the Mountain Lake.

The dogs will like the car ride there too.

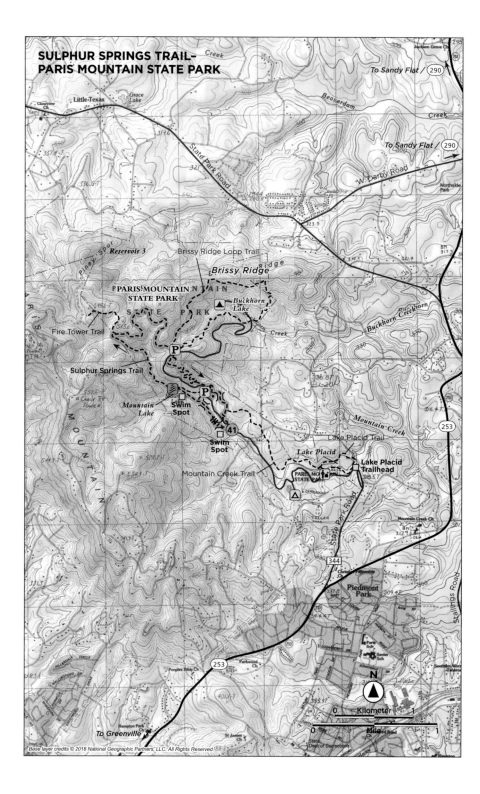

SULPHUR SPRINGS TRAIL–
PARIS MOUNTAIN STATE PARK

0.56 Come to a fork. Bypass the connector trail to the right (east). Stay left (west) on the rocky, rooty path.

0.8 Rock-hop the creek.

1.2 Rock-hop the creek below a pretty rockslide.

1.45 Moving away from the creek, you'll come to a T. Left (west) is the Fire Tower Trail. Go right (east) on the Sulphur Springs Trail.

Option: Extend the hike by following the Fire Tower Trail 0.4 mile to see the fire tower.

2.57 Bypass the Brissy Ridge Trail to the left (north). Continue straight (southeast) toward a parking lot.

2.6 Hike straight (southeast) through a parking lot. Bypass the Brissy Ridge Trail on your left (northeast). Continue hiking southeast on the Sulphur Springs Trail.

2.61 Cross the park road; hike up the stone steps. Continue hiking generally south.

2.7 Come to a T. A social trail leads left (east). Go right (south) on the Sulphur Springs Trail.

3.5 The trail skirts by a parking lot. Continue hiking south.

3.8 Cross a footbridge. Continue hiking generally south.

4.1 The trail ends at the parking lot, near the trailhead.

Surprisingly, people have about five times more taste bud sensors than our furry friends.

Resting up

La Quinta Inn and Suites, 65 W. Orchard Park Dr., Greenville, (868) 233-8018; pet fee required.
Aloft, 5 N. Laurens St., Greenville, (864) 297-6100; no pet fee.

Camping

Onsite.

Fueling up

Karrie's Deli and Pub, 5000 Old Buncombe Rd., Greenville, (864) 235-3033.
The Bohemian, 2 W. Stone Ave., Greenville, (864) 233-0006.

Puppy Paws and Golden Years

Take them on the Lake Placid Trail (see Lake Placid Trail hike). Hike the trail backwards and take them 0.1 mile to the spillway.

Pickens

42 Jones Gap Trail–Jones Gap State Park

Following the Middle Saluda River over its entirety, this portion of the Jones Gap Trail is easily among my favorites. You enjoy the sights and sounds of cascade after wonderfully flowing cascade, while the pups have ample opportunity to safely splash around in several swim holes along this magnificent river. On the way to Ben's Sluice, you'll pass a challenging side trail leading to Rainbow Falls, and an easy spur trail that quickly brings you to view Jones Gap Falls. Without a doubt, you and the dogs are sure to enjoy exploring the Mountain Bridge Wilderness.

Start: 303 Jones Gap Rd., Marietta; west side of the bridge near the trailhead information sign, southwest of the park office
Distance: 3.2 miles out and back
Hiking time: About 1 hour and 45 minutes
Blaze color: Blue
Difficulty: Moderate
Trailhead elevation: 1,341 feet
Highest point: 1,817 feet
Best season: Year-round
Schedule: 9 a.m. to 6 p.m. (extended to 9 p.m. during Daylight Saving Time)
Trail surface: Rocky path, hard-packed dirt
Other trail users: None
Canine compatibility: Leash required

Land status: South Carolina Department of Natural Resources
Fees: Fee required
Maps: *DeLorme: South Carolina Atlas & Gazetteer:* Page 17, C9
Trail contacts: (864) 836-3647; www.south carolinaparks.com/jonesgap/introduction.aspx
Nearest town: Marietta, Greenville
Trail tips: Register at the trailhead before hiking. Bring a hiking stick and lots of drinking water for you and the dogs. Restrooms are located in the picnic area.
Special considerations: The trail closes 1 hour before dark, year-round.

Finding the trailhead: From the junction of US 276 and SC 11 East near Cleveland, drive north on US 276 for 1.4 miles to a right onto River Falls Road. Travel for 3.8 miles to a left onto Jones Gap Road. Drive 1.9 miles to the park at the end of the road.

From the junction of US 276 and SC 11 West, near Caesars Head, drive south on US 276 for 3.4 miles to a left onto River Falls Road. Follow directions above. **Trailhead GPS:** N35 07.523'/ W82 34.459'

The Hike

Before entering the wilderness area, the park requires that you register at a kiosk near the trailhead. Once you've registered, follow the rocky trail into the forest. The trail is easy to follow, and generally follows the Middle Saluda River upstream over the

Left: Autumn adds a splash of color to the magnificent Middle Saluda River.
Right: A challenging side trail leads up to the radiant Rainbow Falls.

length of the hike. There are times the water is out of view, but it's never far. The Jones Gap Trail (JGT) makes up a good portion of the Middle Saluda Passage of the Palmetto Trail. If you're not familiar with it, the Palmetto Trail runs the full width of the state, beginning on the coast, and cutting a diagonal path all the way across the state to the mountains. As you continue hiking generally west, the strong, sturdy river drives you on. Along the way, you'll pass several primitive backcountry campsites. So if you wanted to make an excursion out of it, you could spend the night. The path is wide, and very rocky early on, so watch your footing, although the four-legged hikers seem to breeze right by. When letting the dogs take a dip in the river, please use your own discretion. This is a free-flowing river, solely governed by Mother Nature. The water levels will fluctuate with the seasons, and with each rainfall. At 0.6 mile, you'll come to a fork. The right leads steeply up to Rainbow Falls. To reach the falls is a strenuous 1.1 miles, one way. But if you're up for the challenge, you're in for a treat. The falls are glorious. If you opt out on this side trip, continue following the JGT. As you do, the path follows a subtle climb, and the river is swift and strong. It's full of life, and formed by the many rocks and boulders that fill its bed. The steady sound of water rushing by is spectacular. But the water isn't the only fantastic natural feature along this hike.

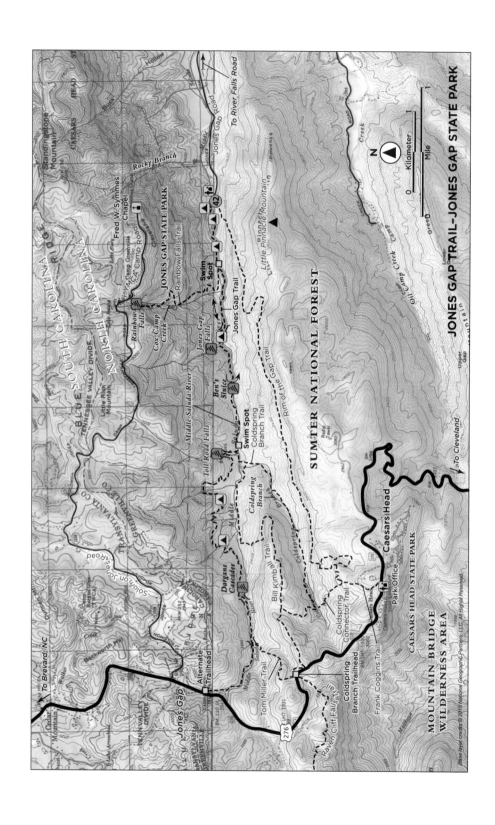

JONES GAP TRAIL–JONES GAP STATE PARK

MOUNTAIN BRIDGE
WILDERNESS AREA

CAESARS HEAD STATE PARK

SUMTER NATIONAL FOREST

JONES GAP STATE PARK

BLUE RIDGE

SOUTH CAROLINA

NORTH CAROLINA

TENNESSEE VALLEY DIVIDE

GREENVILLE CO.
TRANSYLVANIA CO.

To Brevard, NC

To Cleveland

To River Falls Road

Jones Gap Road

Solomon Jones Road

Standingstone
Mountain

Little Rich
Mountain

Little Pinnacle Mountain

Fred W. Symmes
Chapel

Rainbow Falls Trail

Rainbow
Falls

Cox Camp Creek

Jones Gap
Falls

Ben's Sluice

Middle Saluda River

Toll Road Falls

Swim Spot

Coldspring
Branch Trail

Coldspring Branch

Bill Kimball Trail

Coldspring
Connector Trail

Dargans
Cascades

Alternate
Trailhead

Tom Miller Trail

Frank Coggins Trail

Raven Cliff Falls Trail

Coldspring
Branch Trailhead

Park Office

Caesars Head

Jones Gap Trail

Rim of the Gap Trail

Oil Camp Creek

Jones Gap

276

N

Kilometer

Mile

At 0.9 mile you'll pass a tree that is absolutely magnificent. Large burls jutting out from the trunk of this splendid specimen are worth taking note of. When you stop to admire the fabulous figure of this tree, you'll also find the river may be calm enough for the dogs to swim. Beyond the tree, the trail continues to climb, but in short bursts. Just shy of 1.3 miles, you'll reach another fork. The right leads to Jones Gap Falls. A mere 0.05 mile is all it takes to reach this beauty. The falls are tall, slim, and beautiful, with a nice pool at the base for the dogs to cool off. Copper-colored rock accentuates the clarity of the water as it rolls over the surface of the stone. Continuing deeper into the wilderness, you'll reach a spot in the trail where it makes a hard right (northwest). Stay straight here, and a spur trail quickly ends at the river. A short scramble down to the water's edge puts you at the base of Ben's Sluice. At 25 feet, the sluice is slight of stature, but it's absolutely gorgeous. The base of the sluice is a perfect swim hole for the dogs. You may even want to dip your own feet in the cool mountain water. From here, the JGT actually continues on for another 3.7 miles to where it ends on US 276, north of Caesars Head. If you want to extend the hike, feel free. But this is a good turnaround point, with plenty of swim spots for the pups.

Miles and Directions

0.0 Hike north into the forest on the wide rocky path.

0.15 Pass a primitive campsite. Continue hiking generally west.

0.45 Pass a primitive campsite. Continue hiking west.

0.48 Rock-hop a tributary.

0.55 Hike past a good swim spot.

0.6 Come to a fork. Right is the red-blazed Rainbow Falls Trail. Stay left (southwest) on the Jones Gap Trail.

Option: Follow the trail for 1.1 miles to Rainbow Falls (N35 08.027'/W82 35.314'). It's strenuous, but the falls are worth the effort!

0.75 Rock-hop a tributary.

0.78 Rock-hop a tributary.

0.9 Hike past an amazing tree with burls. This is also a good swim spot.

1.15 Cross a footbridge and pass primitive campsite #10. Continue hiking west.

1.25 Rock-hop a tributary.

1.28 Come to a fork. Right leads 0.05 mile north to see Jones Gap Falls (N35 07.489'/W82 35.641'). Left leads southwest toward Ben's Sluice.

Option: I highly recommend the trip to Jones Gap Falls.

1.4 Hike past primitive campsite #12.

1.45 Rock-hop back-to-back tributaries. Continue hiking generally west.

1.6 Come to Ben's Sluice (N35 07.386'/W82 35.921'). Backtrack to the trailhead.

3.2 Arrive at the trailhead.

Option: Continue hiking west on the Jones Gap Trail. It continues for 3.7 miles to an alternative trailhead on US 276 (see Coldspring Branch Trail hike for details).

Left: Dipping their paws in the river along the Jones Gap Trail
Right: Blue, a hound mix, follows the blue-blazed Jones Gap Trail.

Resting up

Best Western, 110 Hawkins Rd., Travelers Rest, (864) 834-7040; pet fee required.

Camping

Backcountry camping onsite.
Table Rock State Park, 158 E. Ellison Ln., Pickens, (864) 878-9813.

Fueling up

Victoria Valley Vineyards, 1360 S. Saluda Rd., Cleveland, (864) 878-5307.

Puppy Paws and Golden Years

Take them to stroll around the day use area. There's a lovely picnic area and the remains of an old fish hatchery.

43 Wildcat Falls Trail–Wildcat Wayside Park

Offering three wonderful waterfalls over the course of a mile-long trail, this unsuspecting roadside park really packs a punch. Make sure you keep the dogs on lead, since the trailhead is near the main road. You'll pass the Lower and Middle Falls before the trail leads up to the remnants of an old picnic shelter. Beyond the charred chimney ruins, you'll be led on a pleasant uphill journey to Upper Falls, where large boulders strewn about add character. The park is part of the Mountain Bridge Wilderness Area, and there are no facilities or amenities onsite, so come prepared.

Start: Wildcat Wayside Park, to the left (west) of Lower Wildcat Falls
Distance: 1.02-mile loop
Hiking time: About 10 minutes
Blaze color: Yellow
Difficulty: Easy to moderate
Trailhead elevation: 1,042 feet
Highest point: 1,085 feet
Best season: Year-round
Trail surface: Stone steps, hard-packed dirt
Other trail users: None
Canine compatibility: Leash required

Land status: Mountain Bridge Wilderness Area
Fees: No fee
Maps: *DeLorme: North Carolina Atlas & Gazetteer*: Page 17, D9
Trail contacts: (864) 836-6115; www.south carolinaparks.com/caesarshead/introduction .aspx
Nearest town: Cleveland
Trail tips: The trailhead and lower falls are right next to the road. Keep the dogs on a leash at all times. Trail map near the base of the middle falls.

Finding the trailhead: From the junction of US 276 and SC 11 South, drive south on SC 11/ US 276 for 0.5 miles to the parking area on the left.

From the junction of US 276 and SC 11 North, drive north on SC 11/US 276 for 4.9 miles to the parking area on the right. **Trailhead GPS:** N35 04.429'/W82 35.811'

The Hike

From the minute you step out of the car, you'll hear the free-flowing water of Wildcat Creek. Once you get the pups leashed up and ready to go, you realize that Lower Wildcat Falls rests right next to the trailhead—and the road. So make sure you keep the dogs on a leash. The waterfall is simply beautiful, and the swimming hole that gathers at the base is a perfect depth for the dogs. It's a bit shallow for people to swim, but you can wade out into the crystal-clear creek, and let the pups splash about. When they've had their fill of the Lower Falls, follow the yellow-blazed path upstream, and you immediately arrive at the Middle Falls. This one also has a small pool collecting at the base. Use caution as you rock-hop the creek, because the Middle Falls sits just upstream from the brink of the Lower Falls. Make sure you keep the dogs on a leash, at least until you reach the fork where the loop begins. Just beyond the falls, a large topographical trail map stands beside the creek, and

WILDCAT FALLS TRAIL–WILDCAT WAYSIDE PARK

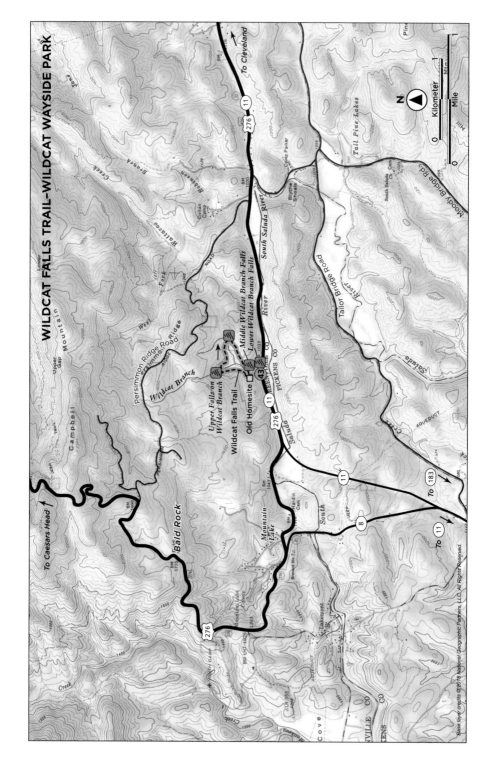

Left: A pristine swim spot sits at the base of Lower Wildcat Branch Falls.
Right: Stepping stones lead across the creek at Wildcat Wayside.

a set of stone steps leads up to the remnants of an old picnic shelter, built by the Civilian Conservation Corps (CCC) back in the 1930s. The foundation and a tall, charred chimney are all that remain today. This wayside park and picnic shelter were built after the advent of the automobile, giving weary travelers a place to stop and take a break alongside the roadway. In its day, this one was known as the Greenville Wayside. Although the name's changed and the shelter is gone, this park still serves its purpose as roadside respite nearly 100 years later. Today, the wayside is part of the Mountain Bridge Wilderness Area. And the hike is a fantastic alternative to some of the more rugged trails found deeper within the wilderness area. Just past the chimney you'll come to the creek and a fork where the loop begins. Bypass the path to the right, and rock-hop straight across the creek. This puts you on a clockwise route around the loop. As you enjoy the shade of the forest, you'll soon be following the trickling waterway upstream. A number of birds serenade you as you hike generally north. In less than a half a mile you find yourself climbing more stone steps, and rock-hopping across the creek at the base of the Upper Falls. Giant boulders litter the base of the falls, as if they've fallen off the flat face of this massive 200-foot waterfall. The boulders have been resting there long enough for trees to grow out of them. And the entire area looks like a colossal patchwork collage of nature. And, there are still plenty of little pools of water for the dogs to dip their paws. After crossing the creek, keep the dogs from wandering. A path leads up toward the brink, and the area can be very dangerous. Looping back toward the trailhead, you can actually feel the air temperature cool off, and dampen down as you near the creek. You'll rock-hop one more tributary with a tiny waterfall on it, and then make a slow steady descent back to the fork where the loop began.

Fields of flowers add a splash of color to the countryside.

Miles and Directions

0.0 Follow the yellow-blazed path up the stone steps.

150' Arrive at the base of Middle Wildcat Branch Falls (N35 04.449'/W82 35.809'). Continue hiking north, and upstream.

0.1 Arrive at an old chimney (N35 04.496'/W82 35.826').

0.12 Come to a fork at the creek. Right (northeast) follows the creek upstream. Go straight across the creek, and continue hiking northeast.

0.4 Arrive at the base of Upper Falls on Wildcat Branch (N35 04.702/W82 35.799). Rock-hop the creek at the base. Continue hiking east.

0.6 Rock-hop a tributary, passing a small waterfall. Continue hiking south.

0.9 Arrive at the fork where the loop began. Backtrack to the trailhead.

1.02 Arrive at the trailhead.

Resting up

Best Western, 110 Hawkins Rd., Travelers Rest, (864) 834-7040; pet fee required.

Camping

Table Rock State Park, 158 E. Ellison Ln., Pickens, (864) 878-9813.

Fueling up

Victoria Valley Vineyards, 1360 S. Saluda Rd., Cleveland, (864) 878-5307.
Bruster's Real Ice Cream, 5152 Calhoun Memorial Hwy., Easley, (864) 306-0401.

Puppy Paws and Golden Years

Take them to the chimney and back. If they can't climb the stone steps, let them play at the base of the lower falls.

44 Coldspring Branch-Jones Gap-Tom Miller Trail Loop— Caesars Head State Park

A number of trails connect with Coldspring Branch, which enables you to make a loop of this wonderfully wooded hike. Tall trees, wildlife, and several creek crossings enhance the experience as you explore the middle portion of the Mountain Bridge Wilderness. You'll begin by making a long, steady descent, dropping down nearly 1,000 feet of elevation. But remember, what goes down, must come up. So be prepared for a steep climb that will challenge your mettle as you return on the Tom Miller Trail. If the loop is too long, simply alter the distance by hiking out and back.

Start: 8155 Geer Hwy., Cleveland; northeast end of the parking lot
Distance: 6.0-mile loop
Hiking time: About 3 hours, 30 minutes
Blaze color: Orange—Coldspring Branch Trail, Blue—Jones Gap Trail
Difficulty: Moderate to strenuous
Trailhead elevation: 3,037 feet
Highest point: 3,156 feet
Best season: Year-round
Schedule: 9 a.m. to 6 p.m. (9 a.m. to 9 p.m. during Daylight Saving Time)
Trail surface: Hard-packed dirt
Other trail users: None
Canine compatibility: Leash required
Land status: South Carolina Department of Natural Resources

Fees: Fee required
Maps: *DeLorme: South Carolina Atlas & Gazetteer:* Page 17, D8
Trail contacts: (864) 836-6115; www.south carolinaparks.com/caesarshead/introduction .aspx
Nearest town: Cleveland, Marietta, Brevard, NC
Trail tips: The trail closes 1 hour before dark. Give the dogs a big bowl of water before you hike; it's over a mile before you reach your first natural water source. Bring a hiking stick, and lots of drinking water for you and the dogs.
Special considerations: The trailhead is near a busy road, so keep the dogs on a leash near here.

Finding the trailhead: From the junction of US 276 and SC 8 near Cleveland, drive north on US 276 for 7.6 miles to the parking area on the right.

From the junction of US 276 and the SC/NC state line, drive south on US 276 for 2.1 miles to the parking area on the left.

Note: Caesars Head State Park office and visitor center is 1.1 miles south of the trailhead on the west side of US 276. **Trailhead GPS:** N35 06.955'/W82 38.287'

The Hike

Many trails intersect with each other here, so make sure you bring a map along. You'll begin by making a long, slow, downhill trek, and the first trail you'll encounter is the Bill Kimball Trail. This path bisects the loop, and reunites with the Cold-

Left: To get this view, stop in at the office of Caesars Head State Park.
Right: Symmes Chapel, known as "Pretty Place," is one of the most popular sightseeing spots in the upcountry.

spring Branch Trail (CBT) in 2.2 miles. Heading deeper into the peaceful forest, a variety of birds sing sweetly to you. It's not until the 1-mile mark that you finally hear some moving water, and the dogs' ears begin to perk up. As you bypass the Coldspring Connector Trail, you can't help but notice how rugged the mountains are. And the plant life is astounding. It's a botanist's dream. There are so many different trees and plants that fill this forest. Keep your eyes peeled for an assortment of mushrooms as well. But make sure the dogs don't take a nibble. Amazingly, you're still going downhill, as the trail drops a full 1,000 feet of elevation over the length of the loop. But remember, what goes down, must go up. At last, you reach the creek and the dogs enjoy splashing about, and sipping from the crystal-clear fresh mountain water, while you cross on a footbridge. Looking upstream, the creek is filled with boulders and rocks covered with brilliant green moss. It's fifty shades of green. And looking downstream, it appears as though a beaver has been busy at work. The wildlife is diverse, ranging from beavers to black bear, and skinks to skunks. And beyond this bridge you'll find swim spot after glorious swim spot, a virtual cornucopia of creek crossings, with the sound of moving water adding to the entertainment. Bypass the Bill Kimball Trail again, and the steep rocky path leads down to and across the Middle Saluda River. After making that long descent, you welcome the cool air that comes along with the river. When you reach a T, the CBT meets the Jones Gap Trail (JGT). Heading left you quickly arrive at the gorgeous, rocky waterfall known as Toll Road Falls. Giant boulders with trees growing out of them rest on one side of the falls, while green moss-covered rocks line the other. It's quite spectacular. Over the next 2 miles the path gently climbs, and you'll cross a series of tributaries, so the dogs have ample opportunities to keep cool. The JGT is loaded with water and natural features. A fantastic forest, impressive rock formations, waterfalls, and an area known as "The Winds" greet you as you hike. When you reach Dargans Cascades, a sandy beach and splendid swim hole welcome you. It's a perfect place to take a break. From the falls, you'll climb up "The Winds," and then continue upstream until you reach your final fork. It's here that you leave the JGT and make the final leg of the loop on the Tom Miller Trail. And this is where the challenge begins. You're about to make a steep, strenuous climb. It'll even have your four-legged friends huffing and puffing as you ascend. When you reach the crest of the mountain, you'll exclaim hallelujah as you wipe the sweat from your brow. You now stand about 0.15 mile from the trailhead. This is a good landmark to put the dogs back on leash if you had them off. After the terrain you just tackled, the remainder of the hike is a breeze.

Miles and Directions

0.0 Hike east into the forest and downhill.

0.15 Come to a T at an old logging road. Right leads west to US 276. Go left (east) following the rocky roadbed.

0.7 Come to a fork. Left (southeast) is the Bill Kimball Trail. Continue straight (southwest) on the orange-blazed Coldspring Branch Trail.

1.05 Come to a second fork about the same time you hear moving water. Right (south) is the Coldspring Connector. Bypass this and stay left (east) on the Coldspring Branch Trail. You'll now parallel the creek from above.

1.2 Cross a footbridge. Continue hiking southeast and downhill.

1.4 At last, you reach the creek. Cross on a footbridge and the dogs enjoy dipping their paws in the crystal-clear fresh mountain water. Continue hiking generally east.

1.7 Rock-hop a trio of tributaries that may be dry. Continue hiking east.

1.8 Rock-hop Coldspring Branch. Continue hiking northeast.

2.0 Rock-hop Coldspring Branch. Continue hiking downstream.

2.2 The trail seems to dead-end at the creek, and you'll see a single blaze on an island in the creek. Ignore the blaze, and follow the creek downstream over roots and rocks, staying on the south side.

2.25 Rock-hop Coldspring Branch. This crossing is near the brink of a cascade. Do not let the dogs wander in this area. Continue hiking northeast.

2.6 Come to a marked fork. The Bill Kimball Trail comes in from the left (west). Go straight following the steep rocky path north.

Option: Return on the Bill Kimball Trail. This would cut 0.6 mile off the hike.

2.65 Rock-hop a tributary, then cross a footbridge over the river.

2.68 Cross a footbridge. The trail makes a quick climb east.

2.7 The Coldspring Branch Trail ends at a T with the Jones Gap Trail. Right leads generally east for 2.2 miles to Jones Gap State Park. Go left (north) on the blue-blazed trail.

Option: Return the way you came, making this hike 5.4 miles out and back.

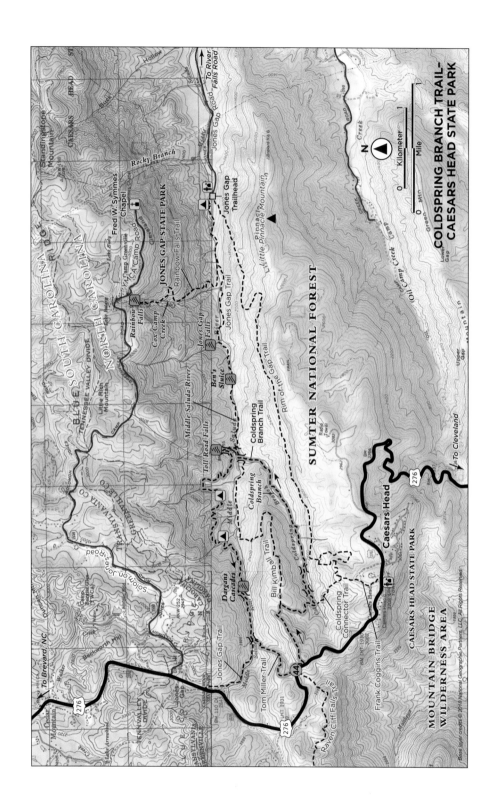

COLDSPRING BRANCH TRAIL–
CAESARS HEAD STATE PARK

MOUNTAIN BRIDGE
WILDERNESS AREA

CAESARS HEAD STATE PARK

SUMTER NATIONAL FOREST

JONES GAP STATE PARK

NORTH CAROLINA

SOUTH CAROLINA

BLUE RIDGE

TENNESSEE VALLEY DIVIDE

GREENVILLE CO.
TRANSYLVANIA CO.

To Brevard, NC

To Cleveland

To River Falls Road

Standingstone Mountain

CAESARS HEAD

Rocky Branch

Fred W. Symmes Chapel

Little Rich Mountain

Little Pinnacle Mountain

Jones Gap Trailhead

Jones Gap Trail

Rim of the Gap Trail

Rainbow Falls Trail

Rainbow Falls

YMCA Camp Greenville
CA Camp Road

Cox Camp Creek

Jones Gap Falls

Ben's Sluice

Middle Saluda River

Toll Road Falls

Coldspring Branch Trail

Coldspring Branch

Bill Kimball Trail

Coldspring Connector Trail

Frank Coggins Trail

Dargans Cascades

Tom Miller Trail

Jones Gap Trail

Raven Cliff Falls Trail

Solomon Jones Road

Caesars Head

276

276

276

N

Kilometer

Mile

Base layer credits © 2018 National Geographic Partners, LLC. All Rights Reserved.

2.8 Cross a footbridge over Toll Road Falls (N35 07.425'/W82 36.519'). Briefly follow the tributary downstream.

3.35 Rock-hop a tributary. Continue hiking south.

3.5 Hike past primitive campsite #14. Continue hiking west as the trail climbs.

3.7 Rock-hop a tributary. Continue hiking south.

3.8 Rock-hop a tributary. Continue hiking south.

4.05 Rock-hop a tributary. Continue hiking southeast.

4.15 Hike past primitive campsite #15. Continue hiking west.

4.25 Rock-hop a tributary. Continue hiking south.

4.65 As the trail makes a hard switchback to the right (east) and uphill, go straight ahead (west) following a spur trail to the river. At the river you'll come to Dargans Cascades (N35 07.319'/W82 37.627'). This is a great swim hole and picnic spot. Return to the switchback, and continue following the Jones Gap Trail east and uphill on an area known as "The Winds."

5.0 After making several switchbacks on "The Winds," cross a log bridge. Continue hiking generally west and upstream.

5.3 Come to a fork. The Jones Gap Trail goes straight (west) over a log bridge, and leads about 0.7 mile to US 276 (not near the trailhead). Do not cross the log bridge. Instead, go left, following the Tom Miller Trail southwest back toward the trailhead.

5.85 You'll reach the top of a mountain, and begin to hear traffic on US 276. This is a good landmark to put the dogs back on leash if you had them off.

6.0 The trail ends at the northwest end of the parking lot.

Option: If the loop is too long, hike this as an out-and-back, altering the distance to suit your needs.

Resting up

Best Western, 110 Hawkins Rd., Travelers Rest, (864) 834-7040; pet fee required.

Camping

Backcountry primitive camping onsite.
Table Rock State Park, 158 E. Ellison Ln., Pickens, (864) 878-9813.

Fueling up

Victoria Valley Vineyards, 1360 S. Saluda Rd., Cleveland, (864) 878-5307.

Puppy Paws and Golden Years

Take them to Wildcat Wayside Park (see Wildcat Falls Trail hike). It's on the north side of SC 11/US 276, 0.5 mile east of the intersection of US 276 and SC 11.

45 CCC Lakeside Trail–Table Rock State Park

Sporting some of the most stunning scenery in the state, this trail finds itself among my favorites. You'll come across a variety of wooded topography, which is a pleasant surprise as you follow a contour around the park's Pinnacle Lake. This one gives you that mountain feel without presenting too much of a challenge. Fantastic views for you, and a few good swim spots for your pups, make this hike ideal year-round: a virtual trail for all seasons.

Start: 158 E. Ellison Ln., Pickens; southeast of the Hemlock Picnic Shelter, near the boathouse
Distance: 1.9-mile loop
Hiking time: About 55 minutes
Blaze color: Purple
Difficulty: Easy to moderate
Trailhead elevation: 1,220 feet
Highest point: 1,257 feet
Best season: Year-round
Schedule: Sun–Thurs 7 a.m. to 7 p.m., Fri and Sat 7 a.m. to 9 p.m.; during Daylight Saving Time, Sun to Thurs 7 a.m. to 9 p.m., Fri and Sat 7 a.m. to 10 p.m.

Trail surface: Hard-packed dirt; small section of gravel and paved path
Other trail users: None
Canine compatibility: Leash required
Land status: South Carolina Department of Natural Resources
Fees: Fee required
Maps: *DeLorme: South Carolina Atlas & Gazetteer:* Page 17, E8
Trail contacts: (864) 878-9813; www.south carolinaparks.com/tablerock/introduction.aspx
Nearest town: Pickens
Trail tips: Trash cans and picnic shelter near the trailhead

Finding the trailhead: From the junction of SC 11 and SC 178 near Sunset, drive east on SC 11 for 4.1 miles to a left onto West Gate Road (SR 25). Travel for 0.4 mile to the west gate entrance of the park on your right. Follow the Table Rock State Park Road for 0.9 mile to a right onto Hemlock Lane. Follow Hemlock Lane for 0.1 mile to the end.

From the junction of SC 11 and SC 8 South, drive west on SC 11 for 6.0 miles to a right onto West Gate Road (SR 25). Follow directions above. **Trailhead GPS:** N35 01.906'/W82 41.868'

The Hike

The CCC Lakeside Trail makes a long simple loop around the park's 36-acre Pinnacle Lake. But this terrific trail does so much more than that. Along the way, you'll pass a historic lodge and spillway. You'll cross crystal-clear tributaries and find several splendid swim holes. Expect a variety of wildflowers, mountain laurel, and even blackberries in summertime. To top it off, you'll get the most spectacular views of Table Rock, better than any other vantage point in the park. All the while, the path undulates up and down, giving you the best of all worlds. At times you'll hike right along the shoreline, while at others you'll see it from up above. The topography is a treat, giving you great views from up high, but not the difficult challenge of many

Left: Hiking at Table Rock State Park is enjoyable year-round.
Right: Some of the most stunning views of Table Rock are seen from the CCC Lakeside Trail.

other trails in this park. The forest keeps you shaded for most of the way. And benches are randomly placed to give you a spot to sit and take it all in. Whether from up above, or right along the banks, the reflection of the clouds, mountains, and trees on the water is incredible, especially in autumn when the leaves are ablaze with color. As you make your way around Lodge Cove, you'll see stone steps leading down to the boat landing. The landing was built so guests could paddle right up to the park's lodge. It doubles as a good swim spot for your happy hounds. Bypass the next set of steps; they lead up to the magnificent lodge. The lodge was built by the Civilian Conservation Corps (CCC) in the mid-1930s. It's definitely worth a visit. The impressive structure has wood floors, stone fireplaces, and vaulted ceilings that are adorned with large wooden beams. The skilled craftsmanship of these industrious individuals is outstanding. Nearly a century ago the CCC also cut a good portion of this very trail, the section from the trailhead to the spillway. And then in 2011, the park system finished the loop. After passing below the lodge, the trail leads you out to a bench that sits in the absolutely perfect place. From this bench, you'll be stunned by the view before you, the lofty, stone face of Table Rock smiling down upon you. With the lake in the foreground, a remarkable reflection of sheer beauty greets you. You won't get a better view of Table Rock from anywhere else in the park. Beyond the bench, you'll continue following the shoreline and within a tenth of a mile come to a stone walled spillway. This too was built by the CCC, and the water at the base gives the dogs another good opportunity to splash around in Carrick Creek. You'll cross

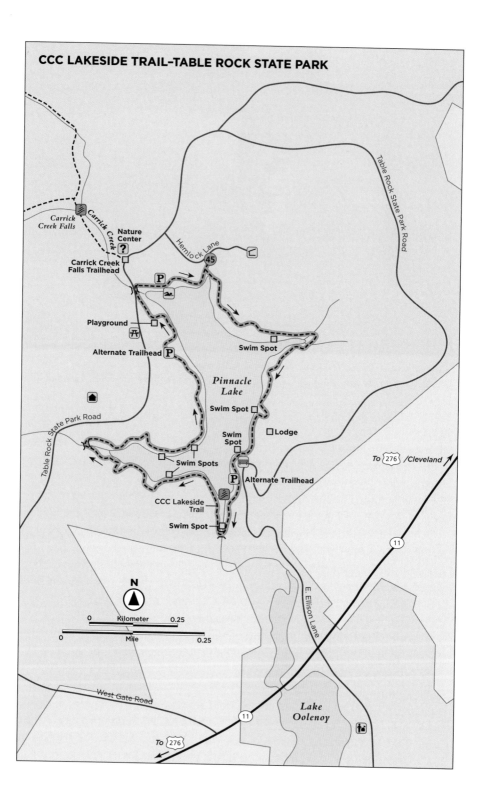

CCC LAKESIDE TRAIL–TABLE ROCK STATE PARK

Carrick Creek Falls

Carrick Creek

Nature Center

Carrick Creek Falls Trailhead

Hemlock Lane

45

Playground

Alternate Trailhead

Table Rock State Park Road

Pinnacle Lake

Swim Spot

Swim Spot

Swim Spot

Lodge

To 276 /Cleveland

Swim Spots

Alternate Trailhead

CCC Lakeside Trail

Swim Spot

Table Rock State Park Road

N

0   Kilometer   0.25

0   Mile   0.25

11

E. Ellison Lane

West Gate Road

11

Lake Oolenoy

To 276

You can explore Pinnacle Lake by land or by water.

the creek over a footbridge and begin to loop back toward the trailhead. Following the shoreline, you'll pass more benches and more swim spots. Oak trees dangling over the water enhance the views, and the variety of plant life surrounding Pinnacle Lake is astonishing. When you reach the 1.5-mile mark, the trail gets a little sloppy, leading you to a parking lot for an alternate trailhead. It then heads on toward the picnic shelter, playground, and over the bridge on the park road. Make sure you follow the Miles and Directions closely. From the bridge, you'll loop around the swim area and boathouse before arriving back at the trailhead.

Miles and Directions

0.0 Hike east into the woods, following the shoreline.

0.2 Pass a swim spot as you hike around a cove.

0.25 Rock-hop back-to-back tributaries. Climb the stone steps; continue hiking southwest.

0.45 Hike past the canoe launch below the lodge. This doubles as a swim spot.

0.5 Bypass the steps leading up to the lodge. Continue following the shoreline.

0.55 Arrive at a bench with stunning views of Table Rock. Agile pups can hop in the lake here too. Follow the shoreline south.

0.6 Come to an alternate trailhead near a stone wall. Hike alongside the wall and the trail leads back into the woods and down some steps.

0.65 Hike past the spillway (N35 01.576'/W82 41.826'). Continue hiking downstream.

0.72 Cross a footbridge. Continue hiking north.

0.8 Come to a T. Right leads less than 100 feet to a bench overlooking the lake. Stay left, following the shoreline.

0.9 Pass another bench with a swim spot. Continue following the shoreline.

1.1 Cross a footbridge.

1.3 The trail leads you back along the lakeshore to another swim spot.

1.35 Pass another bench and swim spot. Continue hiking as the trail passes below the cabins.

1.5 Come to a fork. Right is a narrow overgrown social trail leading north toward the lake. Go left (northwest) toward a parking lot and alternative trailhead.

1.55 Just before you reach the parking lot, follow the trail to the right (east). It leads back toward the water.

1.65 Hike through a picnic area.

1.7 The trail ends at the playground. To make a loop, follow the paved path north to the sidewalk. Hike northeast on the sidewalk.

Option: Extend the hike to 3.4 miles by backtracking to the trailhead from here.

1.75 Cross the bridge on the sidewalk and enter the parking lot.

1.8 Hike past the swim area and concession stand as you head east toward the paddleboats.

1.85 Hike past the paddleboats.

1.9 The loop ends near the trailhead.

Some plants are poisonous to dogs; keep a close eye on them.

Resting up

Laurel Springs Country Inn, 1137 Moorefield Memorial Hwy., Sunset, (864) 878-2252; pet fee required.

Quality Inn and Suites, 5539 Calhoun Memorial Hwy., Easley, (864) 859-7520; pet fee required.

Camping

Onsite.

Fueling up

Victoria Valley Vineyards, 1360 S. Saluda Rd., Cleveland, (864) 878-5307.

Bruster's Real Ice Cream, 5152 Calhoun Memorial Hwy., Easley, (864) 306-0401.

Puppy Paws and Golden Years

Park at the first alternate trailhead and take them down to the bench and swim spot at 0.55 mile. The views are spectacular, and it's less than 0.1 mile to reach from that trailhead.

46 Carrick Creek Falls Trail–Table Rock State Park

What a fantastic treat you're in for as you visit Table Rock State Park. Not only do you get stunning views of the park's namesake, but you'll also find a wonderful little waterfall with an open observation deck built at the base. The dogs enjoy taking a dip in the swim hole here before you delve deeper into the forest on this wooded hike. Several cascades greet you, as the trail stays with Carrick Creek early on, and then picks up Green Creek as you return. With all this lively water, it's easy to see why this is one of my favorites.

Start: 158 E. Ellison Ln., Pickens; north side of the road at the Nature Center, across the street from the parking lot
Distance: 2.0-mile loop
Hiking time: About 1 hour
Blaze color: Green
Difficulty: Moderate
Trailhead elevation: 1,125 feet
Highest point: 1,510 feet
Best season: Year-round
Schedule: Sun–Thurs 7 a.m. to 7 p.m., Fri and Sat 7 a.m. to 9 p.m.; during Daylight Saving Time, Sun–Thurs 7 a.m. to 9 p.m., Fri and Sat 7 a.m. to 10 p.m.
Trail surface: Paved path, hard-packed dirt, with rooty and rocky sections

Other trail users: None
Canine compatibility: Leash required
Land status: South Carolina Department of Natural Resources
Fees: Fee required
Maps: *DeLorme: South Carolina Atlas & Gazetteer:* Page 17, E8
Trail contacts: (864) 878-9813; www.south carolinaparks.com/tablerock/introduction.aspx
Nearest town: Pickens, Easley
Trail tips: Restrooms, trash cans, poop bags, and a water fountain near the trailhead
Special considerations: Use caution when crossing the road from the parking lot to the trailhead.

Finding the trailhead: From the junction of SC 11 and SC 178 near Sunset, drive east on SC 11 for 4.1 miles to a left onto West Gate Road (SR 25). Travel for 0.4 mile to the park on your right. Follow Table Rock State Park Road for 0.8 mile to a parking lot on the right (just after crossing the bridge).

From the junction of SC 11 and SC 8 South, drive west on SC 11 for 6.0 miles to a right onto West Gate Road (SR 25). Follow directions above. **Trailhead GPS:** N35 01.933'/W82 42.024'

The Hike

Sitting at the foot of its namesake, Table Rock State Park gives you the best of both worlds. This fantastic park has scored two trails on the Author's Favorites list. One is the CCC Lakeside Trail, which closely follows the shoreline of Pinnacle Lake, and gives you amazing views of Table Rock Mountain. The other, this fabulous hike, keeps you in the forest, and has the added feature of wonderful waterfalls and lovely cascades. A kiosk with a large map stands at the trailhead, and the park requires

The summit of Table Rock Mountain stands over 3,000 feet tall.

that you stop and register here before hiking into the wilderness. From the kiosk, a wooden walkway leads through the breezeway of the Nature Center, and you immediately get your first taste of Carrick Creek. The water dancing down the boulder-filled creek is simply magnificent. A paved path leads you upstream, and you quickly arrive at a well-built deck overlooking Carrick Creek Falls. A few wide steps lead up to the deck, and there are no railings, and no benches built into it. Instead, it's an open-sided multi-tiered masterpiece. Perhaps what makes it a masterpiece is that it sits alongside a splendid little waterfall. You can step from one level to the next, and then out onto the large, flat stones that frame a spectacular swim hole at the base of the falls. After you've gotten your fill, the paved path continues upstream past the brink. You're greeted by more tremendous, flat rocks that mold and form the creek. Within no time, the paved path transitions into hard-packed dirt. And by 0.2 mile you'll arrive at a fork where the loop begins. You can hike either direction, but it's described clockwise. The climbs are more difficult this way, but it's a gentler descent, which is better on the knees, and easier with the dogs on a leash. As you continue upstream, the trail begins to climb and you'll be following green, white, and yellow blazes for the Carrick Creek, Foothills, and Pinnacle Mountain Trails respectively. While you crisscross from one side of the creek to the other, the dogs have ample opportunity to splash around in the water. You'll pass one stunning cascade after another, watching the water gently slide down the face of this rocky mountain. When you reach a T, the Foothills and Pinnacle Mountain Trails head left. If you wanted to extend the hike, you could go that way, but be forewarned that is a long, rugged,

CARRICK CREEK FALLS TRAIL–TABLE ROCK STATE PARK

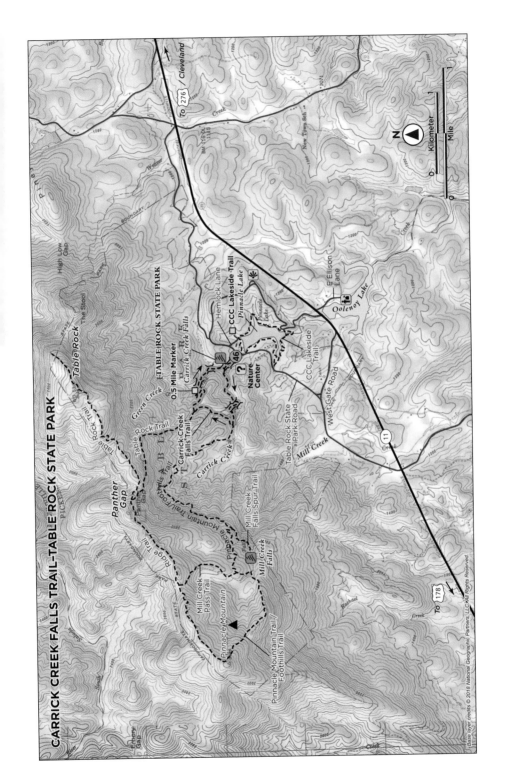

You can view Table Rock and the Table Rock Reservoir from the top of Bald Rock off of US 276.

strenuous hike. Stay right instead, following the green-blazed Carrick Creek Trail. As you move away from the creek, the trail flattens, and soon you notice it smoothes out as well, losing the rocks and roots you hiked over on the way in. When you reach a second T, stay right again. A variety of birds fill the air with song, and you can clearly hear them now that you've moved away from the water. But as you make your way downhill, the sound of the creek begins to build again. You'll soon cross a footbridge over the brink of a waterfall that gracefully drops over rocky ledges. As you continue your descent, you can noticeably feel the air change with the elevation. When you thought Green Creek couldn't get any prettier, you'll pass one last marvelous waterfall. Rock ledges stick out like bookshelves on a wall, and the water drops from one shelf to the next, creating quite a show. A tenth of a mile later, you're back at the fork where the loop began.

Miles and Directions

0.0 Hike through the breezeway at the Nature Center. A wooden boardwalk leads across the creek.

0.07 Come to an observation deck at the base of Carrick Creek Falls (N35 01.966'/W82 42.072'). Continue hiking north on the paved path.

0.18 Cross a footbridge.

0.2 Come to a fork where the loop begins. Go left (northwest).

0.33 Rock-hop the creek. Continue west and upstream.

0.38 Rock-hop the creek. Continue hiking upstream as the trail climbs.

0.55 Hike across back-to-back footbridges. Continue hiking southwest.

0.7 Come to a T. Left (west) is the Pinnacle Mountain Trail/Foothills Trail. Go right (east), now following green, white, and yellow blazes.

Option: Extend the hike on the strenuous Pinnacle Mountain Trail.

0.85 Rock-hop a tributary. Continue hiking north.

1.05 Come to a T. Left (west) is the red-blazed Table Rock Trail. Go right (east), following green and red blazes downhill.

Option: Extend the hike by following the strenuous Table Rock Trail.

1.5 Pass a post indicating that you're 0.5 mile from the trailhead.

1.55 Cross a footbridge over the brink of a cascading waterfall. Keep the dogs on a tight leash here. Continue hiking downhill and downstream.

1.7 Cross a footbridge.

1.8 Come to the fork where the loop began. Go left, backtracking to the trailhead.

2.0 Arrive at the trailhead.

A fantastic multi-tiered deck sits near the base of Carrick Creek Falls.

Resting up

Laurel Springs Country Inn, 1137 Moorefield Memorial Hwy., Sunset, (864) 878-2252; pet fee required.

Quality Inn and Suites, 5539 Calhoun Memorial Hwy., Easley, (864) 859-7520; pet fee required.

Camping

Onsite.

Fueling up

Victoria Valley Vineyards, 1360 S. Saluda Rd., Cleveland, (864) 878-5307.

Bruster's Real Ice Cream, 5152 Calhoun Memorial Hwy., Easley, (864) 306-0401.

Puppy Paws and Golden Years

Take them less than 0.1 mile to Carrick Creek Falls. You won't be disappointed.

47 Twin Falls Trail–Felburn Foundation Nature Preserve

This is such a wonderful hike, I can't help but tout my enthusiasm. Although it's short, I assure you it's worthy. Fall colors in autumn and wildflowers in spring are just a taste of what makes this so inviting. Swim holes with large boulders to sit upon while you watch the dogs play in the creek add to the experience. But then, as you near the trail's end, the falls come into view. Magnificent! If I had only one word to describe Twin Falls, that would be it. A stunning landscape unfolds before you, and you too may call this a favorite.

Start: Northeast end of the parking area
Distance: 0.6 mile out and back
Hiking time: About 20 minutes
Blaze color: None
Difficulty: Easy
Trailhead elevation: 1,037 feet
Highest point: 1,117 feet
Best season: Year-round
Schedule: Open dawn to dusk daily
Trail surface: Wide, hard-packed dirt
Other trail users: None

Canine compatibility: Leash required
Land status: Private nature preserve run by the Felburn Foundation
Fees: No fee
Maps: *DeLorme: North Carolina Atlas & Gazetteer.* Page 17, E6
Trail contacts: None available
Nearest town: Pickens, Easley, Rosman, NC
Trail tips: Let the dogs play in the creek at 0.2 mile, since it's discouraged to hike on the rocks near the falls.

Finding the trailhead: From the junction of US 178 and the North Carolina–South Carolina state line, drive south on US 178 for 7.4 miles. Turn right onto Cleo Chapman Highway (SC 100) and drive 1.9 miles to a T at Eastatoee Community Road (SR 92). Go right and drive 0.9 mile to a right onto Water Falls Road. The road will wind around for 0.4 mile to the parking area at the end of the road.

From the junction of US 178 and SC 11, drive north on US 178 for 3.1 miles. Turn left onto Cleo Chapman Highway (SC 100) (immediately before "Bob's Place"). Follow directions above.

Note: Do not block the gate at the trailhead. **Trailhead GPS:** N35 00.584'/W82 49.274'

The Hike

This hike begins by skirting around a gate, and then following a wide, road-like path into the forest. Although the first impression is rather mundane, the trail quickly puts you alongside a fabulous, clear running creek. You'll enjoy a pleasant stroll that is exponentially enhanced by the lively creek you now follow upstream. The path almost makes a straight line from the trailhead to the falls, with a slight jog in the middle where you find yourself alongside a fantastic swim spot for the dogs. Large boulders are placed perfectly along the banks of the creek, while pools of water gracefully form between them. You can sit atop the rocks, and simply take it all in. The sun glistening on the water and the sound of the creek as it tap dances over

Left: Twin Falls is one of the most spectacular in the state!
Right: Standing in awe of the sheer might of Mother Nature

stones are only surpassed by the grand finale at the end of the trail. While the dogs wade out into the water, you can sit a spell, soak up the sun, and simply take in the scenery as the crystal-clear water passes you by. As you head deeper into the forest, you'll pass a miniature working waterwheel, and the creek continues to present itself with more splendid cascades. Beyond the waterwheel, the trail narrows, but stays with the creek. You'll start to gently climb, and a forest of maple, oak, poplar, and sweet gum keep you well shaded over most of the hike. When you reach trail's end, you'll find an elevated observation deck overlooking Twin Falls. Although it's more commonly referred to as Twin Falls, on maps you may see this one identified as Reedy Cove Falls because the left of the two waterfalls flows on Reedy Cove Creek. The right waterfall is a tributary of the creek, but just as powerful. The scenery here is jaw-droppingly beautiful. Both waterfalls are magnificent, and the scene painted here will leave you speechless. Mother Nature has really outdone herself here. It's picturesque, grandiose, majestic, and simply beyond words. I have no concern that I have set the expectations too high, because I know the second you see this stunning landscape, it won't disappoint.

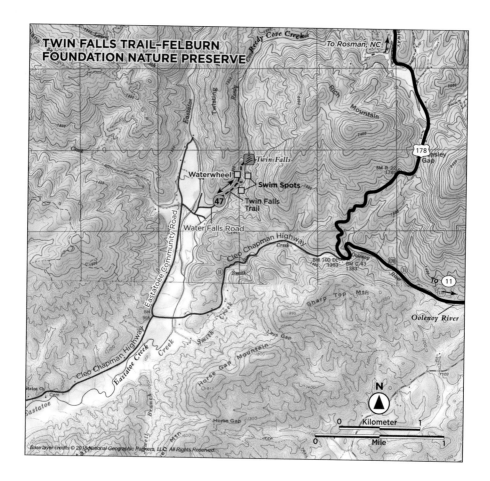

Miles and Directions

0.0   Go around the gate and hike northeast.

0.15 Come to a fork. Follow the spur trail to the right. It leads northeast about 100 feet to a swim hole in the creek. Return to the main trail and hike north.

0.2   Hike past another swim spot.

0.22 Hike north past a small wooden waterwheel.

0.33 Arrive at an observation deck overlooking Twin Falls (N35 00.795'/W82 49.114'). Backtrack to the trailhead.

0.6   Arrive at the trailhead.

Resting up

Laurel Springs Country Inn, 1137 Moorefield Memorial Hwy., Sunset, (864) 878-2252; pet fee required.

Quality Inn and Suites, 5539 Calhoun Memorial Hwy., Easley, (864) 859-7520; pet fee required.

Left: Dogs of all sizes will enjoy the hike to Twin Falls.
Right: There are plenty of large rocks to rest upon near Twin Falls.

Camping

Table Rock State Park, 158 E. Ellison Ln., Pickens, (864) 878-9813.
Keowee-Toxaway State Park, 108 Residence Dr., Sunset, (864) 868-2605.

Fueling up

Victoria Valley Vineyards, 1360 S. Saluda Rd., Cleveland, (864) 878-5307.
Bruster's Real Ice Cream, 5152 Calhoun Memorial Hwy., Easley, (864) 306-0401.

Puppy Paws and Golden Years

Suitable for all dogs. But if 0.6 mile is too long, stop at the first swim spot. Returning from here makes a lovely 0.3-mile hike. But you'll miss out on Twin Falls.

Lake Jocassee

48 Long Shoals Trail–Long Shoals Wayside Park

This fantastic little park is found within a small pocket of Poe Creek State Forest. Although the only amenities are a few picnic tables, trash cans, and a vault toilet, when you take the steep trail down to the water's edge you'll see why I call it fantastic. Little Eastatoee Creek plunges downstream, forming one of the best sliding rocks I've seen in the South. The beige boulder face of Long Shoals is a lovely contrast with the lush green forest surrounding it. The entire family will enjoy taking a dip at this popular local swimming hole.

Start: Northeast corner of the upper lot, at the sign reading "creek access"
Distance: 0.2 mile out and back
Hiking time: About 10 minutes
Blaze color: Blue
Difficulty: Moderate
Trailhead elevation: 936 feet
Highest point: 940 feet
Best season: Year-round
Schedule: Open 6 a.m. to 10 p.m.
Trail surface: Wooden staircase, hard-packed dirt, rock face of the shoal
Other trail users: None

Canine compatibility: Leash required
Land status: Long Shoals Wayside Park within Poe Creek State Forest
Fees: No fee
Maps: *DeLorme: South Carolina Atlas & Gazetteer:* Page 17, F6
Trail contacts: (864) 944-1104; www. visitpickenscounty.com/vendor/88/long-shoals-wayside-park/
Nearest town: Salem, Sunset, Pickens, Easley
Trail tips: Vault toilet, trash cans, and doggy waste bags near the trailhead. No alcohol allowed.

Finding the trailhead: From the junction of SC 11 and US 178 near Sunset, drive south on SC 11 for 6.3 miles to a left into Long Shoals Wayside Park. Park in the upper lot.
From the junction of SC 11 and SC 133 near Keowee-Toxaway State Park, drive north on SC 11 for 2.2 miles to a right into Long Shoals Wayside Park. Park in the upper lot. **Trailhead GPS:** N34 56.919'/W82 51.078'

The Hike

Holy cow this is gorgeous! A beautiful long shoal with a long sliding rock stands as the center of attention at this wonderful "wayside." Locals flock to this popular swimming hole in summertime, and when you see it you'll understand why. It's absolutely perfect, as Little Eastatoee Creek goes rushing by over smooth stone. Use caution when you unload the dogs, since the trailhead is not far from the busy road. You'll begin this very short hike by heading steeply down a wooden staircase. The

Left: Long Shoals is a popular spot to swim, sun, picnic, and play.
Right: Table Rock Mountain can be seen from miles away.

narrow, blue-blazed path then continues on a steep trajectory toward the creek. In less than 0.1 mile you're standing at the brink of Long Shoals. Fortunately, the long shoals are surrounded by large flat rocks that are easy to walk on, so there's no plummet or plunge at the brink. If this trail were longer, it would be rated as strenuous, because the pitch of the hike is substantial. But since it's so short, I opted for moderate. Looking upstream from the brink, massive boulders are propped up on the far side of the waterway, and a bed of smooth, sleek rock forms the creek itself. The rock is tan, beige, bronze, and brown, and the clear water running over it accentuates the rich tones of the stone. As you glance downstream, you'll see kids sliding down the rock, and then hurrying back to the brink to do it all over again. The water at the base is deep enough for the whole family to take a swim. A pathway of rocks cuts directly across the creek downstream from the base. This adds to your options, giving you a place to sit out in the middle of the cool mountain water. This rudimentary rock walkway doubles as a good place to fish from. But make sure you have your South Carolina state fishing license in hand before you bait the hook. From the brink, you can walk up- or downstream on the large flat stone that lines the banks. It's a fantastic place to explore and gives you an ideal place to lay a blanket out to sit a spell. You'll see people sunning themselves, and laying out a picnic lunch. There's a picnic area between the upper and lower parking lots, but when you reach the creek, you won't want

The swimming hole at Long Shoals Wayside is deep enough to do the doggy paddle.

LONG SHOALS TRAIL–LONG SHOALS WAYSIDE PARK

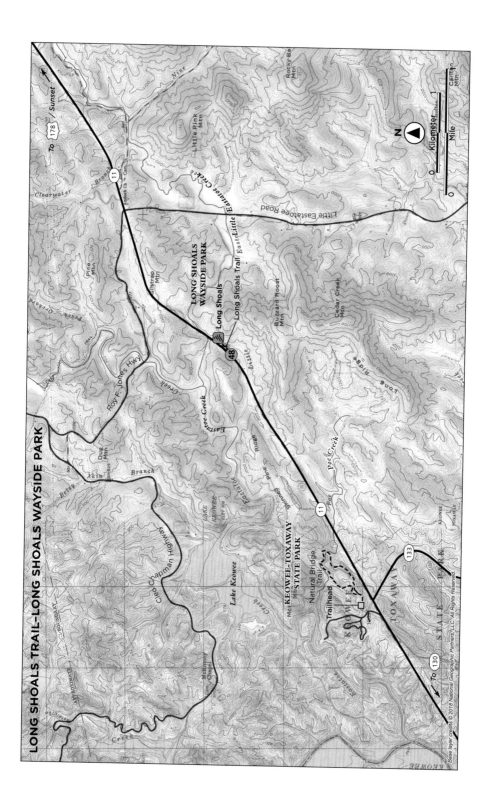

to leave its side. Please be respectful of Mother Nature, and bring a trash bag along if you do picnic. It would be a shame to litter this fabulous little piece of paradise. As the inviting waterway rushes by, you may find it hard to resist its allure. You can take a dip with the dogs in the pool at the base, but bring a friend along too. That way they can hold the dogs while you take a turn at sliding down the rockslide that the long shoals create. It's easily one of the best

The mountain region is loaded with wildflowers.

sliding rocks in the South. Laughter fills the air, and the sound of the water steadily coursing by beckons you back in to do it again. With Lake Jocassee to the west, the mountains to the north, and Greenville sitting to the south, this one has an ideal location for all your traveling needs.

Miles and Directions

0.0 Hike down the wooden steps and follow the blue-blazed trail northeast.

0.05 Arrive at the creek alongside Long Shoals (N34 56.938'/W82 51.058'). Carefully hike down the banks to the base of the falls.

0.1 Arrive at the base of the falls. Backtrack to the trailhead.

0.2 Arrive at the trailhead.

Resting up

Laurel Springs Country Inn, 1137 Moorefield Memorial Hwy., Sunset, (864) 878-2252; pet fee required.
Quality Inn and Suites, 5539 Calhoun Memorial Hwy., Easley, (864) 859-7520; pet fee required.

Camping

Keowee-Toxaway State Park, 108 Residence Dr., Sunset, (864) 868-2605.

Fueling up

Bruster's Real Ice Cream, 5152 Calhoun Memorial Hwy., Easley, (864) 306-0401.

Puppy Paws and Golden Years

This is steep, but very short. If your dogs can't climb stairs or steep grades, take them to the Twin Falls Trail. Dogs of all ages can hike to the fabulous swim hole at 0.15 mile.

49 Natural Bridge Trail–Keowee-Toxaway State Park

A flawlessly flat slab of stone forms the natural bridge for which this trail was named. But that's not the only unique natural feature to be found along this challenging loop. A portion of the hike follows the crystal-clear Poe Creek. As the water tap dances over the rocks, it forms lively cascades and even a small waterfall. An open area at the base of the falls is perfect for the pups to play in the water, and you come to realize that Lake Keowee is not the only amazing waterway within this park.

Start: 108 Residence Dr., Sunset; east of the park office in the upper parking lot
Distance: 1.3-mile loop
Hiking time: About 1 hour
Blaze color: None
Difficulty: Moderate to strenuous
Trailhead elevation: 1,070 feet
Highest point: 1,071 feet
Best season: Year-round
Schedule: Sat–Thurs 9 a.m. to 6 p.m., Fri 9 a.m. to 8 p.m. (extended to 9 p.m. Mon–Sun during Daylight Saving Time)
Trail surface: Gravel path, hard-packed dirt with rooty sections

Other trail users: None
Canine compatibility: Leash required
Land status: South Carolina Department of Natural Resources
Fees: No fee
Maps: *DeLorme: South Carolina Atlas & Gazetteer:* Page 16, G5
Trail contacts: (864) 868-2605; www.south carolinaparks.com/keoweetoxaway/introduction.aspx
Nearest town: Sunset, Pickens
Trail tips: Trail map and trail information sign near the trailhead

Finding the trailhead: From the junction of SC 11 and SC 133, drive west on SC 11 for 0.1 mile to a right onto Cabin Road (SR 347) at the entrance to the park. Drive less than 0.1 mile to a right toward the park office.

From the junction of SC 11 and SC 130 near Salem, drive east on SC 11 for 6.1 miles to a left onto Cabin Road (SR 347). Follow directions above. **Trailhead GPS:** N34 55.968'/W82 53.118'

The Hike

This is not an easy hike, but the rewards are well worth the effort. As you make the loop, you'll pass cascades, small waterfalls, swim holes, and a natural bridge. On top of that, a good portion of the hike places you right alongside Poe Creek. The creek is full of boulders and rocks, and as the water navigates between them, it makes quite a presentation. I recommend doing the loop clockwise, unless you want an even bigger challenge. As you begin, you'll make a long descent, which gets steeper the deeper you get into the forest. When you cross a little culvert, the path briefly flattens out, and you now have the pleasure of following Poe Creek from high above. You soon get down to the level of the creek, and as you rock-hop the waterway, you realize how shallow it is. You'll see a spur trail heading off the main path toward the sound

Lake Keowee-Toxaway offers some of the most picturesque settings in the upstate.

of moving water. Make sure you follow this siren's song. A beautiful little waterfall is waiting in the wings. The dogs can play in the water at the base, and the waterfall is small but precious. When you return to the main trail, it begins to climb as you follow Poe Creek upstream. A second spur trail leads to another little swim spot in the creek. Because this creek is so shallow, and there aren't many places to access it, take advantage of these swim spots while you can. Returning to the main trail, you'll find a dense wall of vegetation stands between you and the water. Rhododendron and mountain laurel bloom from spring to summer. Their blossoms are beautiful, but they keep you from accessing the creek. Not to worry, you'll soon cross the creek, and this crossing is over a fantastic well-placed stone bridge. Now this is not the natural bridge the trail is named for, although it's just as impressive. A large slab of smooth granite stone makes a bridge across Poe Creek as you rock-hop across it. This bridge sits below another beautiful waterfall, and the dogs can dip their paws once more. Enjoy the view, and then continue hiking steeply up the steps to a three-way fork. The left (north) is the Raven Rock Trail. If you wanted to extend the hike, this would add nearly 3 miles. This challenging trail also forms a loop, circling around McKinney Mountain. The right leg of the fork is a social trail that leads to the creek near the brink of the waterfall you just saw from down below. Steer clear of that path to keep the dogs safe. Instead, stay straight at the fork and continue following the unblazed Natural Bridge Trail. The creek is now strewn with boulders forming small cliff walls on the banks. At the 0.75-mile mark, as you hike across one such boulder, you realize you are now hiking over

NATURAL BRIDGE TRAIL–KEOWEE-TOXAWAY STATE PARK

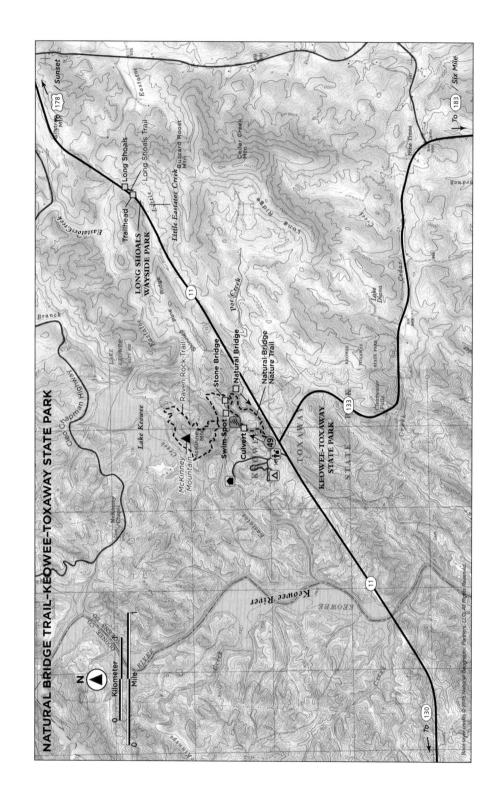

Domestic horses can live up to 25 years.

the natural bridge, for which this trail is named. I think both bridges are fantastic, but the first was man–made. This one, however, was flawlessly forged by Mother Nature. After admiring her handiwork, continue hiking and the trail now leads away from the creek. You'll climb the remainder of the way, as you head back to the fork where the loop began. Overall, this is a great trail! You get a good workout, the dogs have plenty of swim spots, and you get to see some sensational natural features. Mother Nature really did a fantastic job painting the landscape in and around Poe Creek.

Miles and Directions

0.0 Follow the gravel path east into the forest.

0.1 Come to a fork where the loop begins. Go left (north).

0.35 Hike across a culvert.

0.43 Rock-hop Poe Creek and come to a fork. Left leads 50 feet to a beautiful little waterfall and swim spot. Return to the main trail; continue hiking east.

0.5 An obvious path leads to another swim spot. Continue hiking northeast alongside the creek.

0.6 Cross the creek on a stone bridge; this is not the natural bridge. Continue hiking south southeast.

0.65 Come to a three-way fork. Left (north) is the Raven Rock Trail, right (southeast) is a social trail leading toward the brink of a waterfall. Avoid this route. Go straight, following the Natural Bridge Trail east.

Option: Hike an extra 2.9 miles by following the Raven Rock Trail. It leads around McKinney Mountain and back.

0.75 Cross the boulder forming the natural bridge over Poe Creek (N34 56.216'/W82 52.705'). Continue hiking south and west moving away from the creek.

1.2 Arrive back at the fork where the loop began. Backtrack to the trailhead.

1.3 Arrive at the trailhead.

Resting up

Laurel Springs Country Inn, 1137 Moorefield Memorial Hwy., Sunset, (864) 878-2252; pet fee required.

Quality Inn and Suites, 5539 Calhoun Memorial Hwy., Easley, (864) 859-7520; pet fee required.

Camping

Onsite.

Fueling up

Bruster's Real Ice Cream, 5152 Calhoun Memorial Hwy., Easley, (864) 306-0401.

Puppy Paws and Golden Years

Take them to the swim beach at Devils Fork State Park (see map for Oconee Bells Nature Trail hike).

Bandit hikes across Poe Creek at Keowee-Toxaway State Park.

50 Oconee Bells Nature Trail–Devils Fork State Park

Devils Fork State Park is absolutely amazing. It rests on the southern shores of Lake Jocassee, which in itself is enough to impress. Adding to the awe, when you hit the trail, you'll find a variety of rare plant species, among them the trail's namesake, the endangered Oconee Bells. These delicate white flowers typically bloom in March. As you hike through the shady forest, placards help you identify a wide assortment of other plants and trees as well. The fact that you're following a narrow, sandy-bottomed creek is an added bonus.

Start: 161 Holcombe Circle, Salem; northeast end of the parking lot, east of the ranger station
Distance: 1.32-mile loop
Hiking time: About 45 minutes
Blaze color: White
Difficulty: Easy to moderate
Trailhead elevation: 1,141 feet
Highest point: 1,337 feet
Best season: Year-round
Schedule: Late spring to mid-fall, 7 a.m. to 9 p.m.; late fall to mid-spring, 7 a.m. to 6 p.m.
Trail surface: Gravel for less than 0.1 mile, hard-packed dirt

Other trail users: None
Canine compatibility: Leash required
Land status: South Carolina Department of Natural Resources
Fees: Fee required
Maps: *DeLorme: South Carolina Atlas & Gazetteer:* Page 16, F4
Trail contacts: (864) 944-2639; www.south carolinaparks.com/devilsfork/introduction.aspx
Nearest town: Salem, Pickens, Walhalla
Trail tips: Dog waste bags and trash cans near the trailhead. Restrooms are near the ranger station.

Finding the trailhead: From the junction of SC 11 and SC 130 near Salem, drive east on SC 11 for 1.6 miles to a left onto Jocassee Lake Road. Travel for 3.5 miles, following signs to the ranger station. Turn right onto Holcombe Circle and drive 0.1 mile to the parking lot at the end of the road.

From the junction of SC 11 and SC 133 near Keowee-Toxaway State Park, drive west on SC 11 for 4.5 miles to a right onto Jocassee Lake Road. Follow directions above. **Trailhead GPS:** N34 57.126'/W82 56.708'

The Hike

If you've never been to Devils Fork State Park, you must visit! The park rests peacefully along the shores of Lake Jocassee, giving it one of the most desirable locations in the upcountry. A stunning array of mountains keep a watchful eye over the lake, which makes the views from the park spectacular. A large sandy swim beach where the dogs can swim is an added bonus. And although the lake is the highlight, when you head out on this hike, you'll find the park is enjoyable by land as well. You'll begin by heading down some steep steps into the forest. It doesn't look that inviting at first, but trust

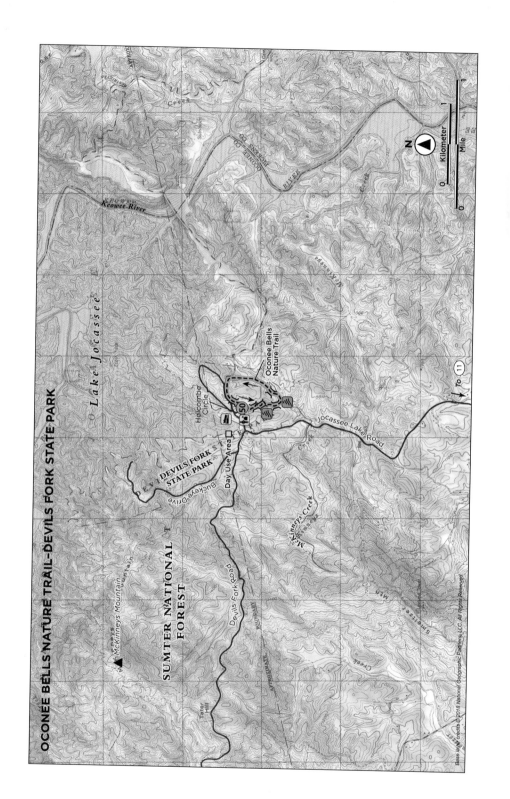

OCONEE BELLS NATURE TRAIL–DEVILS FORK STATE PARK

Keowee River

Lake Jocassee

McKinneys Mountain

SUMTER NATIONAL FOREST

DEVILS FORK STATE PARK

Buckeye Drive

Day Use Area

Holcombe Circle

Oconee Bells Nature Trail

50

Jocassee Lake Road

Devils Fork Road

McKinney's Creek

To 11

N

Kilometer

Mile

Left: The day use area at Devils Fork State Park is a must see!
Right: Even your four-legged friend will enjoy this view.

me, it's well worth a visit. You almost immediately come to a fork where the loop begins, and quickly lose the gravel surface that greeted you at the trailhead, making for happy puppy paws. Tree markers and placards are placed along the path to help you identify the different species of flora. A wide variety of wildflowers, ferns, and trees fill this forest, so it's a very helpful tool. You can also simply test your knowledge by double checking yourself with the markers. Among the plant life, you'll find rare species such as pink lady slippers, wild ginger root, and the trail's namesake, the Oconee Bells. This is a splendid hike year-round, but in springtime it comes to life, as the wildflow-

ers make their delightful debut. The Oconee Bells bloom in March, and the park hosts a big festival each year to celebrate the birth of the showy white blossoms. If you spy them, please look, but don't touch. They are a protected species. Also, it's important to keep the dogs from trampling them, and all the lovely plants within the forest. As you follow a decent grade downhill, you'll arrive at the first of several footbridges. The trail soon follows a narrow stream, and then crosses over it on a second footbridge. This very narrow waterway is quite unique. It's only a few feet wide, at best. But it creates its own little gorge that's as deep as it is wide. And it's heavy with vegetation. Enjoy this splendid show that Mother Nature has put on for you. It just keeps getting better and better. Before crossing your third footbridge, you're treated to a lovely little waterfall. As you cross your fourth footbridge, you'll find interesting rock formations add to the scenery. The easy to follow trail climbs and falls, but on a gentle grade. Just past a bench, another small waterfall greets you. This one is bigger than the last, but still slight in size. The trail is shaded the entire

Cal, a 2-year-old Labra-heeler mix, leads his family out of the forest.

way, and the falls make a great swim spot for the dogs. An interesting phenomenon seems to occur here. As you made your way downhill and into the forest, the trail was well guarded primarily by mountain laurel. But as you climb, you'll find rhododendron has joined forces with the laurel. The creek becomes a bit more lively, and another small waterfall slides over a rock face. On the eastern side of the loop you'll pass a pleasant little pond. Lush green grasses line the shore of the pond. As you hike past the pond, you'll follow the tiny creek that flows into it upstream. When the trail leaves the creek, it climbs and falls several times as you weave through the forest on your way back to the fork where the loop began. With so many natural features, it's no wonder that this is one of my favorites.

Miles and Directions

0.0 Hike southeast down the steps and immediately come to a fork where the loop begins. Left is northeast. Go right (southeast) and downhill.

0.15 Cross a footbridge. Continue hiking south along a fence line and narrow creek.

0.2 Cross a footbridge over the creek. Continue hiking southeast.

0.3 Cross a footbridge near a small waterfall.

0.35 Cross a footbridge. Note the marvelous rock formations nearby. Continue hiking southeast.

0.4 Hike past a bench and small waterfall.

0.55 Hike past a pond and cross another footbridge. Hike upstream.

1.25 Cross a footbridge, continue hiking south.

1.3 Arrive back at the fork where the loop began. Backtrack to the trailhead.

1.32 Arrive at the trailhead.

Resting up

Relax Inn, 109 Windsor St., Westminster, (864) 647-2045; two dogs up to 25 pounds, pet fee per dog, per night. Must call ahead; placed in smoking room.
Quality Inn, 226 High Tech Rd., Seneca, (864) 888-8300; pet fee required.
Quality Inn and Suites, 5539 Calhoun Memorial Hwy., Easley, (864) 859-7520; pet fee required.

Camping

Onsite.

Fueling up

Cornucopia, 16 Cashiers School Rd., Cashiers, (828) 743-3750.

Puppy Paws and Golden Years

Take them to the park's large, sandy swim beach. Dogs are allowed as long as they remain on leash.

Walhalla

51 Station Cove Falls Trail–Oconee Station State Historic Site

As you hike through this diverse forest, make sure you keep your eyes peeled. A number of noteworthy trees rest peacefully alongside the trail, with burls, bracket fungus, and unusual growth patterns keeping you entertained. Toward the latter portion of the hike, you'll follow the gently flowing Oconee Creek upstream. It's hard to believe that this passive creek is fed by a massive and mighty waterfall. A wonderful pool at the base of these photogenic falls is ideal for the dogs to dip their paws. All of these magnificent natural features put this hike among my favorites.

Start: 500 Oconee Station Rd., Walhalla; The trailhead is on the west side of Oconee Station Road, about 0.15 mile past the Oconee Station.
Distance: 1.7 miles out and back
Hiking time: About 50 minutes
Blaze color: Blue
Difficulty: Easy
Trailhead elevation: 1,327 feet
Highest point: 1,327 feet
Best season: Year-round
Schedule: Mar 1–Nov 30, 9 a.m. to 6 p.m.; Dec 1–Feb 28, Fri–Sun only, 9 a.m. to 6 p.m.
Trail surface: Hard-packed dirt
Other trail users: Mountain bikers

Canine compatibility: Leash required
Land status: South Carolina Department of Natural Resources
Fees: No fee
Maps: *DeLorme: South Carolina Atlas & Gazetteer:* Page 16, H3
Trail contacts: (864) 638-0079; www.south carolinaparks.com/oconeestation/introduction .aspx
Nearest town: Tamassee, Walhalla, Cashiers, NC
Trail tips: Trail map and information sign near the trailhead. The trailhead is on a main road. Use caution loading and unloading the pups.

Finding the trailhead: From the junction of SC 11 and SC 183, drive north on SC 11 for 1.9 miles to where Oconee Station Road forks off of SC 11 to the left (at the sign for "Historical Oconee Station"). Go left here and travel for 2.2 miles to a small parking area on your left.
From the junction of SC 11 and SC 130, drive south on SC 11 for 6.6 miles to a right turn onto Oconee Station Road. After turning onto Oconee Station Road, follow directions above. **Trailhead GPS:** N34 50.937'/W83 04.461'

The Hike

A visit to Station Cove has so much to offer, from history, to nature, to hiking on the proud Palmetto Trail. The trailhead is located near the Oconee Station State Historic

Left: You'll find this amazing root burl along the Station Cove Falls Trail.
Right: Several unique natural features greet you on the way to Station Cove Falls.

Site, and named for the Oconee Station House. The station house was built in the late 1700s and is the oldest structure in the upcountry. The old stone building stands as the centerpiece of the park and was built as a military compound to protect against the Creek and Cherokee Tribes. Ironically, years later it became an Indian trading post. The Station House is open to the public on weekends from 1 p.m. to 5 p.m. As you begin this wonderful hike, you'll be following the Oconee Connector Trail, which is part of the state's famous Palmetto Trail. The Palmetto Trail currently covers 350 miles and stretches across the entire state. It begins on the coast at Buck Hall along the Awendaw Passage (see Awendaw Passage hike). It then weaves its way all the way to the mountains. The trail is made up of twenty-six "passages." At 3.2 miles, the Oconee Passage is one of the shortest. It connects Oconee State Park to Oconee Station, so if you wanted to extend this hike, you could continue beyond the fork, following the path for another 2.6 miles to the state park. This wonderful hike is a wilderness wonderland. As you make your way out to the falls, early on you'll pass an overlook off the side of the trail. The mountain views are fantastic from here, especially in the wintertime. The blue-blazed trail is well marked, and easy to follow. Along the way, the trail will climb and fall. But these elevation changes are slow and slight, over gentle slopes. Just after crossing your fourth footbridge, a spur trail forks off of the Oconee Connector. This path follows a passive creek, and leads a mere quarter-mile to the falls. It's hard to believe that this gently flowing creek is fed by the mighty Station Cove Falls. Less than a tenth of a mile from the fork, you'll rock-hop the creek. As you do, stop and appreciate the root burl on the south side of the trail. To say it's noteworthy would be an understatement. This is one of several trees along this hike that have unique figure, fungus, burls, and splits. Each adds its own bit of character to the hike, as does the wide variety of wildflowers found within this area, especially in spring and summertime. When you reach the falls, they are spectacular: tall and mighty, with rock ledges allowing the water to fall from one level to the next. Downed trees rest peacefully at the base and give you a bit of perspective as to how big this waterfall really is. Standing at a full 60 feet, it's perfect. You'll find small pools of water collect in the dips within the smooth rock surface of the base. And the dogs will love keeping cool as they lay in the chilly creek. On the way back to the trailhead, if you had the dogs off the leash, the overlook is a good landmark reminder to put them back on the leash before returning to the trailhead, especially since the trailhead sits right alongside the road.

Left: A pool at the base of Station Cove Falls is just deep enough for the dogs to enjoy.
Right: Dogs can be off leash at Station Cove, as long as they're under voice control.

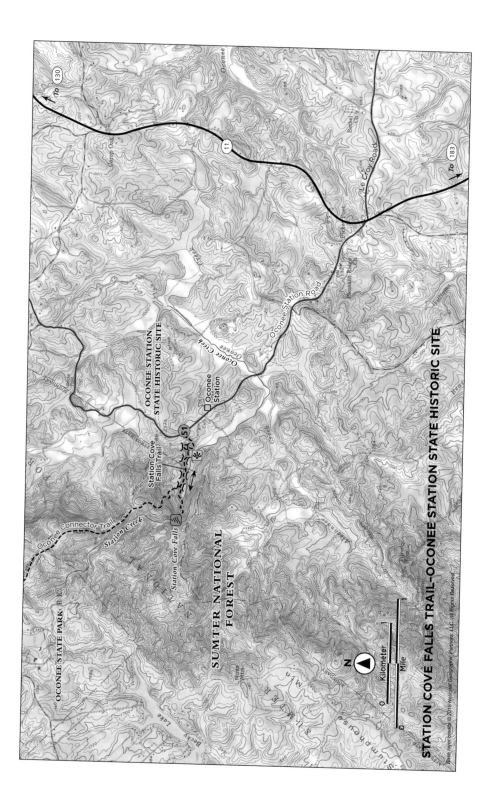

STATION COVE FALLS TRAIL–OCONEE STATION STATE HISTORIC SITE

Miles and Directions

0.0 Immediately bypass the narrow trail to the left (south). Hike straight, following the wide blue-blazed trail west and downhill.

0.15 Hike north past an overlook (N34 50.883'/W83 04.584').

0.25 Cross a footbridge and the trail bends left (south).

0.35 Cross a footbridge. Continue hiking west.

0.5 Cross a footbridge. Continue hiking northeast.

0.6 Cross a footbridge, and quickly come to a fork at a split rail fence. Right is the Oconee Connector Trail and leads to Oconee State Park. Go straight (around the fence); continue hiking west.

These baby bluebirds beg for breakfast.

Option: Extend the hike by following the Oconee Connector Trail. It leads about 2.6 miles to Oconee State Park.

0.8 Rock-hop the creek, and follow it upstream.

0.85 Arrive at the base of Station Cove Falls (N34 50.965'/W83 05.124'). Backtrack to the trailhead.

1.7 Arrive at the trailhead.

Resting up

Relax Inn Westminster, 109 W. Windsor St., Westminster, (864) 647-2045; pet fee required.

Quality Inn Seneca, 226 Hi Tech Rd., Seneca, (864) 888-8300; pet fee required.

Camping

Devils Fork State Park, 161 Holcombe Circle, Salem, (864) 944-2639.

Fueling up

Beyond the Bull, 8095 Keowee School Rd., Seneca, (864) 508-1254.

Puppy Paws and Golden Years

Take them over to Devils Fork State Park. The day use area is fantastic, and they have a wonderful sandy swim beach where dogs are allowed.

52 Yellow Branch Falls Trail–Sumter National Forest

Whether you have four legs or two, you're sure to enjoy this one! You'll find several creek crossings early in the hike, and when you reach Yellow Branch Falls, you'll simply stand in awe of the jaw-dropping beauty before you. A three-dimensional waterfall juts out of its own little cove unlike any other. It's unique and simply stunning. As you take it all in, you'll watch as the water dances over one rock ledge to the next, before finally falling to the base forming catch pools that are perfect for the dogs to splash around in.

Start: Southwest end of the parking lot for the Yellow Branch Picnic Ground
Distance: 3.2 miles out and back
Hiking time: About 1 hour, 40 minutes
Blaze color: Orange
Difficulty: Moderate to strenuous
Trailhead elevation: 1,550 feet
Highest point: 1,558 feet
Best season: Year-round
Trail surface: Hard-packed dirt
Other trail users: None
Canine compatibility: Voice control

Land status: Sumter National Forest—Andrew Pickens Ranger District
Fees: No fee
Maps: DeLorme: North Carolina Atlas & Gazetteer: Page 22, A2
Trail contacts: (864) 638-9568; www.fs .usda.gov/recarea/scnfs/recreation/hiking/ recarea/?recid=47139&actid=50
Nearest town: Walhalla
Trail tips: Trailhead information sign and map at the trailhead. Vault toilet, trash cans, and picnic tables near the trailhead.

Finding the trailhead: From the junction of SC 28 and SC 107, drive south on SC 28 for 2.7 miles and turn right at the sign into the Yellow Branch Picnic Ground. Bypass a road that immediately heads up and to your right, and continue straight ahead for 0.2 mile to where the road dead-ends at a parking area.

From the junction of SC 28 and SC 183, drive north on SC 28 for 5.3 miles. Turn left at the sign into the Yellow Branch Picnic Ground. Follow directions above. **Trailhead GPS:** N34 48.333'/W83 07.728'

The Hike

A decent map of the trail stands at the trailhead, and you get your first introduction to Yellow Branch Creek the minute you begin hiking. Rhododendron and the twisted trunks of mountain laurel line the path. As you begin to follow the narrow creek downstream, you'll quickly come to rock-hop across it through a tunnel of rhododendron. This is the first of several rock-hops as you crisscross from one side of the creek to the other. With each rock-hop, the stream seems to get a little louder, and a little livelier. Let the dogs take as much time as they want playing in the water because you'll soon lose the creek, and won't meet it again for another 0.2 mile. When you cross your first footbridge, it seems to act as a gateway into the forest. Up until this

Left: Little D-O-G needed a little coaxing across the creek.
Right: Yellow Branch Falls is unlike any other.

point, you were surrounded by the low brush of rhododendron, mountain laurel, and ferns. But beyond the bridge, you find yourself in a forest full of tall trees like poplar, hickory, oak, and maple. As the trail gently climbs, you get deeper and deeper into the Sumter National Forest. The Andrew Pickens Ranger District has done a fantastic job keeping the trails well marked, well maintained, and clear of downed trees. While the dogs enjoy another creek crossing, you appreciate the tranquil aspects of the forest: a slight breeze blowing, birds singing in the background, and the trees towering overhead. You'll cross Yellow Branch Creek one last time at 0.7 mile, and the remainder of the hike stays dry for the most part. You'll get one more taste of water when you cross your third footbridge. But this isn't over your typical creek. Instead, this bridge crosses in front of a wonderful weeping rock wall. As the water daintily drips over the face of the stone, you can reach out and touch it. Use caution here. The bridge is somewhat rickety, damp, and the dropoffs are steep. Continuing past the rock wall, it's surprising that there's no sound or sign of moving water yet. But be patient. You'll soon recognize the cues that you're nearing the creek. For one, an obvious change in the air temperature cools you off. And as the air begins to cool, you notice the plant life changes too. You return to the dense flowering thickets of rhododendron and mountain laurel once more. You'll find the trail beyond the last footbridge is narrow

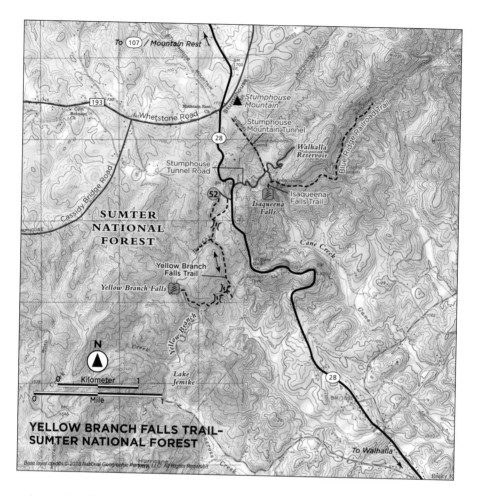

**YELLOW BRANCH FALLS TRAIL–
SUMTER NATIONAL FOREST**

and rugged, with roots, rocks, and steep dropoffs to navigate. If your pup is a puller, you may want to take them off the leash for this part of the hike. Or if they have a harness on, clip it in the front. This helps alleviate the pulling. Please use caution, wear proper footwear, and hike within your limits. The final tenth of a mile brings you steeply down to Yellow Branch Falls. When you arrive at the base of this beauty, you'll simply be stunned and amazed at the scenery that stands before you. This waterfall is unlike any other, and absolutely sensational! A multitude of rock ledges form the falls, and they jut out in such a way that makes it three-dimensional. Words cannot describe this one. Just go! You won't be disappointed. And the four-legged family members will find this a favorite as well. They'll scamper from one swim hole to the next, exploring the many rocks and boulders strewn about at the base.

Miles and Directions

0.0 Follow the path southeast into the forest.

0.13 Rock-hop Yellow Branch.

0.15 Rock-hop the creek. Continue hiking downstream.

0.2 Rock-hop the creek. Continue hiking generally south.

0.25 Come to a fork. The trail you're on goes straight (east) and swings back to the park road. Go right (south), downhill toward a footbridge.

0.28 Cross the footbridge. Continue hiking south.

0.45 Come to a fork. A narrow path goes straight (southwest) and follows Yellow Branch downstream. Go left (east) on the wider trail and rock-hop the creek.

0.7 Rock-hop the creek. Continue hiking south.

0.95 Cross a footbridge and the trail swings left (southeast).

1.0 Come to a fork. Left (southeast) is an overgrown logging road leading downhill. Go right (south), and uphill on the clay path.

Mountain laurel lines the path on your way to Yellow Branch.

1.1 Cross a footbridge near the weeping wall. Use caution, the dropoffs are steep. Continue hiking south as the trail climbs.

1.6 Arrive at the base of Yellow Branch Falls (N34 47.700'/W83 08.052'). Backtrack to the trailhead.

3.2 Arrive at the trailhead.

Resting up

Relax Inn Westminster, 109 W. Windsor St., Westminster, (864) 647-2045; pet fee required.
Quality Inn Seneca, 226 Hi Tech Rd., Seneca, (864) 888-8300; pet fee required.

Camping

Oconee State Park, 624 State Park Rd., Mountain Rest, (864) 638-5353.

Fueling up

Beyond the Bull, 8095 Keowee School Rd., Seneca; (864) 508-1254.

Puppy Paws and Golden Years

Take the pups over to see the Stumphouse Mountain Tunnel or Isaqueena Falls. They're both just north of Yellow Branch, on the east side of SC 28.

53 Lake Trail–Oconee State Park

With no blazes, the Lake Trail isn't the easiest to follow, but as long as you stay with the shoreline you'll be fine. Plenty of tall trees keep you shaded, and this easy waterfront stroll offers lots of swimming spots for the dogs. A levee rests at the south end, and benches are perfectly placed so you can sit and take in the view. At the north end, a marshy area adds diversity. Bring a camera and enjoy the fresh mountain air.

Start: 624 State Park Rd., Mountain Rest; The trail begins at the designated swim area.
Distance: 1.2-mile loop
Hiking time: About 40 minutes
Blaze color: None
Difficulty: Easy
Trailhead elevation: 1,757 feet
Highest point: 1,757 feet
Best season: Year-round
Schedule: Sun–Thurs 7 a.m. to 7 p.m., Fri–Sat 7 a.m. to 9 p.m. (Sun–Thurs hours are extended to 9 p.m. during Daylight Saving Time)
Trail surface: Wide gravel path, and hard-packed dirt

Other trail users: None
Canine compatibility: Leash required
Land status: South Carolina Department of Natural Resources
Fees: Fee required
Maps: *DeLorme: South Carolina Atlas & Gazetteer:* Page 16, H3
Trail contacts: (864) 638-5353; www.south carolinaparks.com/oconee/introduction.aspx
Nearest town: Mountain Rest, Walhalla
Trail tips: Restrooms, trash cans, chairs, and a soda machine that sells water are located near the trailhead.

Finding the trailhead: From the junction of SC 107 and SC 28 near Mountain Rest, drive north on SC 107 for 2.4 miles to the park on the right. Once inside the park, drive 0.1 mile to a stop sign. Go left and follow signs to the office and swimming area.

From the junction of SC 107 and Wiggington Road (SR 413), drive south on SC 107 for 11.4 miles to the park on the left. Follow directions above. **Trailhead GPS:** N34 51.936'/W83 06.289'

The Hike

This is a delightful hike, leading you on a loop around the main park lake. Make sure you pay close attention to the Miles and Directions, since the trail isn't well trodden, or well marked. Early on, you'll pass the designated swim area, which is open seasonally. A fantastic floating dock with a high dive and low diving board sits out in the middle of the inviting water. Unfortunately, dogs aren't allowed. Beyond the swim area, you'll pass below the timber overhang of the bathhouse. This rustic structure was

Swim, paddle, or hike around the lake at Oconee State Park.

built by the Civilian Conservation Corps (CCC) in the 1930s. As you admire their handiwork, you'll cross over a spillway where Jerry Creek flows away from the lake. Next you'll pass the boathouse. You can rent a canoe, kayak, johnboat, or pedal boat by the hour or by the day, and explore the lake by water as well. As you now follow the southern shore, a patch of mountain laurel separates you from the water. The pink and white star-shaped blossoms begin to splatter the trail with color in late May. Even though you're hiking near the shore, there's plenty of tree cover to keep you shaded. Crossing a levee at the south end gives you stunning long-range views of this 20-acre lake. Fishing is a popular pastime here, and the lake is filled with bass, bream, and cat-fish year-round. In wintertime, you can also try your hand at trout fishing, since the park stocks the lake annually. They also participate in the Tackle Loaner Program, so you can check out some fishing gear from the park office. Just bring your own bait, and your state fishing license. On the eastern shore, you'll pass below the park cabins, which were also built by the CCC. The dogs will enjoy popping in and out of the water from one fabulous swim spot to another. At the northeast end of the lake, you'll cross a boardwalk over a marshy area. This terrain adds some unexpected diversity. You'll hear frogs, crickets, and toads here, and you may even spot a great blue heron wading in the water in the warmer months. This adds quite a splendid variety to the wood ducks and Canada geese that live here too. You'll hike below the remainder of the cabins. Again, no dogs are allowed. So you'll have to camp if you want to spend the night here. Along with the campground, the park has volleyball, basketball, and even a miniature golf course to keep you entertained. As you hike past cabin #4, you'll find a lovely little point juts out into the lake, and a perfectly placed bench gives you a spectacular view of the waterway. Geese will come swimming up, begging for

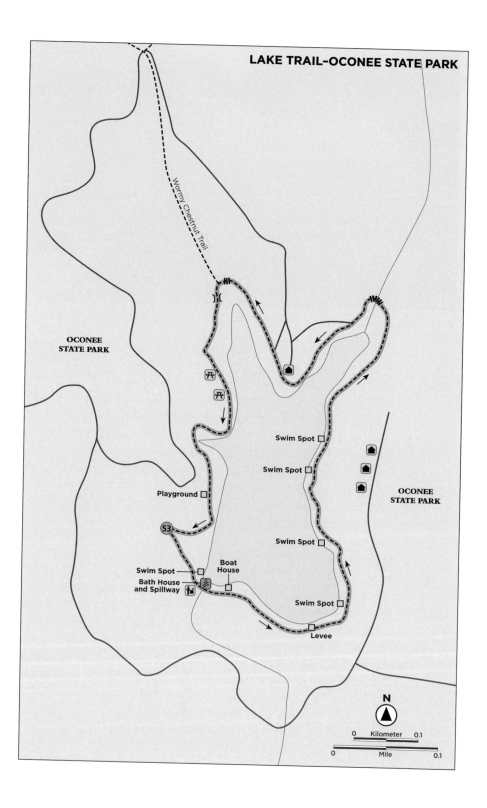

LAKE TRAIL-OCONEE STATE PARK

Wormy Chestnut Trail

OCONEE
STATE PARK

OCONEE
STATE PARK

Swim Spot

Swim Spot

Playground

53

Swim Spot

Swim Spot

Swim Spot

Boat
House

Bath House
and Spillway

Levee

N

0   Kilometer   0.1

0   Mile   0.1

scraps. And surprisingly, they seem fearless of the dogs. After crossing Jerry Creek a second time, you'll pass the Wormy Chestnut Trail. If you wanted to extend the hike, you could follow this lollipop loop out and back to this fork. The western shore of the lake leads you through picnic areas, where benches and Adirondack chairs sit overlooking the lake. For the final hoorah, you'll hike past the playground and return to the swim area where you began. Birds are abundant, and a variety of wildlife inhabit the park—deer, black bear, beavers, and raccoons among them. Hiking early in the morning or late in the day will give you the best chance to spot them.

Miles and Directions

0.0 Hike down the stone steps toward the designated swim area.

0.05 Hike southeast past the swim area, following the fence line to the bathhouse.

0.1 Hike under the overhang of the bathhouse, cross the stone bridge over the spillway, and hike past the boathouse. Follow the wide gravel path east along the shoreline.

0.2 At the south end of the lake, follow the water's edge on a levee.

0.25 Hiking below the cabins you'll pass several good swim spots. Continue hiking north as the trail narrows.

0.5 Cross a boardwalk over a marshy area.

0.8 Cross a boardwalk over a tiny creek.

0.82 Come to a fork. Right (northwest) is the Wormy Chestnut Trail. Stay left, following the water's edge south.

0.9 Cross a footbridge; hike south through the picnic area.

1.1 Hike past the playground.

1.2 Arrive at the trailhead.

Resting up

Relax Inn Westminster, 109 W. Windsor St., Westminster, (864) 647-2045; pet fee required.

Quality Inn Seneca, 226 Hi Tech Rd., Seneca, (864) 888-8300; pet fee required.

Camping

Onsite.

Fueling up

Beyond the Bull, 8095 Keowee School Rd., Seneca, (864) 508-1254.

Puppy Paws and Golden Years

Follow the loop backwards for 0.25 mile, taking them to the picnic area. If 0.5 mile is too long, bring them down to Isaqueena Falls or the Stumphouse Tunnel. They are both south of the park on the east side of SC 28.

54 Pigpen Falls Trail—Sumter National Forest

Simply splendid! Pigpen Falls is just that. Large boulders resting along the banks give you a pleasant place to sit while the dogs romp around in the perfect catch pool found at the base. Compared to other waterfalls in the area, this one is slight in size. But that does not detract from its beauty. As a matter of fact, it's one of my favorites. And as a bonus, to reach the falls, you get to hike along the famous Foothills Trail. Bring a picnic, and a towel, and take a dip yourself.

Start: Northeast end of the parking area, near the trailhead information sign. *Note:* The Foothills Trail also heads out from the steps at the southeast side of the parking lot, but does not lead to Pigpen Falls.
Distance: 1.4 miles out and back
Hiking time: About 45 minutes
Blaze color: White; green blazes from the fork to the falls
Difficulty: Easy to moderate
Trailhead elevation: 1,805 feet
Highest point: 1,811 feet
Best season: Year-round

Trail surface: Hard-packed dirt
Other trail users: None
Canine compatibility: Voice control
Land status: Sumter National Forest—Andrew Pickens Ranger District
Fees: No fee
Maps: *DeLorme: North Carolina Atlas & Gazetteer.* Page 16, G2
Trail contacts: (864) 638-9568
Nearest town: Mountain Rest, Walhalla
Trail tips: A rudimentary trail map is posted near the trailhead.

Finding the trailhead: From the junction of SC 107 and SC 28, drive north on SC 107 for 3.3 miles to a left onto Village Creek Road. Travel for 1.7 miles to a right turn onto Nicholson Ford Road, just before the road makes a hard bend to the left (east). Travel for 2.2 miles to where it ends.

Note: Along the way, Nicholson Ford Road becomes FR 2603 and leads you to drive through a shallow creek twice.

From the junction of SC 107 and Wiggington Road (SR 413), drive south on SC 107 for 10.5 miles to a right onto Village Creek Road. Follow directions above. **Trailhead GPS:** N34 55.510'/ W83 07.336'

The Hike

A rudimentary map at the trailhead gives you a good reference to the area around Pigpen Falls. And although it's very basic, it's accurate, so take a peek before you hit the trail. Delving into the Sumter National Forest, you have the privilege of hiking on two of the most recognized trails in the region: the Foothills Trail and the Chattooga River Trail. This hike begins on the first, which over its full length covers 77 miles of ground. The trail begins and ends in South Carolina, but in the middle it dips into North Carolina as well. The terrain is unique and diverse. If you took the trail north, you'd follow

Left: Hopping on the "selfie" bandwagon.
Right: Boulders at the base of Pigpen Falls are perfect for a picnic.

the Chattooga River, skirt around Lake Jocassee, pass spectacular waterfalls, and take in mountain views that are unmatched. For more information, visit www.foothillstrail .org. To reach Pigpen Falls, follow the white-blazed Foothills Trail into the forest. The pathway leads you on a pleasant stroll, with plenty of tree cover to keep you shaded. A multitude of birds fill the air with song, and wildflowers can be seen here and there. The hard-packed dirt surface is smooth, so it's easy on the puppy's paws. Halfway to the falls, you'll come alongside Pigpen Branch. As you follow the lively creek, you do so from up above. But the sound is sensational. The trail will lead you past a primitive campsite, and then a second that's even larger. This is a fantastic area for backcoun-

try camping, and you're less than a mile from the trailhead, so it's quite convenient. When you reach a fork, the Foothills Trail continues straight ahead, and this is where you'll part ways with it. Heading left at the fork, you'll briefly follow the green-blazed Chattooga River Trail (CRT). Less than 0.1 mile from this fork, you arrive at the base of Pigpen Falls (just before crossing the footbridge). The falls, and the entire area in general, are gorgeous. A large rock near the base is big enough to sit and have a picnic on, and the creek is the perfect depth for the dogs to wade out into. Bring a towel; you may want to take a dip yourself. To extend the hike, you have two options. You could return to the fork, and follow the Foothills Trail/Chattooga River Trail north along the banks of the rustic river. Or, you could cross the footbridge near

The boys patiently wait for mama.

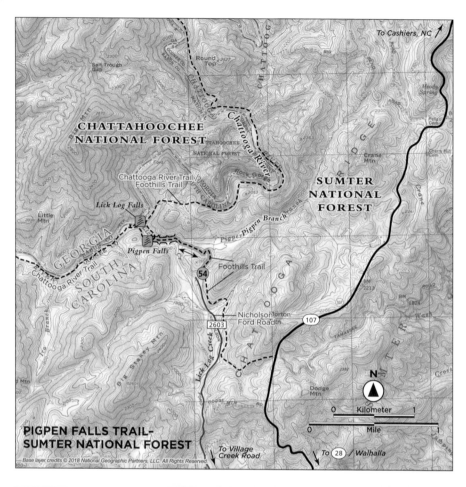

PIGPEN FALLS TRAIL–
SUMTER NATIONAL FOREST

Left: This little box turtle was cruising along with his cracked shell.
Right: You never know what you'll see when you take a scenic drive through the countryside.

the falls, and continue south on the CRT. It too follows the shores of the river, and both options are fantastic. If you take the southern route, you'll also pass by Licklog Falls, though the falls are difficult to see from the trail. Dense vegetation of mountain laurel and rhododendron separate you from the falls. The best option is to hike past the falls, and when the trail makes a hard bend left follow the social trail down to the river. Licklog Creek flows out into the river just downstream of the falls. Use caution with the dogs near the river. This is an untamed Wild and Scenic river, and the current can be very strong in some places. Over the full length, the CRT spans into Georgia, South Carolina, and North Carolina. The leg here in South Carolina stretches 15.5 miles and begins where SC 28 crosses over the river near Mountain Rest. If you followed it the full distance, you'd finish at Ellicott Rock (see Chattooga River Trail). Ellicott Rock forms the border between the three states.

Miles and Directions

0.0   Follow the white-blazed Foothills Trail northeast into the forest.

0.5   Hike past a primitive campsite and cross a footbridge. Continue hiking west.

0.57 Cross a footbridge. Continue hiking downstream.

0.65 Come to a fork where the Chattooga River Trail/Foothills Trail goes straight (north). Go left, following the green-blazed Chattooga River Trail south and down some steps.

0.7   Arrive at the base of Pigpen Falls (N34 55.707'/W83 07.749') on the left (south), just before crossing a footbridge over the creek. Backtrack to the trailhead.

1.4   Arrive at the trailhead.

Option: To extend the hike, continue following the Chattooga River Trail. It follows the river for another 3.5 miles to SC 28.

Resting up

Relax Inn Westminster, 109 W. Windsor St., Westminster, (864) 647-2045; pet fee required.
Quality Inn Seneca, 226 Hi Tech Rd., Seneca, (864) 888-8300; pet fee required.

Camping

Backcountry camping onsite.
Oconee State Park, 624 State Park Rd., Mountain Rest, (864) 638-5353.

Fueling up

Beyond the Bull, 8095 Keowee School Rd., Seneca, (864) 508-1254.

Puppy Paws and Golden Years

Take them down to Isaqueena Falls or the Stumphouse Tunnel. They are both south of here on the east side of SC 28.

55 King Creek Falls Trail–Sumter National Forest

King Creek Falls is simply stunning. And with a perfect sandy swim hole at the base, you and the dogs will both fall in love with this one. The hike leads you through a portion of the Ellicott Rock Wilderness, and then as you near the halfway point, you'll come to King Creek, following it upstream. The crystal-clear creek is one of many that flows out to the Wild and Scenic Chattooga River. The forest is shaded, there's plenty of running water, and when you reach the falls you're sure to be impressed. Bring a camera!

Start: Southwest corner of the parking lot, near the trailhead information sign, and across from the restrooms. *Note:* The trail to the campground is at the north end of the parking lot.
Distance: 1.4 miles out and back
Hiking time: About 45 minutes
Blaze color: White; orange from the second fork to the falls
Difficulty: Easy to moderate
Trailhead elevation: 2,170 feet
Highest point: 2,178 feet
Best season: Year-round
Trail surface: Hard-packed dirt with some rooty and rocky sections

Other trail users: None
Canine compatibility: Voice control
Land status: Sumter National Forest–Andrew Pickens Ranger District
Fees: No fee
Maps: *DeLorme: North Carolina Atlas & Gazetteer.* Page 16, F2-F3
Trail contacts: (864) 638-9568; www.fs.usda .gov/recarea/scnfs/recreation/hiking/ recarea/?recid=47101&actid=50
Nearest town: Mountain Rest
Trail tips: Vault toilet near the trailhead

Finding the trailhead: From the junction of SC 107 and SC 28, drive north on SC 107 for 10.0 miles. Turn left onto New Burrell's Ford Road and travel 2.3 miles to a left turn into the parking area for Burrells Ford Campground.
From the junction of SC 107 and Wiggington Road (SR 413), drive south on SC 107 for 3.8 miles to a right onto New Burrell's Ford Road. Follow directions above. **Trailhead GPS:** N34 58.280'/W83 06.883'

The Hike

The trailhead is in the same parking lot for Burrells Ford Campground. The camping here is fantastic, since you can hear the Chattooga River running by. But you should be forewarned, it's primitive backcountry camping only, and takes a quarter-mile to reach the campsites. The area has an odd and splendid diversity of birdlife. Although the trailhead sits around 2,100 feet, bird species typically found at 4,000 feet are common here. Bring your binoculars. The trail to the campground is at the north end of the parking lot. But you'll begin your hike near the trailhead information sign at the southwest end of the lot. As you head back into the forest, you almost immediately begin following the famous Foothills Trail (FT). The Foothills Trail covers 77 miles over the full length of the trail. Several access points and sections break this down, making it easy to access for a delightful day hike such as this one. For more information on the trail, visit www.foothillstrail.org. The trail seems to make a slow and steady descent down toward the Wild and Scenic Chattooga River. The river is undammed, and completely governed by the will of Mother Nature. Just past the halfway point, you'll come to a fork. Right is where the Chattooga River Trail (CRT) leads north toward Ellicott Rock and the North Carolina state line (see Chattooga River Trail hike). You want to go left, and you'll now briefly follow the Foothills Trail and the Chattooga River Trail where they are conjoined. In less than a tenth of a mile, you'll cross a footbridge over King

One by one, the kids caught up.

Creek and come to another fork. This is where the FT/CRT continues to follow the river south. Stay left again, and you'll now strictly follow the King Creek Falls Trail upstream alongside King Creek. It seems the farther upstream you go, the stronger the flow becomes, and the livelier the creek becomes. The current seems to gain steam, spurred on by the waterfall that feeds it. As the cascades come to life, the dogs seem to get a spring in their step. The path climbs most of the way from the fork to the falls, and the last quarter-mile is a rocky, rooty path. Although the dogs don't even seem to notice, you'll want to watch your footing. The creek is magnificent. It's full of beautiful cascades that make for a good distraction as you climb. But these cascades are far surpassed by the beauty and might of King Creek Falls. It's like royalty. There's no mistaking it when you arrive at this majestic and regal waterfall. The falls stand at a proud height of 60 feet, but seems even taller. Large logs at the base give you perspective into the size of the falls, and a splendid sandy beach offers you and the dogs a perfect access point to wade out into the water. They can dig, splash, and romp around in the water while you simply stand in awe of the spectacular scenery this creek has created. This one will lure you in, so you may want to bring a picnic and a towel and stay a while. It's easily worth the extra weight in your pack, and the pups will thank you for the extra playtime.

Miles and Directions

0.0 Follow the white-blazed trail south into the forest and bypass the steps to the left.

0.1 Cross a footbridge; continue hiking south.

0.4 Come to a fork. Right (northwest) is the orange-blazed Chattooga River Trail. Go straight following the Foothills Trail/Chattooga River Trail (south).

0.41 Cross a footbridge over King Creek.

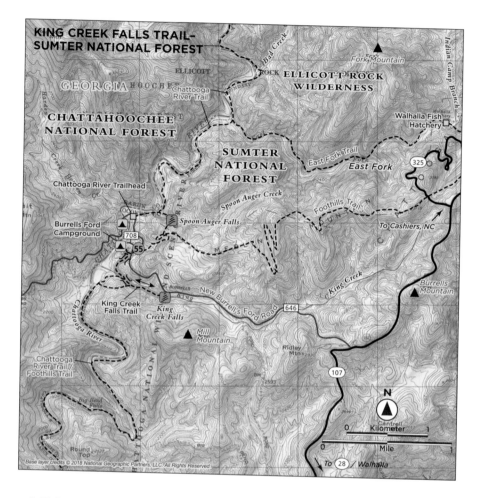

0.45 Come to a fork. Right (west) is the Foothills Trail. Go left (east), climb the steps, and follow the creek upstream.

0.7 Arrive at the base of King Creek Falls (N34 57.974'/W83 06.654'). Backtrack to the trailhead.

1.4 Arrive at the trailhead.

Resting up

Relax Inn Westminster, 109 W. Windsor St., Westminster, (864) 647-2045; pet fee required.

Quality Inn Seneca, 226 Hi Tech Rd., Seneca, (864) 888-8300; pet fee required.

Camping

Backcountry camping onsite.

Oconee State Park, 624 State Park Rd., Mountain Rest, (864) 638-5353.

Top left: Jake is one happy hound, heading out to fish with his daddy.
Top right: Fly fishing is a popular pastime in the mountain creeks of the Carolinas.
Bottom left: King Creek Falls is a spectacular sight.
Bottom right: Large logs at the base of King Creek Falls create a natural playground for the dogs.

Fueling up

Cornucopia, 16 Cashiers School Rd., Cashiers, NC, (828) 743-3750.

Puppy Paws and Golden Years

If you continue driving on New Burrell's Ford Road for another 0.5 mile, cross the bridge over the Chattooga River, and turn left on FR 646A. A green-blazed trail leads from the parking lot about 150 feet to a primitive campsite along the river's edge. There's a perfect sandy beach here, and the water is calm enough for your furry friends to wade into.

56 Chattooga River Trail–Sumter National Forest

As you would expect, the Chattooga River Trail follows the Wild and Scenic Chattooga River over the entire length of the hike. Although at times you'll be standing high above the banks, you'll never leave its side. Large boulders strewn across the waterway create a canvas of nature that was painted perfectly. With calm sandy beaches for the dogs, and stunning scenery, this hike is among my favorites. Whether you find Ellicott Rock or not, it's about the journey, not the destination. To enhance the experience, take the tangent trip to see Spoon Auger Falls.

Start: The trailhead is on the east side of the road before crossing the bridge over the Chattooga River.
Distance: 6.8 miles out and back
Hiking time: About 3 hours, 30 minutes
Blaze color: None
Difficulty: Easy to moderate
Trailhead elevation: 2,074 feet
Highest point: 2,161 feet
Best season: Year-round
Trail surface: Hard-packed dirt with rooty sections
Other trail users: None
Canine compatibility: Voice control

Land status: Sumter National Forest–Andrew Pickens Ranger District
Fees: No fee
Maps: *DeLorme: North Carolina Atlas & Gazetteer:* Page 16, F3
Trail contacts: (864) 638-9568; www.fs .usda.gov/recarea/scnfs/recreation/hiking/ recarea/?recid=47079&actid=50
Nearest town: Mountain Rest
Trail tips: A trailhead information sign is located at the trailhead.
Special considerations: Water levels fluctuate on the Chattooga River. Please use your discretion and caution before letting the dogs swim in the river.

Finding the trailhead: From the junction of SC 107 and SC 28, drive north on SC 107 for 10.0 miles. Turn left onto New Burrell's Ford Road and travel 2.6 miles to a pulloff on the right near the trailhead information sign.

From the junction of SC 107 and Wiggington Road (SR 413), drive south on SC 107 for 3.8 miles to a right onto New Burrell's Ford Road. Follow directions above. **Trailhead GPS:** N34 58.490'/W83 06.882'

The Hike

As you head into the Ellicott Rock Wilderness, early on you'll rock-hop a few tributaries that seamlessly flow into the river. After the third rock-hop, a side trail follows the creek upstream. Although it's only 0.1 mile, the narrow path leads past cascades, through a tunnel of rhododendron, and steeply climbs up to Spoon Auger Falls. A sheer wall of dark brown stone forms the face of the falls. And there's just enough water near the base to let the dogs cool down. Returning to the Chattooga River Trail (CRT), the flat, easy terrain is a welcome break after making the steep ascent

Left: Mikey's coat glistens after taking a refreshing dip in the Chattooga River.
Center: The dogs should be fine crossing this sturdy log bridge over East Fork.
Right: Bandit takes a closer look at the bracket fungus growing on a downed tree.

to the falls. As you follow the river upstream, you'll come to the first of two fantastic sandy beaches, right alongside the river. The dogs will love romping around in the sand as they get a little extra energy out. Returning to the CRT, you'll find at times you're right along the river's edge, while at others you view it from high upon a bluff. This gives you the best of both worlds. Good views, good swim spots, and a few gentle climbs. The sound of moving water and the birds singing in the background is a perfect mix. A barrage of rocks and boulders form the riverbed, and the water dances over these rocks to create one splendid cascade after another. It's crystal-clear, and so inviting. It's hard to believe that this same river touts rapids rated as high as class V and VI. Please use caution and your own discretion at the swim spots. The river levels fluctuate daily. Continuing deeper into the wilderness, you'll pass several primitive campsites. You can picture pitching your tent here, with the soothing sound of the river running by all night long. As you continue hiking, a variety of wildflowers are sprinkled amid the underbrush. Huckleberry, trillium, phlox, and spiderwort are among the common species, adding a splash of color to the trail. At 1.3 miles, a second path leads to a fantastic sandy beach. Silver lines the sand, and it's big enough for the dogs to run, dig, play, and even chase a ball or stick. It's simply spectacular. And the river is usually calm enough for them to wade out into. The water is crystal clear, crisp, and unforgettable. If you haven't gathered by now, this is one of my favorites. Just past the halfway mark, you'll cross a long wooden bridge over East Fork. The East Fork Trail follows this creek upstream for 2.5 miles to the Walhalla Fish Hatchery. Beyond this bridge, the trail seems to transform. Up until East Fork, the path was clear, wide, welcoming, and easy to follow. Beyond the bridge it's narrow, overgrown, and there are lots of downed trees and steep dropoffs. The terrain simply becomes more rugged as you delve deeper into the wilderness. You'll soon rock-hop Bad Creek and two tributaries. Just past the second tributary you'll find one last calm

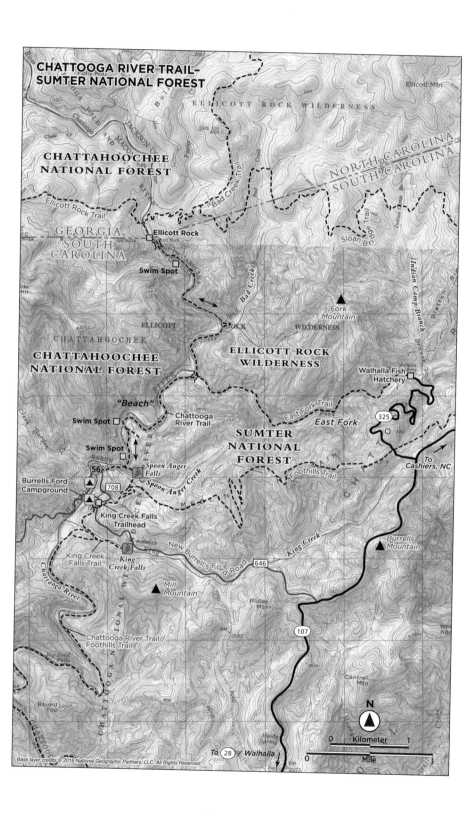

swim spot for the dogs. If you're dog isn't very trail hardy, turn back at the East Fork bridge. When you cross the next footbridge, at 3.5 miles begin looking for surveyor's tape about 100 feet upstream. The tape marks an overgrown path to the river. Unfortunately, viewing Ellicott Rock entails wading into the river, since it's located on the bank near the waterline. So save that for another day, since it's unsafe, especially for the dogs. You can still proudly say that you hiked to the spot where South Carolina, Georgia, and North Carolina meet.

Miles and Directions

0.0 Hike east into the forest.

0.05 Rock-hop a tributary; continue hiking east.

0.1 Rock-hop a tributary; continue hiking east.

0.2 Rock-hop Spoon Auger Creek and come to a fork. The right (south) leads 0.1 mile steeply up to Spoon Auger Falls. Straight is the continuation of the Chattooga River Trail (CRT). Take the side trip to see the falls. It's worth the climb.

0.3 Arrive at Spoon Auger Falls (N34 58.488'/W83 06.602'). Backtrack to the CRT.

0.4 Arrive back at the CRT. Continue hiking northeast following the river upstream.

0.7 Bypass the blue-blazed trail to the right (southeast). Continue hiking north.

0.77 A narrow trail to the left leads to a sandy beach along the river. Take the dogs; they'll love it. Continue hiking northeast on the CRT.

1.1 Hike north past a primitive campsite.

1.3 Another narrow path leads out to an amazing pristine beach on the river.

1.7 Bypass a trail leading left (north) to a large open primitive campsite. Continue hiking east as the CRT moves away from the river.

1.8 Cross a footbridge over East Fork and come to a fork. Right (east) is the East Fork Trail. The right (east) is the East Fork Trail. Go left, hike up the log steps, and continue hiking north past a primitive campsite.

Option: Extend the hike by following the East Fork Trail.

1.95 Hike past a primitive campsite. Continue following the river upstream.

2.4 Rock-hop a tributary and the trail leads to another primitive campsite. Do not hike through the campsite; instead, follow the CRT as it makes a hard bend left (northwest).

2.44 Rock-hop Bad Creek and follow it downstream toward the river. When you reach the river, continue hiking northwest and upstream.

3.0 Rock-hop a tributary. Continue north and upstream.

3.2 Cross a tributary. Just past the tributary is a sandy swim spot for the dogs. Continue hiking north.

3.5 Cross a footbridge. About 100 feet upstream from the footbridge look for surveyor's tape. The tape marks a pathway leading to the river near Ellicott Rock. Do not take the dogs on this path. The river is not safe here, and the dogs could get swept away. Backtrack to the trailhead.

6.8 Arrive at the trailhead.

Resting up

Relax Inn Westminster, 109 W. Windsor St., Westminster, (864) 647-2045; pet fee required.

Quality Inn Seneca, 226 Hi Tech Rd., Seneca, (864) 888-8300; pet fee required.

Camping

Backcountry camping onsite.

Oconee State Park, 624 State Park Rd., Mountain Rest, (864) 638-5353.

Fueling up

Cornucopia, 16 Cashiers School Rd., Cashiers, (828) 743-3750.

Puppy Paws and Golden Years

Continue driving 0.2 mile past the trailhead, cross the bridge over the river, and turn left on FR 646A. A green-blazed path leads from the parking lot about 150 feet to a primitive campsite along the river's edge. There's a perfect sandy beach here, and the water is usually calm enough for your furry friends to wade into.

I highly recommend the side trip to see Spoon Auger Falls.

Westminster

57 Riley Moore Falls Trail—Sumter National Forest

Wow, what a treat! You and the dogs will get a workout in as you make the steady descent to the falls, but when you reach the base you'll be amazed. It's as though you just arrived at the beach, sans the ocean. A large sandy area alongside the creek is perfect for sunning and drying off after you and the dogs take a nice refreshing swim near the base of this beautiful and surprisingly wide waterfall. Bring a towel. When you see the many locals out in the water, you'll find it hard to resist.

Start: If you have a high-clearance, four-wheel-drive vehicle, the trailhead is to the left of the gate at the end of FR 748C. If you don't have this type of transportation, park along FR 748 near FR 748C. The alternate trailhead is where FR 748 and FR 748C meet.

Distance: 2.4 miles out and back if you park at the alternate trailhead; 1.2 miles out and back if you park at the actual trailhead

Hiking time: About 1 hour, 30 minutes (alternate trailhead); 45 minutes (actual trailhead)

Blaze color: Purplish blue

Difficulty: Moderate to strenuous

Trailhead elevation: Alternate trailhead 1,065 feet; actual trailhead 1,021 feet

Highest point: Alternate trailhead 1,065 feet; actual trailhead 1,021 feet

Best season: Year-round

Trail surface: Steep, clay forest road and hard-packed dirt trail with rooty and rocky sections

Other trail users: None

Canine compatibility: Voice control

Land status: Sumter National Forest—Andrew Pickens Ranger District

Fees: No fee

Maps: *DeLorme: North Carolina Atlas & Gazetteer:* Page 22, B2

Trail contacts: (864) 638-9568; www.fs .usda.gov/recarea/scnfs/recreation/hiking/ recarea/?recid=47111&actid=50

Nearest town: Westminster

Trail tips: If you hike from the alternate trailhead, keep the dogs on a leash while hiking along FR 748C. Bring a hiking stick and lots of water.

Special considerations: If you need to hike along FR 748C, make sure you keep the dogs on their leashes until you are past the actual trailhead and well into the woods to avoid traffic.

Finding the trailhead: From the junction of US 76 and US 123 in Westminster, drive west on US 76 for 7.2 miles to a right onto Cobb Bridge Road. Travel for 1.3 miles to a left onto Spy Rock Road (FR 748). Travel for 1.8 miles to FR 748C. Either park here, or drive to the end of FR 748C if you have a high-clearance, four-wheel-drive vehicle.

From the junction of US 76 and the Chattooga River Bridge (Georgia–South Carolina state line), drive east on US 76 for 6.5 miles to a left onto Spy Rock Road (FR 748). Travel for 4.0 miles to FR 748C. Either park here, or drive to the end of FR 748C if you have a high-clearance, four-wheel-drive vehicle.

Note: FR 748C is a very rugged, bumpy forest road. **GPS: Alternate trailhead:** N34 44.423'/ W83 11.468'; **Actual trailhead:** N34 44.453'/W83 11.119'

The Hike

The Chauga River never disappoints. It's full of spectacular rapids, narrows, sluices, and waterfalls. And Riley Moore is no different. The falls are not very tall, but what they lack in height, they make up for in character, and in width for that matter. This fabulous waterfall drops in two tiers and takes up the full width of the river. And the pool at the base is unlike any other. A row of low stones crosses the waterway in front of the falls, forming a shallow wading pool where you can sit with the dogs while the waterfall splashes down at your feet. Just downstream of this perfectly placed rock ledge a deeper pool of water gathers, forming a swimming hole like no other. Locals flock to these falls, using it as a swimming hole, especially on weekends, and in the summertime. When you arrive, you'll find it's like a day at the beach. People have their blankets and towels laid out. Some will be sunbathing, others taking a dip out in the chilly mountain water. People bring coolers, picnic lunches, and beach umbrellas. But remember, if you pack it in, you have to pack it out, trash too. So please bring a bag, so we can keep this pristine place as beautiful as it was when you arrived. The shores along the river's edge are like a sandy beach. Between the beach, the waterfall, and the gently flowing river, you won't want to leave once you arrive. Looking at the map, you'll see I've listed a trailhead and an alternative trailhead. That's because FR 748C is a very rugged, bumpy forest road. Without a high-clearance vehicle, you'll need to park at the alternative trailhead, and hike down the forest road to the official trailhead. This will add an extra half-mile to the hike, but the dogs won't mind the extra mileage. Just make sure you keep them on a leash until you head into the forest, since some people will be driving down this road. From the official trailhead, hike around the gate, and the narrow path makes a steady descent into the forest. Although you can't hear any moving water yet, be patient. This one is well worth the wait, and worth the extra half-mile hike on the forest road as well. It's amazing how populated this one is, because it takes quite a bit of effort to reach, and more specifically to get back out. Ferns, holly, rhododendron, and beech accompany the typical maple and oak trees common to the area. This wide variety of flora is enhanced in springtime, with an array of wildflowers joining the ranks. The closer you get to the falls, the steeper the terrain becomes. You'll also notice that the smooth surface transforms into a rugged, rooty, rocky path. However,

In summertime, locals submerge at the base of Riley Moore Falls.

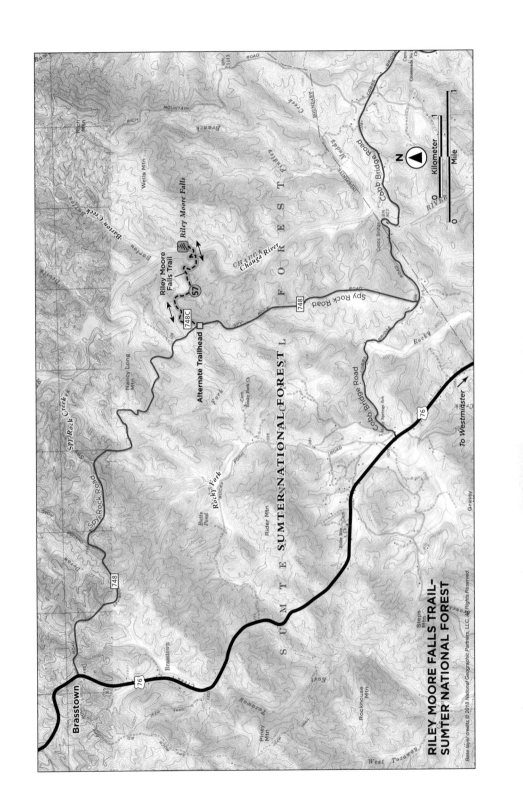

RILEY MOORE FALLS TRAIL–
SUMTER NATIONAL FOREST

Base layer credits © 2018 National Geographic Partners, LLC. All Rights Reserved.

Left: Riley Moore has clear water, a sandy bottom, and an unbeatable beach.
Right: Blue waits upon the long clay path leading down to Riley Moore Falls.

the Forest Service has done an exceptional job establishing a clear, well-marked route to Riley Moore Falls. In years past, this was a scramble at best, with no set trail. It was more of a free for all of social trails making their way down to the falls along any route they could. Bravo.

Miles and Directions

- **0.0** From the alternate trailhead, hike down FR 748C.
- **0.6** Reach the end of FR 748C and the actual trailhead. The trail is to the left (north) of the gate. Hike east into the forest on a steady descent.
- **1.2** Arrive at the base of Riley Moore Falls (N34 44.467'/W83 10.769'). Backtrack to the trailhead.
- **1.8** Arrive back at the actual trailhead. If you parked up on FR 748, continue hiking up FR 748C.
- **2.4** Arrive back at the alternate trailhead where FR 748C and FR 748 meet.

Resting up

Relax Inn Westminster, 109 W. Windsor St., Westminster, (864) 647-2045; pet fee required.
Quality Inn Seneca, 226 Hi Tech Rd., Seneca, (864) 888-8300; pet fee required.

Camping

South Cove County Park, 1099 South Cove Rd., Seneca, (864) 882-5250.

Fueling up

Chattooga Belle Farm, 454 Damascus Church Rd., Long Creek, (864) 647-9768.
Beyond the Bull, 8095 Keowee School Rd., Seneca, (864) 508-1254.

Puppy Paws and Golden Years

Take them to see Falls on Little Brasstown Creek (see Falls on Little Brasstown Creek Trail hike). It's an easy 0.4-mile hike (round-trip). The trailhead is west on US 76, off of Brasstown Road.

58 Falls on Little Brasstown Creek Trail–Sumter National Forest

Although this is a short hike, the prize at the end of the trail makes it a worthy one. Most people visit this trailhead to hike down to Brasstown Falls, a trio of Upper, Middle, and Lower Falls, each with its own unique beauty. Unfortunately, the trail to those falls is simply not safe for dogs. But not to fret. You'll enjoy a beautiful little creek, and the Falls on Little Brasstown Creek easily rivals the splendor of its downstream siblings.

Start: Southwest end of the parking area at the end of FR 751
Distance: 0.4 mile out and back
Hiking time: About 15 minutes
Blaze color: Yellow, only for first 0.1 mile
Difficulty: Easy
Trailhead elevation: 1,015 feet
Highest point: 1,030 feet
Best season: Year-round
Trail surface: Hard-packed dirt with rooty sections

Other trail users: None
Canine compatibility: Voice control
Land status: Sumter National Forest–Andrew Pickens Ranger District
Fees: No fee
Maps: *DeLorme: North Carolina Atlas & Gazetteer*: Page 16, C1
Trail contacts: (864) 638-9568
Nearest town: Westminster, Walhalla
Trail tips: Make sure you head left at the second primitive campsite.

Finding the trailhead: From the junction of US 76 and the Chattooga River Bridge (Georgia–South Carolina state line), drive east on US 76 for 5.6 miles. Turn right onto Brasstown Road and travel 4.0 miles to a right onto FR 751 (just before crossing the small bridge over Brasstown Creek). Follow FR 751 for 0.4 mile to where it ends.

From the junction of US 76 and US 123 in Westminster, drive west on US 76 for 11.6 miles. Turn left onto Brasstown Road. Follow directions above. *Note:* At 2.6 miles Brasstown Road becomes a dirt road. **Trailhead GPS:** N34 43.155'/W83 18.099'

The Hike

Most people take this trail to visit Brasstown Falls. Brasstown Creek is simply amazing. Hiking along that path will lead you to see Upper, Middle, and Lower Brasstown Falls. Unfortunately, to reach these falls, you also have to follow a narrow, muddy path with a steep and dangerous dropoff, not to mention you pass right by the brink of one waterfall to hike on to the next. It's simply not suitable for dogs. So I urge you to stick to the hike as is described. Begin by following the yellow-blazed Brasstown Falls Trail. The path is well trodden and heavily used. As you head into the forest, you'll pass a primitive campsite and then come to a trail information sign. At this sign, instead of following Brasstown Creek downstream, head left, and you'll come to a tiny creek.

Left: Falls on Little Brasstown Creek is a local treasure.
Right: Creekside camping at its best.

This little beauty is Little Brasstown Creek. But when you see the waterfall upstream, you may not call it so little after all. A large log across the creek gives you a place to cross the water, while the dogs traipse right through it. And in the distance, the falls come into view. The path is unmarked, but clearly leads to the base of Falls on Little Brasstown Creek. The falls are tall, and a good amount of water flows over the stone face. The rock seems to make a staircase for the water to run right over as it makes its way down to the creek. At the base, you'll find a deep pool has formed, and the dogs can swim out into the water if they are so inclined. You may want to take a dip yourself. The Brasstown Valley was first explored and inhabited by the Cherokee Indians. They named the area "Itseyi" meaning "place of fresh green." Thanks to a simple misunderstanding, this creek came to be called Brasstown. When the white settlers came along, they confused "Itseyi" with "v-tsai-yi," which means "brass." Soon after, the creek and the area around it came to be commonly known as Brasstown Creek. The Falls on Little Brasstown Creek easily rival the stunning beauty of its downstream siblings. But more importantly, this one is safe for your four-legged friends.

Miles and Directions

0.0 Hike southwest on the heavily trodden path.

0.1 Come to a fork after passing a primitive campsite and trail information sign. Straight (west) is the continuation of the Brasstown Falls Trail. Do not take the dogs that way. It is unsafe for them. Instead, go left, and hike southeast through the large primitive campsite.

0.14 At the far end of the campsite you will reach the creek. Cross on the primitive log bridge. Hike south toward the falls.

0.2 Arrive at Falls on Little Brasstown Creek (N34 43.037'/W83 18.148'). Backtrack to the trailhead.

0.4 Arrive at the trailhead.

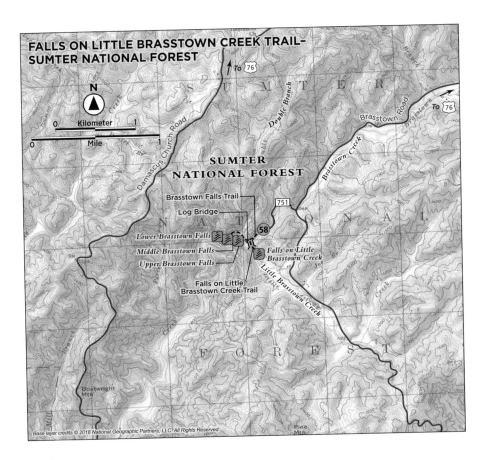

FALLS ON LITTLE BRASSTOWN CREEK TRAIL–
SUMTER NATIONAL FOREST

Resting up

Relax Inn Westminster, 109 W. Windsor St., Westminster, (864) 647-2045; pet fee required.

Quality Inn Seneca, 226 Hi Tech Rd., Seneca, (864) 888-8300; pet fee required.

Camping

Backcountry camping onsite.

Chattooga River Resort & Campground, 110 Blalock Place Rd., Long Creek, (864) 873-7310.

Fueling up

Chattooga Belle Farm, 454 Damascus Church Rd., Long Creek, (864) 647-9768.

Beyond the Bull, 8095 Keowee School Rd., Seneca, (864) 508-1254.

Puppy Paws and Golden Years

Suitable for all dogs.

59 Opossum Creek Falls Trail–Sumter National Forest

Leading to one of my favorite waterfalls in the state, this hike will challenge you physically, but the rewards are well worth the effort. The trail leads you through a diverse forest, before you find yourself on a spectacular sandy beach right on the banks of the famous Wild and Scenic Chattooga River. The views here are outstanding, and the water is calm enough for you and the dogs to take a dip. From the river, the trail follows Opossum Creek upstream to the base of Opossum Creek Falls. The falls are fabulous! Bring a picnic and spend the day.

Start: The trailhead is on the west side of the road, about 200 feet south of the parking area.
Distance: 4.6 miles out and back
Hiking time: About 2 hours, 20 minutes
Blaze color: White
Difficulty: Moderate to strenuous
Trailhead elevation: 1,613 feet
Highest point: 1,618 feet
Best season: Year-round
Trail surface: Hard-packed dirt
Other trail users: None
Canine compatibility: Voice control
Land status: Sumter National Forest—Andrew Pickens Ranger District
Fees: No fee

Maps: DeLorme: North Carolina Atlas & Gazetteer. Page 16, B1
Trail contacts: (864) 638-9568; www.fs .usda.gov/recarea/scnfs/recreation/hiking/ recarea/?recid=47107&actid=50
Nearest town: Mountain Rest, Walhalla
Trail tips: Bring a hiking stick, lots of water for you and the dogs, and a snack for some energy. Also, bring a pack towel if you plan on swimming in the river.
Special considerations: If you decide to take a swim at the beach, use caution. Water levels fluctuate in the river. Currents may be stronger after heavy rain.

Finding the trailhead: From the junction of US 76 and the Chattooga River Bridge (Georgia–South Carolina state line), drive east on US 76 for 4.4 miles. Turn right at the fire station onto Damascus Church Road and travel 0.8 mile to a fork in the road. Go right at the fork onto Battle Creek Road and continue for 1.8 miles. Turn right onto Turkey Ridge Road (FR 755) and travel 2.2 miles to a pulloff on the left next to FR 755F.

From the junction of US 76 and US 123, drive west on US 76 for 12.8 miles. Turn left at the fire station onto Damascus Church Road. Follow directions above. **Trailhead GPS:** N34 46.406'/W83 18.255'

The Hike

Hawks, turkey, and owls are among the birds that may greet you as you hike into the forest. As you begin a long downhill trek, logs embedded in the trail act as steps, helping to ease the descent. And you quickly come to realize that this is a birdwatcher's delight. Woodpeckers, cardinals, and finches join the birds of prey, and the summer tanager makes the cardinal pale in comparison to its bright red plumage. When you

Left: There are plenty of places to sit by the base of Opossum Creek Falls.
Right: Opossum Creek Falls is challenging to reach, but worth the effort.

reach the forest floor, the trail flattens out a bit. As you continue hiking southwest, you'll make your way through a bed of ferns, which is joined by berries, and rhododendron blossoms in the summer months. In fact, this is a trail for all seasons. In fall, the trees are ablaze, full of color and life. In springtime, an outstanding show of wildflowers line the pathway with brilliant-colored blossoms. Summer brings an abundance of lush green hues, and an added variety of birdlife. And in wintertime, the frost transforms the trail into a unique landscape of stunning solitude. Pine, maple, oak, hickory, poplar, and beech are among the amazing array of trees that keep you shaded over the length of the trail. As you follow a tiny tributary through the forest, the faint sound of moving water adds to the ambiance. At about the 1-mile mark, you'll begin to climb, and hear the sounds of a waterfall down below. Ignore this, be patient, and stay on the well-marked path. It's worth the wait. As you make your way steeply downhill, you notice a change in the air, and the closer you get to the river, the cooler the air becomes. You soon find your fitness level being challenged by the steep climbs and drops the path presents you with. But the sound of rushing water urges you on as it lures you in. At last, nearing the 2-mile mark, the river comes into view down below. You'll follow a few switchbacks down to Opossum Creek, where it flows out into the mighty Chattooga River. A downed tree acts as a natural log bridge, leading out to a little island and sandy beach on the shores of the river. This beach is simply amazing. The river is usually calm enough for you and the dogs to wade out into and enjoy the refreshing crisp, clean mountain water. And the beach is big enough for the dogs to romp, run, dig, chase each other, or play fetch. I could pitch a tent and live happily ever after here. It's that perfect. After spending some time at the beach, a narrow footpath follows Opossum Creek upstream and uphill. You'll pass cascades, and cross a little tributary on your way to the falls. Crossing a second tributary brings the falls into view. When you arrive at the base, large boulders are strewn about, giving you a perfect place to perch and enjoy a picnic with the pups. The sound of rushing water adds to the ambiance, and the face of the falls is covered

OPOSSUM CREEK FALLS TRAIL–SUMTER NATIONAL FOREST

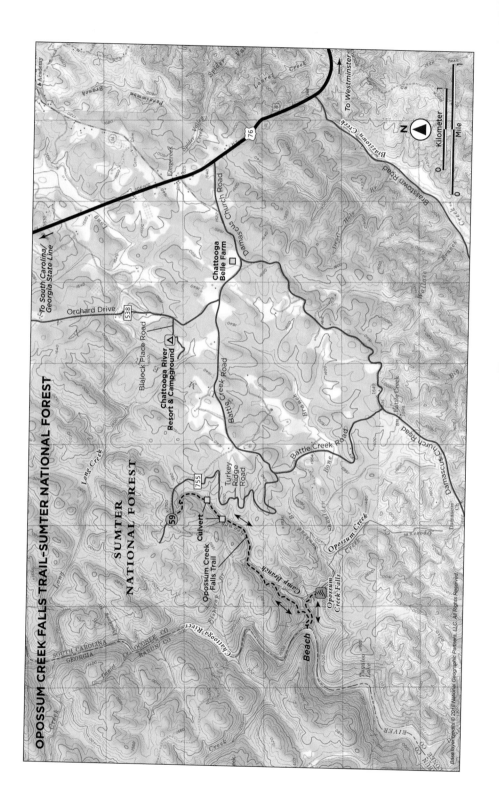

Left: Bandit takes a post-playtime nap near the river.
Right: White-tailed deer are most often seen at dusk and dawn.

in soft spongy moss, giving it a milky white appearance as the water freely flows over it. As you hike back to the trailhead, you realize how steeply you came down into the escarpment. A hiking stick will help ease the ascent.

Miles and Directions

0.0 Hike southeast into the forest.

0.5 Cross a culvert over a tiny creek. Continue hiking southwest.

0.7 Cross a culvert over a tributary. Follow the tributary downstream and southwest.

2.0 Come to Opossum Creek where it flows out to the Chattooga River. To visit the falls, the trail makes a hard left (southeast) and follows the Opossum Creek upstream on a narrow path.

Option: Take a side trip 100 feet to the river first. Cross Opossum Creek here and you'll arrive at a pristine sandy beach on the banks of the Chattooga River (N34 45.477'/W83 19.119'). I highly recommend this side trip! After visiting the beach, follow Opossum Creek upstream.

2.2 Cross a tributary. Continue hiking upstream.

2.25 Cross a tributary and the falls are in view in the distance.

2.3 Arrive at the base of Opossum Creek Falls (N34 45.431'/W83 18.862'). Backtrack to the trailhead.

4.6 Arrive at the trailhead.

Stunning scenery awaits your visit to the upcountry.

Resting up

Relax Inn Westminster, 109 W. Windsor St., Westminster, (864) 647-2045; pet fee required.

Quality Inn Seneca, 226 Hi Tech Rd., Seneca, (864) 888-8300; pet fee required.

Camping

Backcountry camping onsite.

Chattooga River Resort & Campground, 110 Blalock Place Rd., Long Creek, (864) 873-7310, chattoogaresort.com; open year-round.

Fueling up

Chattooga Belle Farm, 454 Damascus Church Rd., Long Creek, (864) 647-9768.

Beyond the Bull, 8095 Keowee School Rd., Seneca, (864) 508-1254.

Puppy Paws and Golden Years

Take them to see Falls on Little Brasstown Creek (Falls on Little Brasstown Creek Trail hike). It's an easy 0.4-mile hike (round-trip). The trailhead is west on US 76, off of Brasstown Road.

60 Falls on Reedy Branch Trail–Sumter National Forest

This short but enjoyable hike leads you down a little-known gravel Forest Service road. When you reach the base of the hill, you are quickly greeted by an alluring waterfall with a wonderful splash pool at the base. The dogs enjoy sniffing about and taking a dip at the base, while the sound and sight of the water dancing on the rocks satisfies your own senses.

Start: The trailhead is located near the stone pillars and gate at the south end of the parking area.
Distance: 0.4 mile out and back
Hiking time: About 20 minutes
Blaze color: None
Difficulty: Easy to moderate
Trailhead elevation: 1,702 feet
Highest point: 1,702 feet
Best season: Year-round
Trail surface: Wide gravel roadbed and narrow dirt footpath
Other trail users: None
Canine compatibility: Voice control
Land status: Sumter National Forest–Andrew Pickens Ranger District

Fees: No fee
Maps: *DeLorme: North Carolina Atlas & Gazetteer.* Page 22, A1
Trail contacts: (864) 638-9568
Nearest town: Westminster, Walhalla
Trail tips: The trailhead sits near a main road. Keep the dogs on leash until you've hiked a safe distance from the roadway. Also remember to leash them up as you make your way back to the trailhead.
Special considerations: The hike is short, but a portion of it follows a gravel forest road. If your merry mutts have sensitive pads, make sure they have their booties on for the first 0.15 mile.

Finding the trailhead: From the junction of US 76 and the Chattooga River Bridge (Georgia–South Carolina state line), drive east on US 76 for 1.7 miles to a pulloff on the right next to a low stone wall.

From the junction of US 76 and US 123, drive west on US 76 for 15.5 miles to a pulloff on the left next to a low stone wall. **Trailhead GPS:** N34 48.438'/W83 16.855'

The Hike

Although the hike is short, it still has many of the wonderful characteristics that come along with a longer hike. You'll find a variety of birds serenade you the minute you pass through the lofty stone pillars that greet you at the trailhead. The pillars were built many years ago, when this area was slotted to become a housing development. The project came to an abrupt halt when the land was thankfully acquired by the Sumter National Forest. The trail itself is basically an extension of FR 2751. As you pass the great pillared entryway into the forest, you'll follow the old gravel road downhill. Although the surface is a wide, gravel roadbed, it hasn't been driven on in years, so there's plenty of grass growing on the sides. This is perfect to protect your pups' paws.

Left: Alley patiently waits for her mom to catch up.
Right: The boys struck a pretty pose for me at Reedy Branch.

If your happy hounds have very sensitive feet, bring booties as a precaution. As you make your descent, the birds' song is joined by the sounds of trickling water on both sides of the road. Tall hardwoods surround the path, and in fall they put on quite a show. They also keep you shaded year-round. When you reach the bottom of the hill, you'll see the remnants of a gorgeous stone bridge. In its day, this stonework once led the gravel road across Reedy Branch Creek as it headed into what would have been a lovely neighborhood. The bridge collapsed several years ago, and today all you see are large pieces of the stone, resting in the narrow creek. This won't affect your hike though. Before reaching the bridge, you'll see a narrow footpath heads left toward Reedy Branch Falls. You can see the falls from the forest road, so you can't get lost. Just as the bridge once stood firm in place, so did a beautiful gazebo near the base of the falls. This too disintegrated over time, and with lack of maintenance. The bridge was nice to look at, but you could do without. The gazebo on the other hand gave you a lovely place to sit alongside the base of the fabulous Reedy Branch Falls. Even without the added allure of the gazebo, this waterfall is quite charming. It's tall, and narrow, and the water seems to bend in the middle as the flow changes direction halfway down. Little pools are formed at the base by a number of rocks resting in the creek at the base. When you sit and stare at the splendid waterfall, you realize how peaceful this place is.

◀ *Reedy Branch Falls: tall, narrow, and worth a visit.*

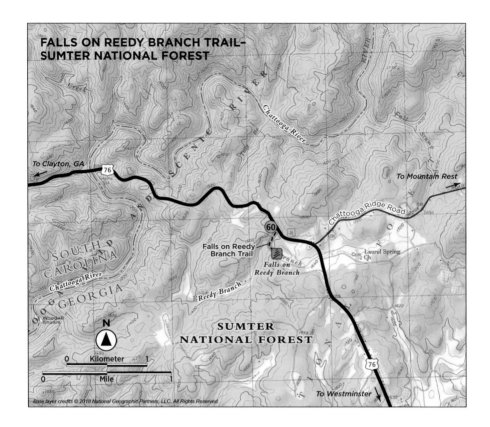

FALLS ON REEDY BRANCH TRAIL–
SUMTER NATIONAL FOREST

Miles and Directions

0.0 Go around the stone pillars and hike south and downhill on the old roadbed.

0.15 At the bottom of the hill, before reaching the remains of an old stone bridge, go left (south southeast), following the narrow footpath toward the falls.

0.17 Cross a tiny footbridge; continue hiking southeast.

0.2 Arrive at the base of Falls on Reedy Branch (N34 48.311'/W83 16.894'). Backtrack to the trailhead.

0.4 Arrive at the trailhead.

Resting up

Relax Inn Westminster, 109 W. Windsor St., Westminster, (864) 647-2045; pet fee required.

Quality Inn Seneca, 226 Hi Tech Rd., Seneca, (864) 888-8300; pet fee required.

Camping

Chattooga River Resort & Campground, 110 Blalock Place Rd., Long Creek, (864) 873-7310, chattoogaresort.com.

Mountain laurel thrives in the South Carolina mountains.

Fueling up

Chattooga Belle Farm, 454 Damascus Church Rd., Long Creek, (864) 647-9768.
Beyond the Bull, 8095 Keowee School Rd., Seneca, (864) 508-1254.

Puppy Paws and Golden Years

Take them to see Falls on Little Brasstown Creek (see Falls on Little Brasstown Creek
Trail hike). It's an easy 0.4-mile hike (round-trip). The trailhead is west on US 76, off
of Brasstown Road.

Hike Index

About the Author

Waterfall hunter, nature enthusiast, tree hugger, and avid hiker, Melissa Watson is truly at her best when she's in the forest. Her passion for waterfalls, hiking, and nature in general stems back to her childhood, and she continues to fulfill that passion to this day. For more than 25 years, Melissa has been exploring the forests of South Carolina, North Carolina, Georgia, and Florida, hiking by day and camping by night, with her beloved canine companions Mikey and Bandit at her side every step of the way. She continues her quest for new trails, new adventures, and new territory to explore.